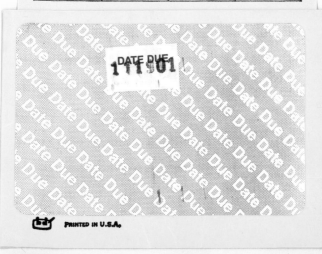

THE FORMATION
OF TENNYSON'S STYLE

THE FORMATION
OF TENNYSON'S STYLE

A STUDY, PRIMARILY, OF THE VERSIFICATION

OF THE EARLY POEMS

BY

J. F. A. PYRE

PHAETON PRESS
NEW YORK
1968

69-5095

Originally Published 1921
Reprint 1968

Library of Congress Catalog Card Number: 68-8979

Published By Phaeton Press

PREFACE

In connection with a few preliminary explanations and acknowledgments, it will not be impertinent, indeed it is almost obligatory, to mention the fact that this study has been in hand, at intervals, for a good many years. Collection of the data which furnished the basis of the study began at a time when I was less sensible than I now am, of the difficulties of the subject; at a time, too, when English metric was even less settled as to theory and nomenclature than at present, and when materials for a study of Tennyson's formative period were less accessible than they have since become. At a later time, these observations were re-tested and some of them, not so much for want of accuracy as of usefulness, were entirely discarded, while, in certain directions, they were very much amplified, and the whole was recast, approximately in the present form. Preparatory to publication, it has been revised and presumably deprived of obvious anachronisms. Although confident that this re-handling, at considerable intervals of time, has not been to the disadvantage of the work as a whole, I scarcely venture to hope I have removed every indication that it is not of a single mintage.

The metrical analyses to which Shakspere and his contemporaries had been subjected, for the purpose of giving exactness to internal evidence on questions of authorship and chronology, first suggested a similar treatment of Tennyson's verse, only here with the different object of providing data for more precise discriminations as to a poetic manner. A start in this direction could be seen in certain chapters of Corson's *Primer of English Verse* and in Mayor's *Chapters on English Metre,* as well as in short passages of Schipper's *Englische Metrik.* No detailed acknowledgments of indebtedness to these sources appear in the notes, I think; for my debt was not of a kind which is capable of such indication, though attempts to reconcile certain detailed analyses of Schipper and Mayor with one another and with my own results furnished, at one stage, a very useful discipline. A preceding metrical study from which I derived many helpful ideas was Bridges' *Milton's Prosody*.

Wherever I have been aware of a definite source for a particular point, I have aimed to record it, either in the notes or in the text, and especially I have aimed to indicate the authority for every statement or opinion attributed to Tennyson himself; but I have not incorporated in the notes references to every known expression, in general criticism, of ideas similar or antagonistic to those expressed in the text. Nor do I believe that a judicious reader will regret, or impute to wilful neglect, the absence of an apparatus which would only encumber this little treatise and tend to obscure its central emphasis.

Much the same might be said regarding the absence of a formal exposition of the scheme of metrical analysis which I have followed and the absence of express definitions of the technical terms employed. These could be supplied, in brief compass, only to the reader for whom they would be superfluous. What special explanation a term requires accompanies its application or is apparent therein. I am aware that the analyses are not all equally thorough-going. Some will seem painfully minute; others, by comparison, may seem superficial or incomplete. I have not, indeed, ground everything through the same mill; but I trust I have not spared industry where it promised to be of service.

For the texts of Tennyson's suppressed poems and for the variants of all, down to and including *In Memoriam*, I have made use, principally, of the editions by J. Churton Collins. Happily, since, in the case of the *Early Poems* at least, these texts were not to be relied on, I was able to collate them all with copies of the original editions. This opportunity I owed to the liberality of Mr. William Allis, of Milwaukee, who very kindly lent me the precious volumes from his private collection.

This study was substantially complete as it stands, about ten years ago. No acceptable means could then be found for its publication as a unit. At least, none *was* found, both pride and poverty interdicting its issue at my own expense, while I preferred indefinite suppression to a dismemberment which would have seriously damaged the connected interest of the whole. I am under peculiar obligation, therefore, to the University of Wisconsin, for the provision which enables me to present these chapters with little to deprecate except my own delinquencies.

To several colleagues acknowledgments are due: in particular, to F. G. Hubbard, who encouraged my first studies of this subject; to John W. Cunliffe, my former chief, whose friendly concern stimulated my return to the subject, at the time indicated above; to Karl Young, for helpful interest in this publication; and to R. E. N. Dodge, for valuable suggestions and for generous assistance with the proofs.

One of the opening sentences of this preface implies that theories of metre have reached a more settled condition since my first studies of Tennyson were made. I had forgotten the disturbance which the votaries of free verse have raised in the temple of poetic art. Perhaps I ought to explain, that the solemn irony of bringing forward, at this late day, an academic discussion of Tennyson's restrained and thorough-paced verse is quite accidental and void of malice.

CONTENTS

			Page
Introductory Note	. . . .		9
Chapter	I	The Age of Imitation	12
	II	Experiments in Metre . . .	23
	III	Revision and Standardization . .	35
	IV	Mastering Blank Verse . . .	68
	V	Maturity: The New Poems of 1842 .	94
	VI	The Blank Verse Poems of 1842 .	113
	VII	The Princess	160
	VIII	In Memoriam and Maud . . .	181
	IX	Tennyson's Later Work . . .	196
Appendix A.		Tennyson's Early Diction . . .	225
Appendix B.		Note on the Origin and Influence of the Locksley Hall Metre . . .	244

For though the poet's matter nature be,
His art doth give the fashion; and, that he
Who casts to write a living line, must sweat
(Such as thine are) and strike the second heat
Upon the Muses' anvil; turn the same
(And himself with it) that he thinks to frame,
Or, for the laurel, he may gain a scorn,
For a good poet's made as well as born.

> JONSON: To the Memory of my
> Beloved Master William Shake-
> speare, and what he hath left us.
> ll. 57–64.

Yet nature is made better by no mean
But nature makes that mean: so, over that art
Which you say adds to nature is an art
That nature makes. . . . . .
> *This is an art*
Which does mend nature, change it rather,
> *but*
The art itself is nature.

> SHAKSPERE: The Winter's Tale,
> IV, iv, 89–97.

INTRODUCTORY NOTE

Tennyson never assumed toward poetry the disposition of the mere skilled workman, or, if one may use the phrase without ambiguity, of the mere artist. "Art for Art's sake! Hail, truest Lord of Hell" implied a creed which he came to hold with something like passion. But, on the other hand, experience taught him the indispensableness of skill in form to one who seeks to express himself in the forms of art. He recognized that a poet must be master of the medium through which he gives his ideas substance. Two years before his death, commenting on a writer's remark of him "Artist first, then Poet," Tennyson said, "I should answer, *Poeta nascitur non fit;* indeed, *Poeta nascitur et fit.* I suppose I was nearer thirty than twenty before I was anything of an artist." He would have agreed, apparently, with Ben Jonson's saying that "a good poet's made as well as born"; only, he would have reversed the emphasis. That he must be born a poet is true; but it is equally true that he must be *made* an artist; not until this is accomplished can the poet *in posse* be considered a poet *in esse.* Probably there is no important English poet whose published works elucidate this principle more impressively than those of Tennyson.

For this reason, and for others less fundamental, there is none whose work affords more profitable matter for technical analysis. Tennyson, first of all, is a derived poet. His practices both in the substance and in the forms of his poetry are educed from a variety of sources, many of which can be identified. We have, moreover, generous illustrations of the work of his periods of apprenticeship; many of his early poems are accessible in their experimental, imitative, and imperfect stage, as well as in their later and revised and improved state. Again, the processes by which his style was

perfected, though superficially patent, do not disclose themselves unreservedly to casual observation. There are no
glaring revolutions of aim or manner. Though distinct, the
processes of his development are not obvious; their delicate
gradations reward the closest scrutiny. Nor are we guided,
in any substantial degree, by external commentary on the
part of the poet. Hardly any modern writer has rested his
case so simply upon his accomplishment in the form and
manner which are exclusively those of poetry. Sparing no
pains to make his creations self-explanatory within the limits
ordained by the laws of their own being, he left them to
confront the reader without exterior aids to their appreciation.[1] Finally, the significance of Tennyson's work, both
vital and technical, is sufficiently great to justify minute inquiry into the processes of its evolution.

The chapters which follow deal primarily with the development of Tennyson's style down to the time when it reaches
its highest perfection, in the poems of the 1842 volumes and
in *In Memoriam*. It is upon this body of work, in all probability, that Tennyson's position among English poets must
finally rest. This, it is assumed, and in some measure shown,
in the following study, is the central, the standard Tennyson.
This study concerns itself, then, primarily with the formation
of Tennyson's style rather than with its later applications.
The poet's early exercises and experiments, the poems of
the formative period in their earlier and their revised versions, and the poems of the central period are examined in
detail with the aim of bringing into prominence the processes
by which the poet's style was evolved. The concluding
chapters of the volume present a more general account of
Tennyson's later and longer works, and voluminous collections, with the view of indicating some of the respects in
which he departed from earlier methods. Particular at-

---

[1] There are, of course, invaluable hints in the *Memoir* and in the notes
appended to the Eversley Edition of Tennyson's poems; but these are, ,
after all, only random observations and provide no considerable body of
commentary when we consider the volume of Tennyson's work.

tention is directed to the poet's practices in versification; but so far as possible these practices have been placed in relation with other elements in his style. The study will be found to contain, therefore, in connection with metrical descriptions and statistics, considerable passages of general criticism and references to the external circumstances which from time to time influenced or conditioned the poet's work. It is hoped that by this means the strictly technical findings of the study may be more conveniently related to other aspects of Tennyson's highly sophisticated art and to broader principles of literary criticism.

CHAPTER I

THE AGE OF IMITATION

Coleridge, in an important passage in his *Biographia Literaria,* places first among the "specific symptoms of poetic power" in a young writer, a delight in verbal melody and a command of the means by which it is produced. He says: "The delight in richness and sweetness of sound, even to a faulty excess, if it be evidently original, and not the result of an easily imitable mechanism, I regard as a highly favorable promise in a young man . . . the sense of musical delight, with the power of producing it, is a gift of imagination."

Judging from the context of this passage, and from the discussion, elsewhere in the same treatise, of the subject of poetic diction, Coleridge may actually have had in mind, here, two elements of poetic effect which frequently go hand in hand, but which, to advantage, may be distinguished from each other. By "sense of musical delight" he apparently meant, first, the love of words for their own sake, that is love for the absolute beauty of words, as such, whether beauty of sound, or beauty of association; but second, and chiefly, he meant the love of such words when their beauty is heightened by their harmonious and expressive position in a rhythmic structure. This primary sense for poetic style is separable into the sense for diction and the sense for metre. Both are, in a degree, sensuous attributes of the poetic imagination, and for that reason are expected to develop in an early stage of any poet's art. They may be expected to exhibit at this stage those crudities which adhere to all the exuberances of adolescence; and they may be expected to give place gradually to other, more austere and spiritual, but not more fundamental, attributes of the imagination. Further, as the intellectual and spiritual elements of the poetic imagination take ground from its physical attributes, we may expect that the sense for diction and the sense for rhythm will shift from mere sensuous pleasure in their color and sound into a delight more proportioned to their expressive significance. Words and imagery will be valued less for their voluptuous appeal, or vague charm, their casual and sometimes irrelevant beauty; they will be more tenderly cherished for their inner faithfulness, their willingness to fall into their appointed places and do their work, their loyalty to the context. Rhythm, also, will be less prized for its cajolery of the senses; more for its expressiveness, its power of controlling the syllabic incidence of speech. In these respects, as Coleridge seems to imply in the passage just quoted, it is well that the poet should be young in his youth. Orderliness, taste, good sense, can afford to wait. Too alert a consciousness of these and a too complaisant obedience to their admonitions may even argue a want of fruitfulness in the youthful poet; they dictate the *forms* of the imagination; but richness and sweetness of speech, "even to a faulty excess," argue the presence of *life*.

Had it been in the nature of Tennyson to submit himself to the discipline, instead of surrendering to the ardors of poetry, he had ample opportunity in the circumstances of his youthful training. His apprenticeship to poetry began early and seems to have continued unwaveringly throughout his boyhood and youth. His father, a clergyman, and a scholar of considerable attainments, interested himself keenly in the education of his sons, who were many and near of an age, and he personally provided the last years of university preparation for a number of them. The mother is said to have possessed spiritual gifts of a rare order. Most of Tennyson's brothers aspired, like him, to be poets, but they early conceded Alfred's call to the poet's career to be the most commanding. Thus, his poetic talent thrived under generous rivalry and encouragement from the beginning. His early preparation for purely poetical achievement is paralleled in thoroughness and singleness of purpose by that of only one or two other

English poets,—Milton perhaps, and Pope. A genuine,
though not transcendent, gift for expression was assiduously
cultivated to make him the artist that he in time became.
The record of his career is one of surprising poetical thrift.
If thousands of lines were sacrificed to the fastidiousness of
later years, we may rest assured that nothing of promise was
permitted to perish. Single verses, passages of description,
prized similes, even single epithets, were sometimes saved
from the refuse, to appear years afterward in new and more
hospitable environments. A device of style or metre, once
discovered, was remembered and called into requisition again
and again. Yet this careful husbanding was no concomitant
of poverty. Tennyson was not without the young poet's pre-
cocious facility. His earliest exercises in verse evince an
inborn turn for both phrase and rhythm, chiefly imitative, to
be sure. He remembered "filling two sides of a slate with
Thomsonian blank verse," at the age of eight. "About ten
or eleven, Pope's *Iliad* became a favorite," and he "wrote
hundreds and hundreds of lines in regular Popeian metre."
"About twelve and onward," he tells us, "I wrote an epic
of 6000 lines *à la* Walter Scott.... with Scott's regularity
of octosyllabics and his occasional varieties"......"Some
what later (at fourteen) I wrote a drama in blank verse which
I have still, and other things. It seems to me, I wrote them
all in perfect metre."

The fragments of a drama, in blank verse, said to have been
written at the age of fourteen, which Hallam Tennyson
printed in the *Memoir*,[2] sustain this estimate. Indeed, one
echoes the wonder of the translator of Plato that "the whelp
could have known such things." The sentiments, characterization, and nature background are an excellent parody of
Byronic "grandeur and gloom"; the diction is surprising
for its precision and adequacy, and the blank verse shows a
notable juvenile instinct for the metre,—an observance, moreover, not only of the normal syllabication and accent, which

[2] *Memoir*, I, 23.

are carried out with due regularity, but also of the usual
licenses such as occasional beginning inversion, double and
weak endings, interspersed short lines of three measures, and
enjambement. All of these variations are managed after the
approved fashion of the older drama. Another early poem,
The Coach of Death, has a considerable stock of horrific
images, with a metre and manner drawn partly from the old
ballads, and may have owed something to such jocular dia-
bolisms as Coleridge's *The Devil's Walk* and Byron's *The
Devil's Drive.* The inclusion of this poem in Tennyson's
Cambridge repertory with old ballads, such as *Helen of
Kirkconnel,* seems to suggest, however, that it was in his own
mind associated with them rather than with more modern
poems of similar aim. The compositions of this period have
echoes, also, of Milton and of Scott.

The facility and correctness in verse-making and the same
literary influences which appear in his earliest compositions,
as far as they have come down to us, mark the contributions
of Alfred Tennyson to *Poems by Two Brothers,* his first
printed issue, made in 1827, in conjunction with his brother
Charles. Alfred Tennyson's compositions were written
''between the ages of fifteen and seventeen''; those of his
brother Charles between sixteen and eighteen. The still
older brother, Frederick, contributed four poems undis-
tinguished by any special qualities. By this time, Alfred
Tennyson had apparently dropped the heroic couplet and
temporarily given up blank verse,—no example of either ap-
pearing among his contributions to this volume, though a
number of the pieces credited to Charles Tennyson are in
''the regular Popeian metre''.

Curiously enough, there is already a differentiation as to
metre in the verses of the two lads. Charles Tennyson is
fond of the heroic couplet, the heroic quatrain, and the octosyllabic couplet; whereas the younger brother employs the
first of these never, and the others seldom. He generally prefers the iambic of four measures with alternate rhyme, or
irregularly rhymed and crossed with other lines of irregular

length. Sometimes he uses the broken septenarius or ballad stanza; sometimes, the septenarius in couplets. He has one poem in the Spenserian stanza; one is in a ten line stanza of two heroic quatrains closed by a couplet, the last line being an alexandrine; one is a sequence of Shaksperean sonnet stanzas except that each fourteenth line is an alexandrine. The anapaestic metres which enjoyed such favor with Byron and Moore are frequently used. Anapaestic trimeter, cross-rhymed, with a couplet to close the stanza, is a favorite; while one of the most noticeable and characteristic metres is the anapaestic of four measures, rhymed in couplets. This metre is obviously derived from Byron. There are not fewer than five poems in the volume which are directly reminiscent in subject, rhetoric, imagery, and movement, of Byron's *The Destruction of Sennacherib*. Compare, for example, the opening couplet of Byron's poem with the following couplet which begins the *Lamentations of the Peruvians:*

> The foes of the east have come down on our shore
> And the state and the strength of Peru are no more.

The following passage concludes a poem on *The Expedition of Nadir Shah into Hindostan:*

> The shriek of the orphan, the lone widow's wail,
> The groans of the children are loud on the gale,
> For the star of thy glory is blasted and wan
> And withered the flower of thy fame Hindostan.

The influence of Byron on the poet at this stage is indicated not only in his choice of metres, but in the character of his diction, his apostrophic rhetoric, his choice of vast, tenebrous, warlike, historical, oriental, scriptural, and Ossianic subjects; his habit of appending classical mottoes and semi-learned annotations to his poems, (the latter, perhaps a Georgian, rather than a merely Byronic, affectation), and finally, most clearly of all, in the gloomy, misanthropic, and remorseful sentiments of a large proportion of the poems.

> Oh 'tis a fearful thing to glance
> Back on the gloom of misspent years,

and

> I would I'd been all heartless, then
> I might have sinn'd like other men.

are among the reflections of this preciously reared lad of ''between 15 and 17 years of age''.

Imaginative power is indicated, if Coleridge is sound when he says, ''A second promise of genius is the choice of subjects very remote from the private interests and circumstances of the writer himself. At least I have found that where the subject is taken immediately from the author's personal sensations and experiences, the excellence of a particular poem is but an equivocal mark, and often a fallacious pledge of genuine poetic power.''[3]

On either of the two grounds which have been adduced from Coleridge, the poems of Alfred Tennyson in this volume may be said to constitute a higher pledge of future poetic achievement than those of his brother. Imitative as the poems of Alfred Tennyson are,—mere parodies of Byron in many instances,—they show a large free interest in remote, grand and unfortunate personages, a turn for the gloomy picturesque in nature and for the significance of great events and enterprises,—and they show an absorbing delight in sweetness and resonance of language, and the roll of rhythm, ''together with the power of producing'' them. In all these particulars, his verses are more impressive and more harmonious with themselves than those of his brother, which show more thoughtfulness, humour, and good sense, and far less fusion and urgency of the poetic spirit. Another feature of Alfred Tennyson's contributions to this volume which is probably worth noting is the almost total absence of poems of amorous origin or design. Tennyson's earliest exercises, then, are indicative of a natural bent toward rhythmical expression, a gift of facile mimicry, and an early appetite for

---

[3]*Biog. Lit.*, Chap. XII, p. 376.

literary fame. They were, of course, too boyish in every
particular to be taken very seriously in a history of his style.
The influence of Byron was destined to pass rapidly away.
Many of the characteristics of the poet's next phase are hardly
to be detected here. Despite unmistakable promise, it was
clearly a fond parent and rash critic who declared upon
such evidence: "If Alfred die, one of our greatest poets
will have gone."

The next section of Tennyson's work, though still immature in taste and largely experimental in manner, is fully
significant and will reward attentive study. We have here
the borderland between boyish mimicry and that rich assimi-
lativeness which characterizes his mature style. This period
embraces *The Lover's Tale*, the prize poem, *Timbuctoo*, the
Poems, Chiefly Lyrical of 1830, and several fugitive pieces.
The Lover's Tale, written in 1827, was printed in 1832, but
not published. This version is accessible in the piratical
reprints of R. H. Shepherd. *Timbuctoo* was published in
1829, and is therefore accessible in an authorized text. These
two poems are in blank verse and, together with *Œnone*,
are discussed in a subsequent chapter upon Tennyson's experiments in that form. The poems of the 1830 volume
seem to have been composed, for the most part, during
Tennyson's residence at Cambridge; a large number of them
were afterward suppressed and therefore do not appear in
the familiar editions of the complete poems.

Of *Timbuctoo* and *The Lover's Tale*, Tennyson declared
near the end of his life that they "are in no way imitative
of any poet," adding, "As far as I know, nothing of mine
after the date of *Timbuctoo* was imitative." In the limited
sense in which he employed the term "imitative", this is perhaps true; but it seems more just to say that Tennyson's
imitative period closes with the volume of 1830. Two or three
pieces in that volume have the specific Tennysonian manner
throughout and are as original as any creation of after years;
but the words of Fitzgerald contain the truth of the matter,
"Two years afterward, he took his ground", that is, in the

volume of 1832-3. The poems of the later volume contain, in phrase and subject matter, more frequent reminiscences of anterior English poetry than ever crept into Tennyson's poems afterward; there are large traces of actual imitation, possibly unconscious, but sufficiently obvious and direct, in *Timbuctoo* and in *Poems, Chiefly Lyrical*.[4]

Most artists commence with copies from specific works by others, only gradually learning to transcribe and synthesize from nature. Tennyson offers no exception to this practice; on the contrary, he is peculiarly one of those poets whose talent owed its inspiration and growth to the influence of others. In his boyish period, as we have just seen, his range was relatively narrow; especially he came under the direct sway of one writer, of Byron. Further, an entire poem frequently resembles a specific composition and resembles it, simultaneously, in several respects, as in subject, in diction, and in metre. In the period we are now considering his method is more synthetic. A particular composition rarely can be traced to a specific model. Items of resemblance are scattered and are mingled with sketches from nature, with original fancies and reflections, the phrases are less frequently reminiscent, and there are more novel and characteristic

---

[4] In entering upon the imitative phase of Tennyson's poetry in this period a word is needed, not of apology, but of caution. It seems difficult for critics to agree upon a proper discrimination between an attribution of literary indebtedness and an accusation of literary theft. And beyond question, in such cases, an obligation of utmost precision of statement lies upon the critic. But when such precision of statement is observed and is met by candor of interpretation, there ought never to be any serious danger of confusion between the kind of literary indebtedness which is entirely creditable to a writer, particularly a young writer, and that mean form of literary freebooting which goes by the name of plagiarism. Tennyson himself was somewhat sensitive, perhaps even "touchy", on this score, and some rather spirited deliverances on the subject are recorded of him. He was of course honest in his indignation, and his indignation may have been justified by the far-fetched parallelisms between his works and those of former writers which were sometimes pointed out, and by the spirit in which such likenesses sometimes were noted. Nevertheless, it would be folly to maintain that there were not, in poems like *Timbuctoo* and numerous poems of the early volumes, many and distinct reminiscences of passages in preceding English poetry. The common method of disposing of such resemblances on the part of those

collocations of sound. In short the poet is beginning to evolve a language and a music of his own,—or at least his own ideal of these. And not only are his literary sources more various and less directly levied upon; they are, also, more remote. Tennyson's indebtedness in this period to his immediate forerunners in English poetry, and to Coleridge and Keats in particular, has had more than sufficient notice by his critics. Since Lockhart's time Tennyson's resemblance to Keats has become a commonplace of Tennyson criticism and the influence of Keats upon his early poems has been too readily assumed. More recently Churton Collins gave currency to this idea, and in addition exaggerated Tennyson's obligation to Coleridge.[5] Now, an examination of the poetic diction which Tennyson employed in these poems and of the parallelisms of phrase in which they abound, indicate that he drew far more copiously from the older English poets, from Milton especially, and from Shakspere, than from his immediate predecessors. The direct influence of Coleridge has been grossly overstated and the likeness to Keats does not become conspicuous until we reach the poems of the 1833 volume. And before any strong influence of Keats became operative, Tennyson was already far advanced toward his own assured style and had gone as far as he was to go in the direct utilization of English models.[6] By that time,

---

who regard the observation of them as invidious or futile, is to treat them as coincidences. (For example, Palgrave remarked that "Not a little ingenious labour has also wasted itself in the attempt to trace supposed previous authorities for this or that passage in Tennyson's poetry." *Personal Recollections,* appended to the *Life.*) Taken individually, such resemblances may easily seem, may indeed actually be, coincidental; it is when reminiscences from the same and similar sources are added to each other in considerable numbers that the theory of coincidence fails, and it becomes plain that one mind or style owes to another a debt of which the most carefully garnered evidence of parallel passages gives but a clumsy record. Every reader who has analyzed literature from this standpoint knows how diffusive such resemblances frequently are, and that actual repetitions of phrase may be only the more ponderable part of the evidence upon which one may rely for a confident ascription of literary influence.

[5] *The Early Poems of Alfred, Lord Tennyson,* etc. N. Y. and Lond. 1900.

[6] For a fuller notice of Tennyson's *Early Diction* and his reminiscences of English poetry, see Appendix A, p. 225.

he was reaching toward sources still more remote from contemporary fashions and interests, toward the ancient classics.
His poems, so far as they resemble those of Keats, resemble
them by analogy, rather than through imitation. Tennyson
and Keats were somewhat similar products of the forces of
Elizabethanism, of mediaevalism, of classicism, and of the
"return to nature" which were at work about them both.
To regard Keats as very much more than an immediate fore-
runner of Tennyson in the midst of a swarm of poets of
similar breed, but inferior vitality, is to falsify historical
perspective. So far as Tennyson's poems previous to 1833
are concerned, they have not even as much in common with
Keats as they have with more nearly contemporary but less
conspicuous writers.

Tennyson differed from countless mediocrities of the period
mainly in the larger scope and the deeper residence of his
talent. In him, as in the poetical world at large, Shelley
was rapidly displacing Byron; the wholesome influence of
Wordsworth was beginning to tell mightily, as yet chiefly on
his subject matter; and he was the focus of a wide diversity
of influences proceeding all the way from Chaucer to Landor,
including poets as unlike as Gray and Burns, including
Chatterton, and including, too, mediaeval ballad and romance,
and even French and Italian versions thereof. His trifling
sensuous knickknackeries may be fairly paralleled in Leigh
Hunt; his idyllic studies had been foreshadowed by Southey;
his ballad and mediaeval studies are not altogether unlike
those of Motherwell; the orientalism of Byron and Moore,
which still held sway over many smaller ones, had not yet
entirely lost the charm for his mind which a dozen contributions to the *Poems by Two Brothers* attested; and the prettiness that weakened his 1830 volume is distinguished only
by occasional genius,—which to be sure is a great deal—
from the milk-and-watery post-Byronism of L. E. L. and other
annualists and magazine nonentities of the time.

But the external force which, above all others, dominated
Tennyson's "Cantab" period was the new style of Elizabeth-

anism then and there regnant. This was an Elizabethanism
closer to Milton than to Spenser, founded on a new and better
understanding of Shakspere and the later dramatists; an
Elizabethanism at once more scholarly and more imaginative
than that of the 18th century; the Elizabethanism of Coleridge, Lamb, and Hazlitt in criticism; of Darley, Beddoes,
Wells, Horne, and numerous others in poetry and drama.
Only, Tennyson signalized his more imaginative absorption
of the Elizabethans—his intrinsic originality one may say—
in that he did not directly imitate them so much as turn
them to his use. His art forms, that is, the designs of his
poems, are not, generally speaking, the art forms of the
Elizabethans. He caught, at times, something of their tone,
and he turned to his own purposes what they could teach
him in devices of diction and metre. And the congeries
of elements which he eventually succeeded in harmonizing
differed from those of any preceding writer. Unlike Keats
and other romanticists, he owed small allegiance to Spenser
who, he somewhere tells us, was not much known or admired
by him. There is little trace of Spenser's diffuse romantic
fashion in the Tennyson of this period or of any other. But
Shakspere affected him mightily. There are traces, also,
of Marlowe, of Chapman, of Fletcher, and of the seventeenth
century lyrical writers, Vaughan, for example; but the
stylistic force mainly supplementary to Shakspere's, if indeed
it was not properly the fundamental, and Shakspere's the
supplemental influence, was that of Milton.[7] The influence
of Milton was lasting, too, and deep, in that he encountered
in Milton, suggestive infusions of still remoter springs from
which both drew,—the fountain-heads of Homer, Theocritus,
and Virgil.

-----

[7] For evidence in support of this thesis, see this study, Chapter IV,
Mastering Blank Verse and Appendix A, *Tennyson's Early Diction.*

CHAPTER II

EXPERIMENTS IN METRE: POEMS, CHIEFLY LYRICAL

To those of us who have become accustomed to the easy fullness of Tennyson's style in the poems of his best period, it is a discipline in the homiletics of art to be confronted with the stages by which he came to this almost too impeccable balance of richness and restraint. One scarcely knows whether he is more astonished by the surprising defects of the earlier work or by the care and artistic intelligence with which these defects were overcome. And, as soon as one examines systematically the metrical characteristics of the three issues of 1830, 1833, and 1842, at least one general principle of the poet's procedure becomes evident. The principle which directed his changes in versification was that which dominated him in the correction of his poetical language. Just as he conventionalized his poetic diction, so Tennyson, in this period, normalized his metres. His most noticeable progress in this direction was during the critical epoch of his artistic life which followed the publication of the 1833 volume. It was after the relative failure of the two earlier volumes that Tennyson settled himself in bitter earnest to conquer the difficulties of his art, and it was then that he seems to have been driven to find the way of his salvation in conformity to some of its fundamental conventions. But there is also appreciable progress in this direction between the collections of 1830 and 1833. This is clearly apparent in his metrical practice.

There is a reference to Tennyson's early poems in the *Table Talk* of Coleridge which has been rather frequently mentioned by commentators on the younger poet, but ordinarily without the marks of respect which it deserves. This passage is referred to by Lord Tennyson and a portion of it is quoted,[1] but in such a manner as to indicate that the author of the Life held it somewhat cheaply. And he repeats, apparently with approbation, a comment made by his father in which the substance of the passage is waved aside as if it were merely a casual old gentleman's literary twaddle, based upon insufficient observation and unintelligent reading. This is the passage in which Coleridge referred to Tennyson as a young man who "has begun to write verses without very well understanding what metre is". Extraordinary folly, one might think off-hand, concerning a writer whom we have come to regard as nothing if not a master in the modulation of poetic speech. And yet if this off-hand remark of Coleridge's be considered curiously in connection with the facts which are brought to light by a close study of the poems with which they are concerned, not, probably, the *Poems, Chiefly Lyrical* of 1830, but the still later volume of 1833, they will be found to be laden with critical wisdom. They are in fact a signal example of that flashing insight which now and then enlightens us from the midst of much dull and unprofitable prosing in the utterances of the Sage of Highgate. According to the report of H. N. Coleridge, S. T. Coleridge said, in full[2]: "I have not read through all Mr. Tennyson's poems, which have been sent to me; but I think there are some things of a good deal of beauty in what I have seen. *The misfortune is, that he has begun to write verses without very well understanding what metre is.* Even if you write in a known and approved metre, the odds are, if you are not a metrist yourself, that you will not write harmonious verses; but to deal in new metres without considering what metre means and requires, is preposterous. *What I would, with many wishes for success, prescribe to Tennyson,—indeed, without it he can never become a poet in act,—is to write for the next two or three years in none*

---

[1] *Memoir*, I, 50.
[2] *Table Talk*, p. 445.

but one or two well-known and strictly defined metres, such
as the heroic couplet, the octave stanza, or the octosyllabic
measure of the *Allegro* and *Penseroso.* He would, probably,
thus get imbued with a sensation, if not a sense, of metre,
without knowing it, just as Eton boys get to write such good
Latin verse by conning Ovid and Tibullus. As it is, I can
scarcely scan his verses."

Tennyson was perhaps justified in his statement, "Coleridge did not know much about my poems." It is quite
possible that the venerable critic was, in giving the advice
italicized above, making a somewhat off-hand application
of a general principle with which he had been long acquainted.
At any rate, the principle was sound, and the advice, good.
But Tennyson, always sensitive to adverse criticism, seems
to have developed in his old age the habit of taking the de-
fensive whenever his earlier poems were concerned, and in
this frame of mind, he failed to see, perhaps, how both just
and prophetic the words of Coleridge had been. We have
noticed Tennyson's own statement late in life, when ap-
proached on a different tack, that he had been "nearer
thirty than twenty" before he "was anything of an artist."
If, now, we examine his actual practice during the years
under discussion we shall see that he did actually follow,
longo intervallo, very much the course which Coleridge "prescribed" in the conversation recorded above, although it is
not probable that he could have had, at this time, any knowledge of the old man's remarks.

Regarded from this point of view, the metres of the three
successive volumes of 1830, 1833, and 1842, furnish a significant contrast with each other. For sake of brevity and
clearness, I will first state generally these relations. The
1830 poems are, as a whole, strangely and rashly anarchic.
There is, throughout, the most admired disorder of wild and
irregular metres. Scarcely any two poems are in the same
metre with each other, and only a small proportion of the
individual poems are systematically strophied throughout.
Such stanzaic schemes as are adopted are usually the in-

vention of the poet and are frequently anything but simple.
Again, when two poems are more or less parallel in theme
and are, roughly, in the same form, the parallelism of form
is seldom respected, but is rudely and, as a rule, damagingly
infringed upon—that is, the poet loses more than he gains
by his sacrifice of the self-imposed system. It is not altogether accidental that in two or three conspicuous instances
in this volume where the poet adopted and adhered to a
systematic and comparatively simple pattern of verse, he
was rewarded for his faithfulness by an unusual and lasting
success, as in the case of *Mariana*. But in a large proportion
of the individual poems, the metre is quite unregulated
except by the caprice of the poet's ear, and even when a
provisional strophe has been adopted, it is no uncommon
occurrence for it to be violated in some unsystematic or
unexpected manner. The poet lays a rude hand even on the
sonnet and mutilates it most Gothically. Tennyson could
hardly have been ignorant; he must, therefore, have been
either remarkably careless, or remarkably impatient of the
ordinary restraints of metrical and stanzaic form, restraints
which were the legacy of centuries of the experience of genius,
and which the most distinguished of his predecessors in the
art of English poetry had seldom neglected with impunity.

But that he soon tired of "this unchartered freedom" and
made way to escape "the weight of chance desires" is clear
from the evidence of the 1833 poems. There are far fewer
really "wild" metres in the 1833 volume. The poet is still
inclined to invent his stanzaic system for each new poem
rather than to accept any settled and well-known form, but
having once adopted a strophe, he is more disposed to observe
it consistently throughout a piece and he is far more faithful
to the metre in which the poem chances to be composed.

The new pieces which were added to the collection brought
out in 1842 carried this development a step farther, and the
tendency was equally pronounced in the selection and revision
of the old pieces which were reissued at that time. Practically
every new poem in the 1842 edition was in some standard and

well-known metre and observed a definite stanzaic order of construction. The conventional form was usually modified in some minute particular, but this modulation was always simple, organic, and consistently observed. Correspondingly the revision of the earlier poems made for the regulation of metrical vagrancies and the standardization of strophic form.

The volume entitled, *Poems, Chiefly Lyrical,* contained 56 poems of varying, but none of considerable, length. Of these 56 poems somewhat less than half, 24, to be exact, were reissued in 1842. Of the poems not reprinted in 1842, 8 were restored in subsequent editions of the collected works, under the division, *Juvenilia.* All but two of these last were first reprinted in 1872; but *The Deserted House* and *The Sea Fairies* were restored in intervening editions, *The Deserted House* in 1848, and *The Sea Fairies,* greatly altered and improved, in 1853. One other poem, the *National Song* ("There is no land like England"), was by Tennyson inserted in *The Foresters,* 1892. At that time, a chorus appropriate to the new environment was substituted for the old one; otherwise the poem was reproduced without change.[3] There remain, then, 23 poems whose reissue was never authorized by the poet. Except in commentaries, they were never reprinted during his life.[4]

Of the 24 poems that were again brought out in 1842, 10 have some strophic form, 1 is roughly strophic, and 13 have rambling rhyme schemes frequently combined with irregular metres and can, in no sense, be considered strophic. Of the 10 stanzaic poems, 6 are in patterns based on the four stress iambic movement, as may be seen in the accompanying table.

---

[3] Particularity is indulged in regard to this poem, for the reason that Collins failed to note the fact of its reappearance in *The Foresters.* Also in the list of the poems, *Introd.* p. viii, he fails to place the appropriate mark after the poem, *We Are Free;* although the fact of its revival in the *Juvenilia* of 1872 is duly recorded in the note on the poem, p. 296. Thackeray's cartoon on the lines from this poem,

> There are no maids like English maids
> So beautiful as they be.

deserves to be remembered.

[4] They have since been reprinted by Collins, *Tennyson's Early Poems,* London, 1900, and by J. C. Thomson, *Tennyson's Suppressed Poems,* N. Y. and London, 1907.

STANZAIC TABLE (1830)

In Regular Metre

Metre	Title	Regular Scheme	Systematic variation
4 x a.....	*Mariana*.....	ababcddc $\overline{efef}$ R	
"	*The Owl*......	aba $\overline{bb}$ cc	
"	*Second Song*.	"	Initial truncation.
"	*A Character* .	abcbca	
"	*Oriana*.......	a R a R aa R a R................................	
"	*The Sleeping Beauty*.....	ababcdcd	
5 x a.....	*Sonnet to J. M. K*.....	$\Big\{$ abbacaac................................... dededd	
		In Irregular metre	
Troch ...	*A Dirge*......	a^4 b^4 b^4 Rc^2 a^4 c^4 Rc^2	catalectic
Iamb....	*The Poet*	a^5 b^3 a^5 b^2	
Ia a) Anapaest	*Song* ("*A spirit haunts*")	a^4 a^4 b^2 c^4 c^4 b^1 b^4 a^2 $\overline{s^4\ d^4\ s^4\ d^4}$ R	Beg. inversion in refrain.

Not all of the poems in the four stress verse need be discussed, but certain pieces deserve particular mention.

The strophe of *Mariana* is an excellent invention, and it is admirably managed. We have first a quatrain with cross-rhyme, then, a quatrain in which the middle pair are spanned by the rhyme of one and four, (exterior-interior rhyme) and finally another quatrain, cross-rhymed, as refrain. The refrain is slightly and subtly modified in the final stanza of the poem.

> With blackest moss the flower-plots
> Were thickly crusted, one and all:
> The rusted nails fell from the knots
> That held the pear to the garden-wall.
> The broken sheds look'd sad and strange:
> Unlifted was the clinking latch;
> Weeded and worn the ancient thatch
> Upon the lonely moated grange.

> She only said, "My life is dreary,
>   He cometh not," she said;
> She said, "I am aweary, aweary,
>   I would that I were dead!"

It may be noticed that in the second quatrain of this strophe, we have Tennyson's first systematic use of the enclosed rhyme arrangement which he afterward adopted for the stanza of *In Memoriam* and many of the shorter poems.. As early, however, as some of the *Poems by Two Brothers,* he had shown a marked liking for this arrangement, and it crops out frequently in his irregular poems of this volume.

The Ballad of Oriana is unusual with its strophe of five verses on one rhyme, set off by the word, *Oriana,* introduced as a refrain after the first, second, fourth, and fifth lines, as follows:

> My heart is wasted with my woe,
>   Oriana.
> There is no rest for me below,
>   Oriana.
> When the long dun wolds are ribb'd with snow,
> And loud the Norland whirlwinds blow,
>   Oriana,
> Alone I wander to and fro,
>   Oriana.

The *Sonnet to J. M. K.* suggests the Italian model; but the rhyme scheme is imperfectly followed.

The strophe of *The Poet,* in iambic movement, with the scheme $a^5 b^3 a^5 b^2$, points forward to the stanzas afterward invented for *The Palace of Art* and *A Dream of Fair Women.*

> The poet in a golden clime was born,
>   With golden stars above;
> Dower'd with the hate of hate, the scorn of scorn,
>   The love of love.

The *Sleeping Beauty* in four stress iambic, with two cross-rhymed quatrains joined to make the strophe, anticipates favorite strophe forms of the 1842 volume.

The most complicated stanzaic pattern among the poems of this group is that of the *Song* ("A spirit haunts the year's last hours"). The poem consists of two strophes of twelve lines each, of which the last four, as in *Mariana*, constitute a refrain. But, in contrast to the stanza of *Mariana*, the verses are of irregular length, the rhyme scheme is involved, and the rhythm is changeable. There is a complicated movement of iambs and anapaests, modulated by inversions and spondees, and there is a modified balance between the strophes. So involved a plan can hardly be made clear without an illustration; the first stanza follows.

> A spirit haunts the year's last hours
> Dwelling amid these yellowing bowers:
>   To himself he talks;
> For at eventide, listening earnestly,
> At his work you may hear him sob and sigh
>   In the walks;
>   Earthward he boweth the heavy stalks
> Of the mouldering flowers:
>   Heavily hangs the broad sunflower
>   Over its grave i' the earth so chilly;
>   Heavily hangs the hollyhock,
>   Heavily hangs the tiger-lily.

This was one of Tennyson's poems which was extravagantly admired by Edgar Poe. The irregularity of the stanza is justified by its effectiveness; but such triumphs are rare among Tennyson's departures from simple forms.

The composition characterized above as "roughly strophic" is the well-known *Recollections of the Arabian Nights*. This poem is marked off by a changeable refrain into divisions of eleven lines, but the rhyme within these divisions is unsystematic. The metre is four-stress iambic, with free initial truncation after the manner of *L'Allegro* and *Il Penseroso*.

Little need be said of the non-strophic poems. Nine of the thirteen are mainly in iambic movement; of these *Claribel* is in trimeter with much double-rhyme; *Isabel, Love and Death, Circumstance,* are in five-stress metre; the remaining poems are irregular both in rhyme and in verse length. The

Ode to Memory deserves some comment. It is in what is sometimes called "irregular ode form." Collins thought this
poem was "modelled on" Coleridge's *Song of the Pixies*.
The suggestion, if not absurd, is certainly too strongly phrased.
Most readers will find the influence of Milton more obvious
than that of Coleridge. The versification is suggestive of the
five-stress and three-stress iambics of *Lycidas*. That poem
unquestionably influenced the phraseology.[5] At times the
cadences of the metre seem reminiscent of Wordsworth's *Intimations*.[6] The following extract is a favorable example of
Tennyson's style and metre in this poem :

> Whilome thou camest with the morning mist,
>   And with the evening cloud,
> Showering thy gleaned wealth into my open breast,
> (Those peerless flowers which in the rudest wind
>   Never grow sere,
> When rooted in the garden of the mind,
>   Because they are the earliest of the year).
>   Nor was the night thy shroud.
> In sweet dreams softer than unbroken rest
> Thou leadest by the hand thine infant Hope.
> The eddying of her garments caught from thee
> The light of thy great presence; and the cope
>   Of the half-attained futurity,
>   Though deep not fathomless,
> Was cloven with the million stars which tremble
> O'er the deep mind of dauntless infancy.
> Small thought was there of life's distress;
> For sure she deem'd no mist of earth could dull
> Those spirit-thrilling eyes so keen and beautiful:
> Sure she was nigher to heaven's spheres,
> Listening the lordly music flowing from
>   The illimitable years.

The trochaic movement appears in *Lilian, Adeline,* and *The
Poet's Mind,* though the last mentioned poem becomes anapaestic toward the close,—a shift of movement frequently
affected by Tennyson at this time. Frequently he combines

---

[5] Cf. Appendix A, p. 236.

[6] *Ibid.,* p. 238. It is not unlikely that the *Intimations* may have helped
to suggest, as well, the germ-thought of this poem.

with the change of movement an increase of verse-length toward the end of a poem. A very irregular metre of general anapaestic effect is employed in *The Merman,* and practically the same movements are reproduced in *The Mermaid;* but perfect balance is not attempted and there is no genuine strophic effect.

Some distinctions as to versification are to be noted between those poems which were retained in the 1842 collection and those which were either temporarily, or finally suppressed. Seven of the thirty-two suppressed poems observe a regular scheme of rhyme and metre, with a few sporadic freedoms. In this class I include *Elegiacs,* republished in *Juvenilia,* 1872, with the title *Leonine Elegiacs.* Three songs, "I' the glooming light," "The lintwhite and the throstle-cock," "Every day hath its night," have each an exceedingly complex pattern, and not one of these was ever reprinted. *Chorus* (*in an unpublished drama written very early*) was also excluded from later publications. Two others, *We are Free* and *National Song,* are simple; they were revived, the former in the *Juvenilia* of 1872, the latter twenty years after that, or sixty years after their first publication, in *The Foresters.*[7]

The sonnets, with the one exception noted above, were remorselessly excised, and with them went a number of other poems in 5xa metre. Perhaps nothing reflects so unfavorably upon Tennyson's "sense for metre"[8] at this period as the hodge-podge of heroic lines which he frequently lumped together in masses resembling the sonnet shape. It is rash to conjecture on such a matter, but it is hard to resist a speculation that in many of these cases the poet started to make a sonnet, and then, like a hasty or unskilled potter, finding a misshapen vessel on his hands, impatiently finished it off or set it regretfully aside. Later, he tossed such specimens with less compunction to the shards. One sonnet, that *To J. M. K.,* and two of the other poems of this class, *Circumstance,*

---

[7] See above, p. 27.

[8] At almost the same age and stage, Keats wrote *On First Looking into Chapman's Homer.*

and *Love and Death,* he re-exhibited in 1842; later, in 1872, he made salvage of *The Kraken.* Eight others, including four imperfect sonnets, and the poem, *Love,* which is roughly, a sonnet sequence in three parts, he preferred that the public should forget. The same was true of *The Mystic,* his one blank-verse poem in this collection, if we except six lines at the beginning of *The Sea Fairies,* which was likewise held back till much later.[9]

There remain fifteen poems in irregular movements and without systematic rhyme-scheme. Some of these are roughly, but none of them perfectly, strophic in form; all are very imperfect. Some of them Tennyson saw fit to restore in his later issues of the *Juvenilia,*[10] but the rest deserved the oblivion which he was content should overtake them. An attention to the metrical characteristics of this group gives the touch of confirmation to one's impression of the unsettled state of Tennyson's taste at this period, its restless ambitiousness and impatience, its curious complex of elaborateness on the one hand with imperfection on the other.

The heterogeneity of theme in this collection has not escaped comment. In part, this was the mark of the era. The Muse of the period was "a capricious elf", with diverse fleeting fancies. The apathy of the counter-Revolution had set in. The most thrilling personalities of the decades just past had been suddenly stilled, or had turned their strength in less inspiring directions. Byron and Shelley and Keats were silent in the grave. Wordsworth, Coleridge, and Southey no longer led where young and ardent minds might follow. Carlyle, who was to challenge the time and of its spiritual perplexity and unrest was to give so telling a characterization in his *Life of Sterling,* had not yet lifted his manly voice to audibility, and Ruskin was a child at Herne Hill. To be sure Byron still held sway in some quarters, and Shelley and

---

[9] See above, p. 27.

[10] These are, *Supposed Confessions of a Second Rate Sensitive Mind Not In Unity With Itself; Nothing Will Die; All Things Will Die; The Deserted House; The Sea Fairies;* the last, much changed.

Keats were coming to be much admired; but all these writers had died before reaching their acme, and they lacked the compelling force of living and growing personalities. In this interregnum, many young poets fell by the way, dissipating themselves in romantic folly and outworn Elizabethanism, not having in them the poetic valour and volition which might strike the keynote of a new age. In Tennyson himself the poetic urge was, as yet, vacillating; its direction indeterminate. Just as he beat about for themes and manner, was by turns trifling and earnest, now reaching for the trumpet of the masters, and now dandling aesthetic fripperies of style, so, in the apparently remote concern of choosing his forms of poetic expression, he was loose, fickle, and uncertain. The succeeding chapters will undertake to give some insight into the methods by which Tennyson improved the design and enriched the substance of his poetry; but, particularly, they will endeavor to show how, by industrious experimentation and keen self-criticism, he gradually arrived at a standard of style together with a practice in versification which seemed to him best suited to sustain it.

CHAPTER III

REVISION AND STANDARDIZATION

The volume, entitled *Poems by Alfred Tennyson,* (printed in December 1832, but dated on the title page, 1833) added thirty new titles to the list of Tennyson's early poems. They were, on the average, of greater length and more substantial in content than the poems of the preceding issue. But that Tennyson was far from satisfied with the execution of his more ambitious designs in a number of these poems is indicated by his drastic revisions of style and metre before their reissue in 1842, and by his suppression of such poems as seemed of insufficient value, or as proved recalcitrant in the reviser's hand. Fourteen of the poems in the 1833 collection were kept back when the new selections were made for the 1842 issue. Most of the suppressed poems were short. All of the 1833 sonnets, seven in number, were held back, though all except two of these saw the light in subsequent collections. One was included in the *Juvenilia* of 1871, and four were republished among *Early Sonnets* in the edition of 1872. The lyric *To—* ("All good things have not kept aloof") was altered slightly and added to *Juvenilia,* in 1871; in 1884, *Rosalind* was included, and *Kate*[1] in 1895, after the poet's death; but the last mentioned poem does not appear in the more recent editions. *The Hesperides* was reprinted in the *Memoir.* Thus, only four of the original 1833 poems failed of authorized republication.

Except *The Hesperides,* all the longer poems were retained in the 1842 collection; most of these longer poems were greatly changed, and, in parts, practically rewritten. The poems treated so were *The Lady of Shalott, Mariana in the South,*

---

[1] Collins's note, *E. P.,* p. 306.

The Miller's Daughter, Œnone, and *The Palace of Art. A Dream of Fair Women, The Lotus Eaters, The May Queen,* and *New Year's Eve* received important alterations and additions. The poems which were reissued with comparatively few changes were *Eleanore, Fatima, The Sisters, To*—(introducing *The Palace of Art*), *Margaret, The Death of the Old Year,* and *To J. S.*

There is a clear advance toward regularity in the metres of the 1833 volume and a further clear advance is observable in the suppressions and revisions by which its contents were subsequently modified. The appended table will afford the reader a conspectus of the metrical phenomena of which the descriptions that follow will be complicated and necessarily somewhat tedious.

Not counting *Œnone* and *To*—(introducing *The Palace of Art*) which were in blank verse and have subsequent consideration, there remain twenty-eight poems, of which only six were wanting in definite strophic form.   These were *Eleanore, Margaret, The Lotus Eaters, The Hesperides, Rosalind,* and *Kate.* Of these, the first three, as we have seen, were retained in 1842.   Of the suppressed poems, *Rosalind* and *Kate* like most of the early poems of similar content are mainly in 4xa metre and mainly in couplets, but, the first especially, variegated by plentiful license of movement, verse-length, and rhyme arrangement.   Of *The Hesperides* Tennyson probably would have said, as he sometimes wistfully did of his partial failures, that it contains "many good things".   In addition to the flowing blank verse with which it opens, there are numerous passages in it of considerable rhythmic beauty: but it is so irresponsible in movement, verse-length, and rhyme-scattering as to be perplexing, and, at times, irritating, to the ear.   This alone would be sufficient to account for its permanent exclusion from the collected poems.   Tennyson, evidently, did not consider it worthy of the laborious rehandling which he gave to the other long poems of the same volume.

METRICAL AND STANZAIC TABLE (1833)

Metre	Title	Rhyme-scheme	First republication
5 xa	Œnone	blank verse	1842
5 xa	To—(Introducing The Palace of Art)	blank verse	1842
Irreg	Eleanore	non-strophic	1842
Irreg	Margaret	non-strophic	1842
Irreg. 4xa	Rosalind	non-strophic	1884
Irreg. 4xa	Kate	non-strophic	1895
Iambic	The Hesperides	blank verse ⎫	Memoir
Irreg	Song	non-strophic ⎭	
5 xa	Seven sonnets	various arrangements	4 in '71; 1 in '72.
Iambic	Song -(Who can say)	$a^2\ a^2\ a^4\ b^2\ b^2\ c^5\ c^3\ c^4$	Never repub.
4 xa	O Darling Room	a a a a a a	Never repub.
Trochaic catalectic	To Christopher North	$a^4\ R^2\ a^4\ R^2\ b^4\ b^4\ R^2\ a^4\ R^2$ (R: '- x'-xx)	Never repub.
4 xa	To—(All good things)	a b a h b	1871
Iambic	The Lotus Eaters	Spenserians ⎫	1842
Irreg	Choric Song	Irreg. ⎭	
Iambic	The Palace of Art	$a^5\ b^4\ a^5\ b^3$	1842
Iambic	A Dream of Fair Women	$a^5\ b^5\ a^5\ b^3$	1842
Ballad	The May Queen	$a^7\ a^7$	1842
Ballad	New Year's Eve	$a^7\ a^7$	1842
4 xa	Fatima	a a a a b b b	1842
Iambic	The Lady of Shalott	$a^4\ a^4\ a^4\ a^4\ R^4\ b^4\ b^4\ b^4\ R^3$	1842
Iambic	The Sisters	$a^4\ a^4\ R^4\ b^4\ b^4\ R^3$	1842
4 xa	To J. S.	a b a b	1842
4 xa	The Miller's Daughter	a b a b	1842
Iambic-anapaestic	The Death of the Old Year	$a^4\ b^4\ a^4\ a^4\ b^3\ \overset{R}{c^3\ d^3}\ d^3\ c^3$	1842
4 xa	Mariana in the South	a b a b c d d c $\overline{ef}$ef	1842

Like their companions of the earlier volume all the sonnets of this one were denied a place in the 1842 collection;
but a greater number, five in all,[2] were republished at a later
time.   The sonnets of 1833 show considerable progress toward
an observance of the conventional form.   The rows of couplets which frequently formed the closing six lines of the
earlier group now give way to the regulation sestet, usually
the three-rhymed form; but the octave has in only two cases
the prescribed rhyme scheme and in the seven sonnets there
are six different arrangements of the octave.   The modelling
of the thought, too, approximates more nearly, in a number
of instances, to that which we are accustomed to expect in
compositions which adopt this form.   But Tennyson never
mastered the sonnet; it baffled him to the end of his days.
Though it is only fair to say that he rarely returned to it
after this early period, it still remains a fact, that no single
composition by him in sonnet form takes a high rank among
his poems.

Of the remaining poems which failed to reappear in 1842,
one, the *Song* ("Who can say"), is only a catch in the manner of some of the trifling lyrics in the earlier volume.   Tennyson never saw fit to reprint it, and it may be considered
as negligible here.   Practically the same may be said of *O
Darling Room,* an ill-considered trifle of three six-line staves,
in octosyllabics, which made a Roman holiday for contemporary critics and continues to furnish merriment for
ghoulish commentators, who still, from time to time, insist
upon dragging it forth.   So slight a thing, so speedily with-
drawn, scarcely deserves the derision lavished upon it.   The
first and third stanzas are indeed sufficiently inane; but the
middle stave is not without charm of tint and melody:

> For I the Nonnenwerth have seen
> And Oberwinter's vineyards green.

Needless to say, these are not the verses generally chosen for
quotation, though Lockhart, with questionable generosity,

---

[2] See above, p. 35.

quoted it in full. *To Christopher North*, again, a nine-line quip, has had more than its due share of emphasis and may be set aside as of no particular importance to this history.

One only of the suppressed poems remains, and this is of some interest to the student of Tennyson's versification, *viz.*, the poem *To—*, which had for its first line in 1833,

> All good things have not kept aloof.

It consisted of seven five-line stanzas in four-stress iambics with the rhyme-scheme a b a b b.[3] When Tennyson revived this poem for insertion in the *Juvenilia* of 1871, he improved the shapeliness of the piece as a whole by excising the last two stanzas; and he improved the emphasis and the thinking of the first stanza by shifting the last line to the beginning, making only the necessary verbal changes of "my" for "but" and "but" for "all" in the first and second lines, respectively, so that now the poem opens:

> My life is full of weary days
> But good things have not kept aloof.

In making this shift, he violated the rhyme scheme of the first stanza, and this remains *absolutely the sole example* in which a later version of a revised poem is less consistent in its rhymed structure than was the original. But by 1871, it should be observed, Tennyson could afford to indulge a liberty which he would not have allowed himself in the revisions of 1833 to 1842.

Of the 16 poems which were reissued in 1842, then, two as we have noted were in blank verse. Two, *Margaret* and *Eleanor*, are of little significance, being reminiscent of the 1830 volume in substance, style, and metre; both were mainly in the four-stress iambic, the former regular in movement and tolerably so in rhyme distribution, the latter, in both respects, exceedingly free. There remain a dozen poems, all, except

---

[3] Another poem which must have been written about this time, though not published until 1865, is in the same stanza, *viz.*, *To a Mourner* ("Nature so far as in her lies"). See *Memoir*, II, 19.

the *Choric Song* which formed the bulk of *The Lotus Eaters,*
in definite strophic form.

The Lotus Eaters is *sui generis* as to form. The four
Spenserian stanzas with which it opens constitute Tennyson's
one published undertaking in that stanza after *Poems by Two
Brothers.* These are followed by a *Choric Song* which is
basically five-stress iambic in rhythm. Possibly we may
trace a continuation of the Spenserian rhythm in the frequency with which the rhythmic periods conclude with the
alexandrine,—a device for retardation in movement opposed
to Tennyson's usual practice in strophe building. The movement is varied by frequent initial truncation which produces
a trochaic effect and more rarely by anapaestic substitution,
and the rhyme arrangement is of the freest. But the poet's
ear is here at its best; the rhymes fall at happy intervals,
sometimes prolonging dreamily a single strain, sometimes
concluding it with a drowsy fall, and again linking a forward
swaying period to a preceding movement. Since no structural
system has been even remotely suggested, none is violated,
and we lend our hearts and spirits wholly "To the influence
of mild-minded melancholy" and to the eddying stream of
melody on which we are borne softly and irresistibly forward.
Supremely excellent, as he himself once confessed, only "in
slow metres", Tennyson finds himself in this poem and makes
his supreme use of the *rallentando* principle.

For the purpose of making this statement more intelligible,
let us note in detail the metrical scheme of the first stave
and then, more generally, the succeeding movements of the
poem. The scheme of the first stave is as follows: a^5 b^5 a^5
b^5 c^5 c^5 c^6 d^3 d^4 d^5 d^6. Familiar though the lines are, doubtless the reader will be glad to have under his eye the text of
this remarkably modulated passage:

> There is sweet music here that softer falls
> Than petals from blown roses on the grass,
> Or night-dews on still waters between walls
> Of shadowy granite, in a gleaming pass;
> Music that gentlier on the spirit lies,
> Than tir'd eyelids upon tir'd eyes;

Musiç that brings sweet sleep down from the blissful skies.
Here are cool mosses deep,
And thro' the moss the ivies creep,
And in the stream the long-leaved flowers weep,
And from the craggy ledge the poppy hangs in sleep.

Beginning with the five-stress iambic, the poet pursues this
movement steadily through six verses, then slows to an alexandrine, at the same time breathing-in the third successive
"*c*" rhyme; then he drops back to three stresses, hurrying-
in a new rhyme sound which he employs *four* successive times,
in each successive verse retarding the fall of the rhyme by one
beat, until finally, the fourth occurrence of the sound falls at
the end of the second alexandrine of the stave and thus
closes this movement.

In the second stave, the five-stress movement begins again
and persists through several verses; then a three-stress verse
drops in, then two three-stress verses; but ever the five-stress
theme recurs and finally the stave breathes its last in an alexandrine. The next opens with four-stress movement and
this continues throughout the stave, occasionally interrupted
by a five, and the stave closes on a four-stress line.   The fourth
stave opens boldly on a trochaic four-stress movement, subtly
anticipated by an initial truncation in the preceding. But
soon the original five-stress movement takes possession, and
the stave closes on an alexandrine.   Five, again, is mainly
five-stress with occasional four, and comes to rest with an alexandrine. Six does the same; only, here, the 1833 version
ended with the five-stress verse, lacking the fine concluding
alexandrine:

And eyes grown dim with gazing on the pilot-stars.

Seven has much the same movement, except that double rhymes
are more freely used and an additional suspension is given at
the end by doubling the alexandrine.

The 8th and last stave of the poem was subjected to one of
those masterly revisions by which Tennyson re-created so
many passages of the earlier poems while preparing them for

the re-issue of 1842. Originally, among numerous minor
blunders of style and metre, the poet had made the mistake
of dropping back to shorter movements and to the irregular
frequent rhyme, with the result of a complete breakdown both
in movement and in style. A dozen lines of the conclusion
will suffice for comparison with the improved version:

> We'll lift no more the shattered oar,
> No more unfurl the straining sail;
> With the blissful Lotos-eaters pale
> We will abide in the golden vale
> Of the Lotos-land till the Lotos fail;
> We will not wander more.
> Hark! how sweet the horned ewes bleat
> On the solitary steeps,
> And the merry lizard leaps,
> And the foam-white waters pour;
> And the dark pine weeps,
> And the lithe vine creeps,
> And the heavy melon sleeps
> On the level of the shore:
> Oh! islanders of Ithaca, we will not wander more,
> Surely, surely slumber is more sweet than toil, the shore
> Than labour in the ocean, and rowing with the oar,
> Oh! islanders of Ithaca, we will return no more.

As it stands now, the eighth stave is, as it were, the culminating movement of a fugue. Opening upon the basic five-
stress theme, soon, through initial truncation, the iambic gives
way to a trochaic rhythm, the rhymes are massed in *trios*, and
the verse is prolonged to a seven, and, in some cases, to an
eight-stress movement.[4]

Let us swear an oath, and keep it with an equal mind,
In the hollow Lotos-land to live and lie reclined
On the hills like Gods together, careless of mankind.
For they lie beside their nectar, and the bolts are hurl'd

---

[4] The capacities of the eight-stress, trochaic-catalectic line Tennyson
first systematically explored in *Locksley Hall*. Whether he first invented
the line for that poem or stumbled upon it during his revision of *The
Lotos Eaters*, it is probably impossible to discover. I incline to the latter
view. (See below p. 110 and Appendix B, where the origin of this metre
is discussed at length.)

Far below them in the valleys, and the clouds are lightly curl'd
Round their golden houses, girdled with the gleaming world:
Where they smile in secret, looking over wasted lands,
Blight and famine, plague and earthquake, roaring deeps and fiery
    sands,
Clanging fights, and flaming towns, and sinking ships and praying
    hands.
But they smile, they find a music centred in a doleful song
Steaming up, a lamentation and an ancient tale of wrong,
Like a tale of little meaning tho' the words are strong;
Chanted from an ill-used race of men that cleave the soil,
Sow the seed, and reap the harvest with enduring toil,
Storing yearly little dues of wheat, and wine and oil;
Till they perish and they suffer—some, 'tis whisper'd—down in hell
Suffer endless anguish, others in Elysian valleys dwell,
Resting weary limbs at last on beds of asphodel.
Surely, surely, slumber is more sweet than toil, the shore
Than labour in the deep mid-ocean, wind and wave and oar;
Oh rest ye, brother mariners, we will not wander more.

Each massive trio breaks forward with a plunge and goes staggering on with a long resounding roll precisely suited to the ideas with which the poem concludes.

This is one of Tennyson's triumphs in unsystematic verse. Nowhere else, among the early poems at least, does he control the irresponsibilities of irregular rhyme and metre with a success even approximating that of *The Lotus Eaters*.

The remaining poems are composed in definite strophes. For two, *The Palace of Art* and *A Dream of Fair Women*, Tennyson adopted stanzas which may be treated as modulations of the cross-rhyme *five-stress* iambic. The stanza of *The Palace of Art* is arrived at by reducing the second and fourth verses of the quatrain to four and three beats respectively. To produce the stanza of *A Dream of Fair Women* the only modification is in the fourth line, which has three beats. Both movements had been anticipated in principle by the stanza of *The Poet* in the 1830 volume.[5]

---

[5] See above, p. 29. The text implies that these stanzas were of Tennyson's invention; but this is far from certain. There is an exact analogue for two of these stanzas among the poems of Henry Vaughan, the Silu-

The Palace of Art and *A Dream of Fair Women* are, in more than one respect, companion pieces. Each is a dream fabric for the presentation of more or less miscellaneous descriptive studies drawn from art and story, backgrounded in both cases by studied sketches from nature. The former is by far the more miscellaneous in plan and has the profounder theme and, significantly enough, gave the designer by far the greater trouble of the two. *A Dream of Fair Women* was reissued with very little modification in 1842. Its companion craved and received a very thorough rehandling. Since the metrical schemes adopted for the two poems exhibit the same parallelism as the two plans, these facts are of considerable interest and suggest a minute comparison of metrical characteristics. First, however, the history of the two poems deserves some consideration.

A Dream of Fair Women is noted by Collins among the poems that were "greatly altered"[6] for the 1842 issue; but on examination the facts do not justify this classification. With the exception of two important excisions and a few slight

---

rist. The *Palace of Art* stanza appears in one of Vaughan's best and best known poems:

> They are all gone into the world of light
>   And I alone sit lingering here;
> Their very memory is fair and bright,
>   And my sad thoughts doth clear.

The stanza of *A Dream of Fair Women* duplicates the stanza employed by Vaughan in his paraphrase of *Psalm* 104:

> The beams of thy bright Chambers thou dost lay
>   In the deep waters, which no eye can find;
> The clouds thy chariots are, and thy path-way
>   The wings of the swift wind.

George Herbert, whose stanzas Vaughan imitated, has numerous stanzas composed like these of combinations of the *five-stress* iambic with shorter lines. The closest approximation to Tennyson's formulas is found in *The Temper*, which has the scheme, $a^5b^4a^4b^3$, and in *Content* and *Divinity*, both of which have the scheme $a^5b^4a^5b^4$. This little point may have some slight bearing on the much discussed question as to whether Tennyson owed to seventeenth century poets the suggestion of the *In Memoriam* stanza.

[6] *Early Poems,* Introduction, p. ix. In his note, *Early Poems,* p. 115, Collins speaks of the poem, as "very extensively altered on its republication in 1842", and again, "perhaps no poem proves more strikingly the curious care which Tennyson took", etc., an odd example of a critic's infidelity to the information which he himself has gathered.

verbal changes, the poem was issued without alteration in 1842. Subsequently, in 1843, one of the five stanzas in which Cleopatra lamented Mark Antony was excised and the others rewritten and greatly improved, while further changes for the better were made in 1845. The Iphigenia passage made notorious by the ridicule of Lockhart,

> One drew a sharp knife through my tender throat
> Slowly, and nothing more.

remained unaltered until 1853, when the excellent change was made to the present reading,

> The bright death quivered at the victim's throat,
> Touched; and I knew no more.

We return to the excisions of 1842. A curious introduction of four stanzas about "a man that sails in a balloon" was deleted,[7] as were two diffuse stanzas, amplifying the magnificent

> Beauty and anguish walking hand in hand
> The downward road to death.

These stanzas have a certain interest, as anticipating with considerable distinctness the theme of *The Princess*, and for this reason may be recorded here.

> In every land I thought that, more or less,
>   The stronger sterner nature overbore
> The softer, uncontrolled by gentleness
>   And selfish evermore:
>
> And whether there were any means whereby,
>   In some far aftertime, the gentler mind
> Might reassume its just and full degree
>   Of rule among mankind.

---

[7] The partiality of Fitzgerald is well illustrated by his observation upon these irrelevant stanzas. "They make a perfect poem by themselves without affecting the 'Dream'." (See *Memoir*, I, 121, where the stanzas are reprinted.) Collins quotes Fitzgerald's sentence with apparent approbation though he notices the irrelevancy of the verses.

The Palace of Art received much more fundamental alteration. With the possible exception of *Œnone*, no poem of this volume was so radically remodelled. When we compare the present text with that of 1833, it is easy to see that the piece was at that time in no condition to leave the artist's hand. Many of the beauties of language and versification which the poem still possesses were already present in it; but, not only was the piece marred by the most astonishing crudities of detail; it was exceedingly faulty in general construction. The poet seems to have been embarrassed by the abundance and the miscellaneity of his materials,—an embarrassment of riches which resulted in his appending two considerable passages in notes, outside the scheme of the poem, and in incoherence of plan. A comparison of the plot of the present piece with that of the piece out of which it was composed serves doubly to reveal the lucidity of the one and the confusedness of the other. It will be clearest to begin with an outline of the thought scheme of the poem as it stands in the collected editions.

The poem consists of 74 stanzas. The first 13 of these present the general and external view of the Palace. The first five stanzas present the most general description of the Palace, its situation and foundations and the purpose of the soul there to dwell. Then we have more particulars of the quadrangles and fountains (6), cloisters (7), galleries and view (8), the great stream and "torrent bow" (9), statues and "incense steam" (10), then the triumph and pride of the artist soul (11), and finally a summary of the exterior brilliancy of the palace (12), ending with the gleaming windows and shadowy arches (13). Now, we pass within and have first a general description of the rooms (14) and corridors (15); then follows the long series of symbolical arras pictures; 16 to 23 are landscapes: the hunter (16), a lone figure in a tract of sand, "lit with a low large moon" (17), an "iron coast" in storm (18), a meadow, "full-fed river," and herd, in rain (19), reapers at work (20), a foreground of slags, with heights on heights, light-smitten, beyond (21),

an English home, "a haunt of ancient peace" (22) ; finally,
closing this group, a general and summary stanza (23). Next
follows a series of religious and legendary paintings (24-32),
the maid-mother by a crucifix (24), St. Cecily (25), the
Houris and the dying Islamite (26), Arthur and the weeping
queens (27), Egeria and Numa (28), Cama (29), Europa
and the Bull (30), Ganymede and the Eagle (31), and again
a general and summary stanza (32). The next movement,
33-42, is ushered in by a great chime of bells (33) and we
pass to history and a series of paintings of the wise and great
in literature, philosophy, and affairs. Milton, Shakspere,
and Dante are done off in one stanza (34), Homer has a
stanza to himself (35), the treatment slips into complete
symbolism with the description of a ceiling of carven angels
(36), and the "mosaic" of history (37), the populace emerges,
now a tiger (38), now an athlete (39) ; over all this the soul
makes its way in triumph (40), and closes with Plato and
Verulam, "the lords of those who know" (41), and again we
have a general and summary stanza (42).

Now the soul begins its revel of intellectual and aesthetic
delight, (43-53), symbolized in Memnonian music (43), compared with the nightingale (44) and culminating in sensuous
triumph (45) ; night comes on divinely (46), only that she
may joy in artificial lights of "precious oils" in "moons of
gems" (47) and she is "flattered to the height" by her
"mimic heaven" (48) ; (the next three stanzas were added
in 1857) she boasts of the joys of sense and the fellowship of
"the Great and Wise" (49), in her God-like isolation (50),
her superiority to the common herd (51), and, glib of abstract
morality and metaphysics (52), holds no form of creed, but
contemplates them all (53). From 54-72 we proceed through
disillusion, to despair and utter remorse. For three years
the soul keeps "her solemn mirth, and intellectual throne"
(54), but "on the fourth she fell" (55) ; she looks inward
and finds only hollowness (56), 'mene, mene,' is written,
(57), loathing and self-scorn possess her (58), there is a
last half-hearted attempt to make the most of the Palace (59),

and then follows a wonderful series of images to symbolize or characterize her dread and despair: phantasms and nightmares haunt her (60), ghosts and corpses (61), stagnation without light afflicts her in the midst of a moving and purposeful universe (62); she is a land-locked pool cut off from the tidal sway (63), a star outside "the choral starry dance" (64); her own pride stings her and she is horrified at the stillness (65); decay follows and exile from God (66); she hates life, death, time and eternity (67); her "dismal tears" bring no comfort (68), she is as if shut in a tomb (69), a traveler perplexed in a strange land (70), among awful and inexplicable sounds (71), and goes mad with terror and remorse (72). Here the poem culminates, and it then concludes swiftly but not abruptly in two stanzas, depicting the soul's humility, her determination to leave the horrible palace for "a cottage in the vale", where she "may mourn and pray" (73); but, unlike Spenser's "Bower of Bliss", the Palace is not to be pulled down:

> Perhaps I may return with others there
> When I have purged my guilt. (74)

The comparative incoherence of the earlier poem may be indicated by a sketch of its contents with continual reference to the position of the various stanzas in the present clearly arranged and well proportioned scheme. The opening passage of general description and exposition was of six stanzas, in 1842 reduced to five by excising the fifth, which was mere amplification of the present fourth; then instead of completing, as in the newer arrangement, the description of exterior and surroundings, we passed within to the rooms and corridors, present 14 and 15; then followed five landscape stanzas; of these, four became the present 16, 22, 17, and 21; while one was excised, probably because too like 22. The maid-mother, present 24, followed, and, appended to it was the note: "When I first conceived the plan of the *Palace of Art,* I intended to have introduced both sculptures and paintings into it; but it is the most difficult of all things to *devise*

a statue in verse. Judge whether I have succeeded in the
statues of Elijah and Olympias.'' The note concluded with
two stanzas descriptive of ''the Tishbite'' and two of Olympias
and the snake, with the fragment of a verse trailing after.
In the main text there followed a picture of Venus rising from
the sea, excised in 1842.[8] Then came 25 to 27; here a stanza
on Kriemhild was excised in 1842; present 28 to 30 followed;
a second Europa stanza was excised in 1842; 31 and 32 concluded this series of pictures. There followed 6 stanzas on
the state and reflections of the soul of which three were excised in 1842. One became present 53. Two were shifted,
in 1842, so as to follow the present 48; these were excised in
1851.

At this point the 1833 poem took up again the description
of the exterior of the Palace: ''Four ample courts there
were,'' present 6,-7,-9,-8,-10,-11,-12,- and 13. Then the pictures began again with present 33 and 34, followed by five
stanzas concerning great men of history, art, literature etc.;
in 1842 all these were excised, while Homer was taken out
of present 34 and given a stanza to himself, present 35; 36,-
37,-38,-39,-40,-41,-42,-43, and 44 followed. Then came 8
stanzas delineating the sensuous revel and over-weening pride
of the soul; these were mostly excised in 1842; but some of
the best things were made over into the present 45,-46,-47,
and 48; while the present 49, 50, and 51, added in 1851, are
a restatement of some of the ideas excised with these stanzas
and the three mentioned above. At this point, a note was
appended to the effect that ''if the poem were not already
too long'' the poet would have inserted the following stanzas
expressive of the joy wherewith the soul contemplated the

---

[8] Collins prints the Venus stanza as if it had been a part of the note, a
very misleading error since it conveys the impression that Venus, too,
was described as a statue, an error perpetuated by A. C. Benson, *Alfred
Tennyson*, Appendix, p. 221. Collins' notes on this poem are full of errors
and confusion. His plan of treating the text is such as to make it practically impossible for a reader to gain any clear or correct idea as to
the manner in which Tennyson revised the poem. For one thing, he
notes passages as "excised" or "added" which were merely shifted from
one position in the poem to another.

results of astronomical experiment. He then printed three stanzas and a fragment:

Hither, when all the deep unsounded skies.[9]

The remaining stanzas of the poem are essentially the same as in the present text, except that one stanza, following the present 58 and amplifying it, was excised in 1842.

To summarize: the rearrangements made the poem much more coherent in plan; the excisions and additions improved the substance of the descriptions for variety, contrast, and orderly relation; they improved the proportion of the various divisions of the poem, each to each; the exterior description of the palace gathered together at the beginning of the poem now balances fairly with the three great groups of paintings which rise steadily in the intellectual scale, while each is made to balance with its neighbor and rendered consistent within itself. The landscapes are increased from five to seven and are made to contrast finely with one another; one being excised as not sufficiently individual and three new ones besides a stanza of summary and transition added. As in the landscape group, each of the sacred and legendary subjects occupies a stanza, Venus and Kriemhild are excluded, the tentative studies in statuary are banished, the Houris and Cama are added, and the picture of Europa which had been allowed to over-run into a second stanza is restrained to one. At this point, instead of returning to a description of externals, we pass directly on to history and the great and wise; Homer is removed into a complete stanza, and this makes room for a more adequate mention of Dante; but the tedious list of historical characters is cut down to a stanza on Plato and Verulam; the images and the symbolism are made more intelligible; we pass on by easy and regular stages to the next general section, which deals with the delights of the soul in the palace that has been reared for it. This, formerly, was one

---

[9] Reprinted, *Memoir*, I, 120; Eversley Ed. I, 368; Collins, *Early Poems*, p. 95. The vanity of the device by which Tennyson sought to include and yet not to include in his poem this passage and the preceding one descriptive of the statues was very harshly, and on the whole justly, ridiculed by Lockhart.

of the most defective portions of the poem; now, the exposition of the soul's sensuous enjoyments and its pride of pleasure and intellectual isolation, instead of being divided between two passages, is massed into one and forms a full and natural transition to that movement of the poem which deals with the soul's disillusion and remorse. Formerly, too, the delight of the soul in its self-indulgent solitude was almost purely physical; it is now more spiritually delineated; the element of voluptuousness is less emphasized, the element of pride and self-flattery more, and the preparation for the culminating exposition of the soul's despair is much strengthened thereby. This final section of the poem was more successfully executed and remains practically unchanged.

From the metrical standpoint no significance can be attached to the few changes made in *A Dream of Fair Women*. The chief idiosyncrasy is the long streaming movement of the verse, which not only overrides the interior pause but the verse end as well and with unusual frequency overflows the strophe itself. A further idiosyncrasy which does much to establish the metrical character of the piece is the unusually plentiful beginning inversion, and particularly its frequency in the closing verse of the strophe. There are 69 such inversions in the 76 stanzas, distributed as follows: 10 in the first verse of the strophe, 17 in the second, 15 in the third, and 26 in the last.

But the most striking feature of the verse is the constant pressure by which the onward streaming syntax is made to overbear the normal pauses of the structure. Reduced to statistical statement these characteristics are summarized as follows: there are 66 run-on lines (first, 24; second, 20; third, 22), this, if we apply the strict construction of the run-on line. There are 11 cases of the run-over strophe, again according to strict construction. Definite pause falls 32 times in the exceptional positions, 7 times after the first syllable, 6 times after the second, 5 after the third, 8 after the seventh, 6 after the eighth. Finally an unusual number of the lines are without interior pause (72 exclusive of the fourth verse), and this is often accompanied by failure of the end pause as well. Other modifications of the normal rhythm are exceedingly rare. The metrical *differentiae* of this poem are, then, free enjambement, long intervals between pauses, great diversity in the placing of the same, and much beginning-inversion, the last artfully bestowed and particularly marking the closing verse of the strophe. The full significance of these facts will appear as we proceed with the comparison of this poem and the two versions of *The Palace of Art*.

The changes in *The Palace of Art* furnish such striking illustrations of the various means by which Tennyson created master-pieces out of mediocrity that we can hardly scrutinize it too closely, hardly afford to neglect any resource of analysis or comparison which can give us an insight into the methods by which he went to work. As noted above, this poem has in general the same metrical characteristics as *A Dream of Fair Women*. The stanzas are identical, except for the second verse, which is reduced from five to four stresses. The variations of the fundamental movement are the same in kind as in the preceding poem and similar in extent, *viz.*, unusual freedom of enjambement, variety of pause, and beginning inversion. A strong idiosyncrasy of the movement is the alternation of the inversion between the third and last verses of the strophe. In the 74 stanzas of the 1842 version, beginning inversion falls 5 times in the first, 8 times in the second, 13 times in the third, and 13 times in the concluding verse of the strophe, a total of 39, against 69 in *A Dream of Fair Women*, which has practically the same number of stanzas. But *The Palace of Art*, it should be remembered, was thoroughly rehandled, and an examination of the revised passages reveals the significant fact that while 16 examples of inversion were removed in the process of revision, only one case was added. In fine, *The Palace of Art* of 1833 was much closer to *A Dream of Fair Women* in its proportion of this license than is the present version.

A parallel relation is found in the treatment of pause.

Here a slight difference of treatment was imposed by the fact of the second line of the stave having four instead of five beats. This, in itself, introduced a uniform variation of the movement which involved an answering restraint upon such discursive variation as was successfully practiced in the companion stanza of *A Dream of Fair Women*. It also complicates somewhat the comparison of the two poems from the standpoint of pause; a complication which is partly compensated by considering positions 5 and 6 in this verse to be parallel with 7 and 8 of the corresponding verse in the other stanza. One striking feature of the movement is the frequency of the run-on line in the last verse but one of the stanza; the first and second verses furnish each 12 cases of run-on, but the third verse 23 cases, a total of 47 in the poem, against 66 in *A Dream of Fair Women*. In this particular there is no significant difference between 1833 and 1842. In the run-over stanza, on the other hand, there is a considerable change. For while only 4 cases remain in 1842, 8 cases were removed by revision; so that the total of 12 in 1833, it will be seen, was close to the 11 of the other poem. Again, the number of exceptional pauses was greatly reduced in revision. The most striking illustration of this change is the removal of 9 cases of pause after the second syllable alone (5 of these in the closing verse of the strophe) while in the entire text of 1842 only 2 cases remain. Altogether 18 exceptional pauses disappeared in revision and only 11 remain. Now with the decreased frequency of beginning inversion in this poem, the greater regularity of the end-pause, the increased firmness of the strophic close, and the decreased frequency of the exceptional interior pauses, place the additional observation that the number of lines with no interior pause is nearly one-half greater than in the companion poem (106 in *The Palace* against 72 in *A Dream*), and one readily perceives that by a great number of comparatively trifling changes the poet has secured, accumulatively, a very considerable alteration in the character of his metre. What he has secured is a more fluent movement within the verse and within the stanza while preserving a strong sense of the integrity of both; he has secured the effect of a more measured movement with a consequent access of dignity and without a sacrifice either of ease or expressiveness. We do not enjoy in this stanza quite the same luxury of movement which the freer handling of the other stanza confers upon the verse; the stanza of *The Palace of Art* must be held to be, on the whole, a less successful stanza than that of *A Dream of Fair Women;* but it combines to a remarkable degree precision and fluency of movement; its terser and firmer handling well adapts it to the contents of the poem, which are at once more miscellaneous and more thoughtful than those of the sister piece.

We may best conclude this discussion with a few illustrations of the passages which were rehandled in the manner which the foregoing pages have described. One example of the greater precision of treatment in the later version of the poem is the change of "some" to "one" in two of the landscape descriptions. The following is one of the landscape pictures as set forth in the 1833 version:

> Some were all dark and red, a glimmering land
> Lit with a low round moon,
> Among brown rocks a man upon the sand
> Went weeping all alone.

In 1842 this reads:

> One seemed all dark and red—a tract of sand,
> And some one pacing there alone,
> Who paced for ever in a glimmering land,
> Lit with a low large moon.

The following stanza was excised in 1842. (Note the caesural inversion in the first verse, the beginning inversion in each of the others, the hovering accent in "sunshine," and the trace of early diction, "bunchy").

> Some showed far-off thick woods mounted with towers
> Nearer, a flood of mild sunshine
> Poured on long walks and lawns and beds and bowers
> Trellised with bunchy vine.

Now compare the foregoing in movement with the following stanza, much like it in substance, which was retained:

> And one an English home—gray twilight poured
>   On dewy pastures, dewy trees,
> Softer than sleep—all things in order stored
>   A haunt of ancient peace.

The following from the description of Olympias is worth citing, (excised 1842) :

> Round by the shoulder moved: she seeming blythe
>   Declined her head: on every side
> The dragon's curves melted and mingled *with*
>   The woman's youthful pride
> Of rounded limbs.

This is characteristic of the earlier poem in its inversions, in the rhyme-stressed preposition "with", in the broken movement of the lines, in the run-over stanza; and it is anti-characteristic for the revised poem in all these particulars. The two versions of the Arthur stanza are interesting. The earlier version reads:

> Or that deep-wounded child of Pendragon
>   Mid misty woods on sloping greens
> Dozed in the valley of Avilion
>   Tended by crowned queens.

Note, in the later version, the disappearance of the hovering accent in the first verse, the evasion of the two beginning inversions, the smoothing away of the "ed" cacophony in the last verse with the gain of a fine alliteration, and the purer flow of the syntax mirrored in the softer movement of the syllables:

> Or mythic Uther's deeply-wounded son
>   In some fair space of sloping greens
> Lay, dozing in the vale of Avalon,
>   And watched by weeping queens.

In the two lines which follow, the revision has got rid of an inversion in the first verse and a weak first measure in the second, and has increased the fluency of both:

1833:   Europa's scarf *blew in an arch*, unclasped,
          From her bare shoulder backward borne.

1842:   Or sweet Europa's mantle blew unclasp'd,
          From off her shoulder backward borne.

Note the smoother syllabling in the later version of the following:

1833:   Four ample courts there were, East, West, South, North.
1842:   Four courts I made, East, West, and South and North.

and the following:

1833:   While day sank low*er or r*ose higher,
1842:   And, while day sank or mounted higher.

Perhaps the worst stanza in the 1833 text, all things considered, is the following:

        Full of her own delight and nothing else,
          My vain-glorious, gorgeous soul
        Sat throned between the shining oriels
          In pomp beyond control.

For bad syllabling it would be hard to outdo the second verse; the rhyme of "else" and "oriels" is almost as barbarous; while the first line is incredibly silly as to sense, occurring as it does just before the poet proceeds to enumerate all the appetizing eatables with which the soul was pampered:

        With piles of flavorous fruits in basket-twine
          Of gold, upheaped, crushing down
        Musk-scented blooms—all taste, grape, gourd or pine—
          In bunch, or single grown—

> Our growths, and such as brooding Indian heats
>   Make out of crimson blossoms deep,
> Ambrosial pulps and juices, sweets from sweets
>   Sun-changed, when sea-weeds sleep.

Small wonder Lockhart thought this was "Keats turned imbecile." Needless to say, these three stanzas did not escape the pruner's hook.

Two poems, *The May Queen* and *New Year's Eve,* form in reality one composition, and they are in the same form, as is the *Conclusion*, which was added in 1842. The metre is the free seven-stress verse, rhyming in couplets, sometimes known as the ballad form, though it is by no means the only metrical form in the old English and Scottish ballads and is there "broken" into four and three stress verses. Both stress and syllabication are freely handled by Tennyson. The unstressed syllable frequently drops out entirely and an alexandrine is occasionally admitted in place of the fourteener.

The remaining strophes of the volume are based on the four-stress iambic. Two poems, *Fatima* and *The Lady of Shalott,* are constructed of massed rhymes. The rhyme scheme in *Fatima* is a^4 a^4 a^4 a^4 b^4 b^4 b^4; in *The Lady of Shalott* the same scheme is modified by adding a line of refrain after the *a* part of the scheme and another, rhyming with it, after the *b* section, so that the plot runs a^4 a^4 a^4 a^4 R^4 b^4 b^4 b^4 R^3. Similar but simpler is the stanzaic design of *The Sisters,* which may possibly be regarded as a modification of the cross-rhyme quatrain with the silent first and third doubled and the second and fourth converted to refrain lines. The scheme is a^4 a^4 R^4 b^4 b^4 R^3, thus:

> We were two daughters of one race:
> She was the fairest in the face:
>   The wind is blowing in turret and tree.
> They were together and she fell;
> Therefore revenge became me well.
>   O the Earl was fair to see!

This could have been a modified form of the tail-rhyme stanza frequently employed in mediaeval metrical romances and satirized in Chaucer's *Sir Thopas;* but it was very likely Tennyson's independent invention.

To J. S. is in the simple cross-rhyme quatrain of four-stress iambics and the norm is faithfully adhered to throughout. *The Miller's Daughter* has an eight line stanza made by printing together two cross-rhyme quatrains of four-stress iambics. *Mariana in the South* is in the same stanza as the first *Mariana*, a twelve verse stanza constructed out of four-stress iambic quatrains, the first and third quatrains cross rhymed, the second quatrain with exterior-interior rhymes, the final quatrain being a refrain.

The Death of the Old Year has a tolerably complex stanza, reminding us somewhat of the more complicated stanzaic systems of the earlier volume.

> Full knee-deep lies the winter snow,
> And the winter winds are wearily sighing:
> Toll ye the church-bell sad and slow,
> And tread softly and speak low,
> For the old year lies a-dying.
>   Old year, you must not die;
>   You came to us so readily,
>   You lived with us so steadily,
>   Old year, you shall not die.

It will be seen that each stanza falls into two distinct parts: the first composed of four four-stress verses followed by a three-stress verse with the rhyme running a b a a b; the second, a repetend of four three-stress lines with exterior-interior rhyme, the interior rhymes triple. The rhythm is basically iambic, but there is free anapaestic substitution, and occasional truncation, and one line has two compensating pauses. The system is consistently observed throughout.

It will be seen from the foregoing survey that, though the poems selected for republication in 1842 furnish still a sufficient variety of stanzaic forms and though these stanzaic forms

are for the most part of the poet's own invention, (a number
of them embodying the refrain principle) there is nevertheless
a tendency toward the adoption of *some* stanzaic system and
an adherence to it.   Further, unquestionably, a larger proportion of the poems are in a comparatively simple form and
a uniform metre, and the process of selection has tended
to bring those poems into a relatively greater prominence.

If we turn now to a more detailed observation of the changes
wrought in the versification of certain of these poems by the
revision which preceded their re-issue we may note yet more
striking evidences of a progress toward regularity of strophe
and metre.   It is not until we compare with their 1833 versions the accepted texts of such poems as *Mariana in the
South, The Palace of Art, A Dream of Fair Women, The
Miller's Daughter,* and *The Lady of Shalott,* that we thoroughly realize how impeccable is their execution in the form
in which we know them.   Such variations from normal rhythm
as .occur in them seem inevitable, and it is not until we
notice earlier irregularities which were not in taste and tune
that we realize how easy it is to err in such matters and how
infallible was the hand that altered them.

We are distressed, as if we had stumbled upon some dire
moral delinquency when we find the earlier version of *Mariana
in the South* marred by two violations of the stanzaic system,
the very opening strophe containing four quatrains instead
of three, the concluding strophe containing the same irregularity and marred by a false rhyme in the first quatrain.
That such delinquencies should have been atoned for, by correcting them, is not remarkable; but in much minuter
and less obvious ways the metre was amended, and
this invariably in the direction of a more conscientious observance of the established rhythm.   As the poem now stands
we can see that regularity of rhythm is of the very essence
of its being; the persistent monotony of the unvarying
iambics; their slow but persistent fluency of progression; the
persistent close of a thought with the close of each quatrain;

the persistent return of the repetend every third quatrain;
the subtle modulations of the repetend, uniform even in its
variations; the invariable recurrence of the anapaestic substitution in the third measure of the third and fourth lines
of each concluding quatrain; the absence of anapaestic substitution everywhere else; the utter regularity of it all.
Six times, in the ninety-six verses that compose the poem,
initial inversion[10] forces itself upon the rhythm, and twice
initial truncation visits the last line of the refrain.[11]   The
result seems magical; for, as has been suggested, the particular
changes are very minute which in the sum total of their
effect produce this result.   Through the revision, seven cases
of weak first measure and one of anapaestic first measure
disappear, leaving not one of either in the present version,
and making for greater regularity and fulness of rhythm.
Numerous cases of initial inversion are likewise smoothed
away.   What so much as fulness and regularity of stress
(stress of metre and stress of meaning) dictated the following
change, for example?

1833:   Shrank *the* sick willow sere and small.
1842:   Shrank *one* sick willow sere and small.

Only a side by side comparison of the two versions entire
could make explicitly patent the accumulative effect of a
series of minute alterations of this kind.   Such treatment is
forbidden by limitations of space; but we must find room
for the texts of the concluding strophe of this poem in the
two versions.   Almost all the technical points noted above,
including the matters of stanzaic integrity, regularity of
rhythm, and the conformity of thought scheme to verse scheme
are here illustrated.   It is hardly necessary to emphasize in
addition, the superiority of the language both rationally and
poetically in the later version of the passage.

---

[10] That is, one in sixteen.   Note that in blank verse Tennyson's ratio is
usually about one in ten.

[11] The cases of truncation are in successive stanzas and are accompanied
by two striking examples of initial inversion.

1833:   One dry cicala's summer song
         At night filled all the gallery.
    Backward the lattice-blind she flung,
         And lean'd upon the balcony.
    Ever the low wave seemed to roll
         Up to the coast: far on, alone
         In the East, large Hesper overshone
    The mourning gulf, and on her soul
    Poured divine solace, or the rise
         Of moonlight from the margin gleamed,
         Volcano-like, afar, and streamed
    On her white arm, and heavenward eyes.
      Not all alone she made her moan,
         Yet ever sang she, night and morn,
      "Madonna! lo! I am all alone,
         Love-forgotten and love-forlorn."

1842:   At eve a dry cicala sung,
         There came a sound as of the sea;
    Backward the lattice-blind she flung,
         And lean'd upon the balcony.
    There all in spaces rosy-bright
      Large Hesper glitter'd on her tears,
      And deepening thro' the silent spheres,
    Heaven over Heaven rose the night.
      And weeping then she made her moan,
      "The night comes on that knows not morn,
      When I shall cease to be all alone,
         To live forgotten, and love forlorn."

The changes wrought in *The Miller's Daughter* are less sweeping and the improvement is not so remarkable as the improvements made in other poems. There is somewhat more reason to regret, as Fitzgerald regretted, the disappearance of some of the old stanzas which were removed to make room for new ones. It would be hard to find in the revised poem a more charming quatrain than this one which Tennyson sacrificed, perhaps as too remote from the immediate foreground of his picture, perhaps as too much retarding the progress of his narrative, perhaps for the imperfect rhyme, and perhaps for all these reasons:

      Each coltsfoot down the grassy bent
        Whose round leaves hold the gathered shower,
      Each quaintly-folded cuckoo pint
        And silver-paly cuckoo flower.

But most of the omissions were undoubtedly well-advised, and when we come to those passages which were not omitted but in which the phrasing and metre were rehandled, there can be no doubt that the revised is invariably the improved form.

Like *Mariana in the South,* this poem observes with great precision its iambic norm, and except for rare expressive effect or for occasional variety, the thought nestles cosily within the quatrain. Again, the revised poem is far more careful of the full regular stress than was the original; weak first measures with the spondee following frequently disappear with excised passages as do initial inversions, and these "kinks" in the metre seldom or never occur in the displacing verses. Frequently verbal changes seem made for little other purpose than to be rid of these peculiarities of metre. The list of these changes is not a very long one and may be given in full.

Revised for fuller stress:

1833:   His mem*ory* scarce makes me sad
1842:   His mem*ory scarce* can make me sad.

1833:   Thick-studded ov*er with* white cones
1842:   In masses thick with milky cones.

1833:   *Like' the* long mosses in the stream.
1842:   Like those long mosses in the stream.

1833:   *And the* green chestnuts whisper near
1842:   While those full chestnuts whisper near

1833:   *When in* the breezy limewood shade.
1842:   The day, when in the chestnut shade.

1833:   *To the* old mill across the wolds.
1842:   To yon old mill across the wolds.

1833:   *Down from* the wold I came and lay.
1842:   From off the wold I came and lay.

1833:   *I was* a long and listless boy   (excised)
          In the back-current—   (excised)
          And the marred chestnut—   (excised)
          Of his sweet eyes that—   (excised)
          Like the moon in an ivy-tod   (excised)

Finally, as an example of Tennyson's improvement in that even fluency which he evidently sought in this metre let us put side by side the early and the revised reading of a single quatrain.[12]

1833:   How dear to me in youth, my love,
               Was everything about the mill;
          The black and silent pool above,
               The pool *beneath that* ne'er stood still.

Note particularly the easier movement of the last verse:

1842:   I loved the brimming wave that swam
               Through quiet meadows round the mill,
          The sleepy pool above the dam,
               The pool *beneath it* never still.

The metre of this poem is simple, and Tennyson caught its spirit from the start; so that the changes here are less numerous and less radical than in some of the other poems; but they are consistent and are ample to give further proof, if that were needed, of the direction in which the poet's metrical technique was developing.

The metrical changes effected by the revision of *The Lady of Shalott* are less remarkable than the changes wrought in its substance and diction. Still, here too, close inspection reveals the regulating hand of the reviser. As the poem now stands, the characteristic variation of the metre is initial truncation; there is a marked tendency to mass the truncations distinctively in certain passages; the poet is particular to preserve the truncation in connection with the double-rhymes, thus emphasizing the trochaic character of these passages; and this effect is still further enhanced by frequent feminine pause within the verse. Finally, few other variations of the movement are admitted and, except in the last line preceding the refrain, the thought closes with the

---

[12] This example was noted by Collins, *Early Poems*, Introduction, xiii; but by one of those errors in which this volume is so fruitful, the point of the comparison is largely lost through the misquotation of the last line of the 1833 quatrain.

verse so that within the limits set down the rhythm is very firm and consistent. Apparently, these advantages of rhythm were not clearly perceived when the earlier draft was made; certain it is they were not executed with anything like the precision which characterizes the poem as we now have it.

Let us, then, examine the poem in the foregoing respects. The poem is divided into four parts of four, four, five, and six stanzas respectively. In the first and fourth parts initial truncation is plentiful; in the second and third parts, it is rare. Now, in the 1833 version of Part I, the proportion of lines with initial truncation to those without it was 13 to 25; in the later version it is 21 to 15. In Part IV, the proportion was: 1833, 18 to 36; 1842, 24 to 30. In Parts II and III, however, where truncation is not characteristic, (there being only one case in Part II, and five cases in Part III,) there was no change between 1833 and 1842. Turning now to the matter of initial inversion, the chief license admitted in the 1833 poem, we may note that the 21 examples of this variation are reduced to 11 in the 1842 text; but we note further that 8 of these 11 cases occur in Part III, where the variation is characteristic and expressive of the somewhat bolder movement which marks the entrance of Sir Lancelot, and that, here, there is no change between 1833 and 1842; while the 13 examples in the other three parts have been reduced to 3, 2 of which are doubtful. Nor should we do justice to the subtlety of this technique did we fail to note that the remaining case occurs at the very close of the poem and is indicative of Tennyson's further nicety in the 1842 version, of admitting a delicate modulation of the metre at the close of each section of the poem. It may not be amiss at this point to call attention to the fact that each section of the poem is made to end on a quotation with a run-on between the last verse and the refrain:

> "The curse is come upon me," cried
> The Lady of Shalott.

an ingenuity of construction which was not consistently carried out in the earlier version of the poem. Finally, in the earlier version of the poem, Tennyson continually abuses the run-on principle and this he brings within bounds in the process of revision, using the privilege only rarely and then with graceful and expressive effect. No part of Tennyson's work was more marvelously reclaimed from imbecility by his revision than numerous passages in this poem. Not only did he improve the diction of such passages, expunging affectations and sillinesses of phrase and substituting simple and rational and truthful expressions; but he improved the continuity of the thought even more than the fluency of the metre, besides immeasurably ennobling its imaginative content. Compare the following,

> A pearl garland winds her head
> She leaneth on a velvet bed,
> Full royally apparelled,

—its atrocious syllabication of "pearl", its affected diction, and its vulgarity of decorative accessories,—with the simple, fluent, and imaginative lines that now occupy the same room in the poem:

> But who hath seen her wave her hand?
> Or at the casement seen her stand?
> Or is she known in all the land,
> The Lady of Shalott?

Or for improvement in fluency of sound and rhythm, clarity, continuity of thought, compare the two stanzas about the reapers.

> 1833:   Underneath the bearded barley
> The reapers, reaping late and early,
> Hear her ever chanting cheerly
> Like an angel, singing clearly
> O'er the stream of Camelot.
> Piling the sheaves in furrows airy,
> Beneath the moon, the reaper weary,
> Listening whispers, "'tis the fairy
> Lady of Shalott."

5

1842:   Only reapers, reaping early
             In among the bearded barley
             Hear a song that echoes cheerly
             From the river winding clearly
                 Down to towered Camelot:
             And by the moon the reaper weary,
             Piling sheaves in uplands airy,
             Listening whispers, "'tis the fairy
                 Lady of Shalott."

Lines choked in their movement by too full syllabling or by
the juxtaposition of sibilants, were lightened and smoothed
so as to give freer play to the pulse of the metre. Thus, for
the following heavy lines:

> They crossed themselves, their stars they blessed
> Knight, minstrel, abbot, squire and guest.

we have the lighter movement of the following verses, opening
the last stave of the poem:

> Who is this? And what is here?
> And in the lighted palace near
> Died the sound of royal cheer.

The verse,

> A pale, pale corpse *she* floated by

becomes

> A gleaming shape she floated by.

A characteristic piece of treatment is that of the lines,

> Till her eyes were darkened wholly,
> And her smooth face sharpened slowly,
>   Turned to towered Camelot.

where the second line is completely transformed and the
order reversed so that in addition to improvement in pictorial
detail and flow of thought we get greater smoothness of
versification:

> Till her blood was frozen slowly,
> And her eyes were darkened wholly,
>   Turned to towered Camelot.

George Eliot preferred the earlier reading[13], and it must be admitted that something in imaginative poignancy was sacrificed for the greater softness of the present line.

No line in the present version of the poem is so obstructed by consonants as the following:

> From dying swans wild warblings come.

and in the final draft of the poem, we shall look long for any such inept enjambement and such misplacement of rhymes and pause as we find in the very false gallop of verses that follows:

> Though the squally east wind keenly
> Blew, with folded arms serenely
> By the water stood the queenly
>   Lady of Shalott.

These passages disappeared altogether in the reorganization of the poem. What Tennyson might have made of them had he chosen to preserve their substance we may not know; but we have ample proof before us as to the nature of the changes he would have made.

---

[13] Eversley Ed. Vol. I, p. 353.

CHAPTER IV

MASTERING BLANK VERSE

We turn now to the early experiments in blank verse. Tennyson's first published composition in this form, of which he was destined to win a mastery unequalled by any other poet of his generation, was his prize poem, *Timbuctoo,* and this was, with the exception of *Œnone,* his only important experiment in blank verse which saw the light previous to the issue of the 1842 volumes. The list of his published examples of blank verse, down to that time, is as follows: (1) *Timbuctoo* (1829); (2) in *Poems, Chiefly Lyrical* (1830), a short poem, afterward suppressed, entitled *The Mystic,* and a few lines introductory to *The Sea-Fairies;* (3) a few lines, entitled *A Fragment,* published in *The Gem, A Literary Annual* (1831); (4) in *Poems* (1833), *Œnone,* and the short introductions prefixed to *The Hesperides* (suppressed) and *The Palace of Art.* In addition to these, *The Lover's Tale* was printed for the 1833 volume, but was not published. It will be seen that three substantial items stand out as of especial importance. *Timbuctoo* and *Œnone* obviously deserve careful attention. So does *The Lover's Tale,* which is somewhat aside, in a place by itself. Tennyson states that it had been written as early as 1827; but from what we know of his methods, we may infer that it received alterations down to 1832, when it was printed with a view to its inclusion in the 1833 volume.[1]

Although Tennyson's publications in blank verse are few in this period, he began early to "learn the great horse." Already in his "Cantab" days, he was a careful, we might

---

[1] See below, p. 76.

even say, a technical student of blank verse.[2]   His command
of it matured slowly, but from this time on, until 1842, he
experimented busily and in due time developed a style in
this greatest of all English metres which was distinctly his
own creation.

Tennyson departed from academic convention in submit-
ting for competition a poem in this metre.   A contemporary
writer who greatly admired the poem noted the unusualness
of the form, declaring that *Timbuctoo* was the first poem in
blank verse which had ever been selected for highest honors.
And indeed the poem was a most creditable performance
in a form "which affords no shelter for mediocrity."[3]   The
blank verse of *Timbuctoo* is, on the whole, flexible and melodious and shows exceptional variety and resourcefulness for
so young a writer.   Here and there devices appear of which
the poet never tired, such as the "run-on" followed by beginning inversion and emphatic pause after the monosyllabic
verb at the beginning of the second line:

> As when in some great city, when the walls
> Shake,

directly imitative of the same device in Milton, e. g.,

> And over them triumphant Death his dart
> Shook.[4]

---

[2] "Mr. Tennyson us't in his undergraduate days, to read the genuine
parts of *Pericles* to his friends in college. He read them to me last
December, 1873. He pickt them out by his ear and his knowledge of
Shakspere's hand. Last April, Mr. Fleay sent me, as genuine, the same
parts, got at mainly by working metrical tests." (F. J. Furnivall, *The
Succession of Shakspere's Works, N. S. S.* 1876.) Furnivall adds that
Tennyson also "pointed out Fletcher's hand in *Henry VIII,*" and that this
idea, "pooh-poohed by Hallam, was afterward tested and made the subject
of a published paper by Tennyson's friend, Spedding." (Spedding's paper
is in the publications of the *New Shak. Soc.*) This critical display on the
part of the Laureate may have been in the mind of Mr. Fleay when, in
1876, he dedicated his *Shakespeare Manual* "To Alfred Tennyson, who, had
he not elected to be the greatest poet of his time, might easily have become the greatest critic."

[3] Shelley, Preface to *The Revolt of Islam.*

[4] *P. L.* XI, 491.

Much the same character is found in the following,

Wide Afric, doth thy Sun
Lighten, thy hills enfold.

The blank verse of the poem is considerably unlike that of Tennyson's mature period. The influence of Milton is much more obvious in it. In pause scheme, the verse is very like that of *Paradise Lost*. For example, an uncommon number of the lines, (23 per cent), have the pause after the seventh syllable, a phenomenon probably determined by the fact that Tennyson was imitating some exceptional cadences in Milton's verse of which his ear was temporarily enamored. Again, in the extent to which enjambement is practiced, the poem resembles *Paradise Lost* and differs from the blank verse poems of 1842. In *Timbuctoo* 39 per cent of the lines run-on; the blank verse idylls average nearly 10 per cent less than that proportion, while it is about the normal proportion for *Paradise Lost*. The effect of sustained rhythm produced by enjambement and obviously an object of effort in *Timbuctoo* and some of the early fragments is further enhanced by the extraordinary number of lines without the interior pause, *viz.*, 100 lines out of 244 which comprise the poem, or a proportion of 41 per cent. The combined frequency of pause-failure at the end and in the interior of the verse may be mathematically expressed by computing the average number of measures to the pause throughout the poem. This relation is expressed by the ratio 4.25 to 1. That this is an extraordinary effect of deferred pause may be shown by a comparison with later poems. In *Œnone* (1833), for example, the ratio is 3.29 to 1; in *Ulysses* (1842), 3.24 to 1; *Tithonus* 3.27 to 1; *Dora* 3.07 to 1. As to syllabication, the verse resembles that of *Paradise Lost* in a number of respects. Words like "Heaven", "spirit", "towers", are treated after the manner of Milton,—falling in 9 cases out of 15 at the end of the verse and twice at the caesura. Extra syllables are more freely admitted than in Tennyson's mature idyllic type of verse; there are 24 of the "slurred" variety and

14 "unslurred", and not all these last come strictly within the laws of Miltonic elision,[5] *e. g.*, "o' the city." Double-endings are sparingly admitted; there are five exclusive of the "Heaven" class. There are two examples of epic-caesura, as follows:

> Oh ci*ty, oh* latest throne where I was raised

> How changed from this fair ci*ty.*
> > *Thus* far the Spirit.[6]

The use of the epic caesura at the transition from quotation to narration, as in the second instance above, is characteristic of Milton in *Paradise Regained.* For the weak prepositional verse-end, of which Tennyson allowed six cases[7] in this poem, he had no precedent in the blank verse of Milton's late poems, but he was familiar with the phenomenon in Shakspere, in whose later plays it is a salient characteristic of the verse structure. It is possible, too, that Byron's slip-shod treatment of the verse-end may have had some influence.

Numerous light endings are also admitted.[8] The recession of accent in the line

> And odors rapt from *remote* paradise,

also smacks of Shakspere, though it is a license practised by Milton in *Comus.*[9] The general treatment of stress in this

---

[5] See Bridges, *Milton's Prosody.*

[6] The first of these is of the type, exceedingly common in *Paradise Lost,* in which the open vowel elision collides with the caesural pause, as in

> Wallowing unwield*y,* enormous in his stride.

Mr. Bridges prefers to explain this phenomenon by the doctrine that, theoretically, epic caesura does not occur in *Paradise Lost.* My own sense of these collisions is that Milton felt them as a *hurrying of the caesura* through the invitation to elision, an effect that may be readily perceived in such a line as

> Damasco and Marocco *and* Trebisond.

I should be as well satisfied by the explanation that epic caesura, though admitted in *Paradise Lost,* is almost exclusively confined to this type.

[7] On, from, through (three times), in.

[8] Such are the verses ending in, "buildeth up", "wherefrom", "wherewith", "not", "I", etc.

[9] Nor am I satisfied that Mr. Bridges explains away all the seeming examples of the license in *Paradise Lost.*

poem will be noted later in connection with some of Tennyson's improvements in his early blank verse.

Doubtless mechanical coincidences of the kind here noted are insufficient ground upon which to base an assertion that Tennyson's blank verse at this period was modelled after Milton's; and, at any rate, there are sufficient variations from the Miltonic practice to destroy most of the force which attaches to such argument. Specific passages will be found more convincing. Let us then consider broadly the traces of outside influence which may be detected by other means.

Timbuctoo is an interesting composite, and well illustrates the formative state of Tennyson's style at this period. Its spectrum shows Milton, Byron, Shelley, with flecks of Shakspere and perhaps other Elizabethans, while one recognizes, here and there, distinct anticipations of the genuine Tennysonian manner. In the syntax, in the diction, in some of the archaic spellings, in occasional reminiscent phrases, as well as in the pause and accent of the verse, we are frequently reminded of *Paradise Lost*. To show these resemblances conclusively, large extracts are needed, but the following brief ones will be at least illustrative. For phrasing and syntax we may notice,

> Divinest Atalantis whom the waves
> Have buried deep, *and thou of later name*
> *Imperial Eldorado, roofed with gold.*

Here, the balance of construction and rhythm, together with the fertile device by which both are varied and, so to speak, disguised, are Miltonic in manner and source. Another device of Milton's style, which Tennyson copied early, and later learned to manage in a way more truly his own, is studied repetition and word play, with the repeated syllables artfully disposed in the verse structure so as to bestow upon them a variable emphasis. The following is an example from *Timbuctoo:*

                              chrystal pile
Of rampart upon rampart, dome on dome,
Illimitable range of battlement
On battlement, and the imperial height
Of canopy o'er-canopied.

An examination in detail of the distribution of weak stresses
and slurred extra-syllables in this passage will reveal the
devices by which Tennyson has given to the measures something of the Miltonic carry and swiftness. In the following,
the phrase, "interpenetrated arc", and the construction,
"scan definite round", are Milton-like, as in fact are the
grammar and prosody of the entire passage, except the first
five measures.

                        The eye in vain
    Amid the wild unrest of *swimming shade*
    Dappled with hollow and alternate rise
    Of interpenetrated arc, would scan
    Definite round.

The visual content of the lines hardly requires comment from
this standpoint and the same may be said of the following
extracts, each of which bears one or more marks of Miltonic
thought, style or metric.

                        as with visible love
    Filled with divine effulgence, circumfused

                            showering circular abyss
    Of radiance,

                            If gold it were
    Or metal more etherial

                            Yon river whose translucent wave
    Forth-issuing from darkness

                            Compassed round about his brow
    With triple arch of everchanging bows.

                            Thus far the spirit:
    Then parted heaven-ward on the wing: and I
    Was left alone on Calpe, and the Moon

the streets with ghastly faces thronged.

Blaze within blaze, an unimagin'd depth
And harmony of planet-girded suns
And moon-encircled planets, *wheel in wheel*,
Arch'd the wan sapphire.

Miltonic, likewise, though also post-Miltonic, are such particles and phrases as ''nathless'', ''what time'' ''there where'', and the spellings, ''th' Atlantick'', ''Afric'', etc.

Next to Milton's, Byron's is the strongest influence to be descried in this poem; and this fact may receive its explanation from the circumstance that, for this competition, Tennyson ''patched up an old poem on *The Battle of Armageddon*,''[10] possibly one of those early studies, in the Byronic manner, upon remote or historical subjects, in which *Poems by Two Brothers* abounded. Some such explanation is required, for we are informed that, at this period, ''Byron's 'comet blaze' was on the wane.''[11] Curiously enough, it is those poems in which Byron himself owed a debt to Milton that seem to have haunted Tennyson at this time. There are a few reminiscences of certain of Byron's blank verse poems, for example, *The Dream, Manfred,* and *Cain.* The rhetoric is frequently like Byron's, and sometimes the diction. Each of the following has its Byronic tinge:

To be a mystery of loveliness
Unto all eyes.

Or is the rumor of thy Timbuctoo
A dream as frail as those of ancient times?

At midnight in the lone Acropolis,

Adown the sloping of an arrowy stream.

One, and perhaps two, of the finest passages of *Cain,* must have been floating near the surface of the subconscious, in the youth who wrote,

---

[10] *Memoir,* I, 46.
[11] *Memoir,* I, 36.

> Then with a mournful and ineffable smile
> Which but to look on for a moment, fill'd
> My eyes with irresistible sweet tears.[12]

Apostrophic appositions like those of Byron give the tone to these lines:

> Where are ye
> Thrones of the Western wave, fair Islands green,
> Where are your moonlight halls, your Cedarn glooms?

"Gone—glimmering through the dream of things that were,"[13] one is tempted to continue.

Byron had an idiosyncrasy for intensive "do" and "did", whereby at times he gave a peculiar artificial poignancy to his rhetoric. Tennyson seems to have felt about the same value in the syllables at the time he composed *Timbuctoo* and *The Lover's Tale;* in both of these poems "do" and "did" are used with the Byronic accent. This and a certain violent simplicity in the diction, and in the incidents narrated, with the air of saying a tremendous thing in words of one syllable for the sake of intense explicitness, give a Byronic sound to the lines.

Shelleyan influence is discernible in the conception and spirit of the poem, in the quality of its mythology and ideas rather than in style or versification. One seems to find a Shelleyan form of thought insisted upon, by a boyish imagination, in such a passage as the following:

> I am the Spirit
> The permeating life which courseth through
> All th' intricate and labyrinthine veins
> Of the great Vine of *Fable*.

or in

> My thoughts which long had grovell'd in the slime
> Of this dull world, like dusky worms which house
> Beneath unshaken water, but at once
> Upon some earth-awakening[14] day of Spring

---

[12] Cf. *Cain*, I, i, 517 ; II, ii, 255 ff.
[13] *Childe Harold,* Canto II, st. II.
[14] Cf. Shelley, *Ode to Liberty*, st. VI.

> Do pass from gloom to glory, and aloft
> Winnow the purple, bearing on both sides
> Double display of starlit wings which burn
> Fan-like and fibred with intensest bloom.

Here "earth-awakening", and "winnow the purple" may be reminiscent of Shelley; that the simile has a Shelleyan quality few will dispute. Other phrases suggestive, at least, of Shelley, are "translucent wave", "odorous winds", "frequent with".[15] Some of the passages of self-analysis in the poem are not unlike parts of Browning's *Pauline*, a poem written about the same time under strong Shelleyan influence.

Of Shakspere there are a few verbal reminiscences, as in the phrase, "yeasty waves", "impleached twilights," "passing loveliness", "The time is well-nigh come when I must render up". Such orthography as "o' the elder world", "o' the city", etc. was probably owing to Shakspere. I find no trace of Keats in this poem, but here and there are passages whose qualities of sensuous description and tone coloring anticipate the Tennyson of a later date. Such passages as,

> Your flowery capes and your gold-sanded bays
> Blown round with happy airs of odorous winds,

particularly the second line, are thoroughly Tennysonian; a few such lines and some longer passages of the same quality might be pointed out; but they are not many, and seldom is the manner sustained for many phrases in succession. We seem to see the poet in this exercise, groping among various styles, taking something here, something there, and occasionally, almost by accident, hitting upon the style which is to be precisely his own.

The Lover's Tale holds a peculiar position among Tennyson's early poems. Probably earliest written of all the poems of considerable length which were included by him in his collected editions, it must have undergone considerable changes when prepared for the press in 1832. Suppressed at that

---

[15] All three in *Alastor*, and the first two also in Milton.

time, it was afterward revised again and again before assuming the form in which it was published in 1879 and still appears in the authorized editions of the poet's work. The poem, as it was printed in 1833, is accessible in two ways. First, there were various pirated reprints from one of the early copies, by R. H. Shepherd from 1866–76. Second, the early version of the poem is most readily accessible in the reprint of *Tennyson's Suppressed Poems* by J. C. Thompson, 1903. Thompson does not mention the source of his text, and his version of the poem differs in some slight particulars from the reprint by Shepherd which I have examined. Tennyson himself mentioned that the imprint passed about by his friends, (from which Shepherd must have made up his text) was ''without the omissions and amendments'' which he had ''in contemplation''.

The Shepherd reprint therefore does not accurately represent the state of Tennyson's art and taste in 1833; the poem, in that form, must be assumed to bear about it certain crudities, the relics of an earlier stage, which would have been removed at that time had the revision of the poem been complete. Though Tennyson himself in his account of the matter gives no hint of such a reason, it may be assumed, with probable truth, that his lack of ability or leisure to give the poem at that time the needed rehandling contributed to his determination to suppress it.

We have, in a comparison of the two chief versions of the poem, then, that of 1832-33, and that of 1879, an important source of information concerning the changes which Tennyson consciously brought about in his style. But for two reasons: first, because the earlier version must be regarded as having many crudities belonging to the boyish period, and second, because the later version was so very late, this composition must be regarded as occupying a somewhat different position among the early poems from any other considerable piece of which we have knowledge. It has been assumed by some critics that *The Lover's Tale* was written under strong Shelleyan influence; but this was vigorously denied by

Tennyson himself, who assures us that he was not at that time acquainted with Shelley's poetry.[16]   This may be presumed to dispose of the matter, though it is difficult to believe that Tennyson's memory did not in this case play him false, so many features of the poem remind us of Shelley.

For our purpose it will be sufficient to compare the earlier and the revised versions of Part I.   This portion of the poem, as reprinted by Shepherd, consisted of 848 blank verse lines. In the revision of 1879 Tennyson excised 174 lines and added 126 new ones, besides making a great many verbal changes in the parts that were allowed to stand.   By means of these changes many bathetic, irrational, or otherwise unsuccessful expressions were removed from the poem; nor did the reviser refrain entirely from the addition of passages, here and there, which were beyond the scope of the art that fashioned the earlier version.   Many of the changes were ob viously made for the purpose of strengthening the blank verse and bringing it closer to the standards of the poet's later practice.   As a result of these changes, the poem is artfully made more uniform in execution and brought to present fewer oddities and crudities of thought, phrase, and versification than did *The Lover's Tale* of 1833, while at the same time, the original tone, that of youthful verve and floridity, is tolerably sustained. "The expression," Tennyson once said approvingly of this work of his nonage, "is very rich and full."   This quality he preserved in the revision, at the same time lopping off many of the excrescences that originally went with it.

A few illustrations somewhat systematically arranged and a statistical presentation of the most important characteristics of the verse will most clearly delineate Tennyson's change of taste and his re-creative method as exemplified in the revision of this poem.

Many oddities of language were removed: "crisping" is *excised* in two out of three cases; "landskip" gives way to "landscape", "afeard" to "afraid"; "revin" to "ravin";

---

[16] *Memoir*, II, 285.

"gan rack and heave" to "began to heave"; "battailing with" becomes "to battle with"; "airily built" displaces "airy-fashioned"; "agglomerated swiftness", "lethargised discernment", "swift conceits", "mighty evocation", "honey-dews of orient hope", "ghastful brow", "half-bursten from the cerecloth", and many similar strained or unnatural phrases disappear. Numerous cases of intensive "do" or "did" and syllabic "ed" were lopped away, to make place for more natural expressions. The language is frequently much simplified and thereby invigorated, the simpler expression being frequently attended by condensation and increased definiteness of thought, or originality and swiftness of imagination. "Lapt in seeming dissolution" becomes "seeming due to death"; "after my refluent health made tender quest" becomes "something she asked, I know not what"; the two lines referring to "her hair",

> And onward floating in a full dark wave,
> Parted on either side her argent neck,

are reduced to one,

> And floated on and parted round her neck;

where the manner of coupling the successive preterites is peculiarly that of mature Tennyson. The passage

> To stand within the level of their hopes
> Because my hope was widow'd, like the cur
> In the child's adage,

(a confused set of images, where "level of their hopes" is vague and obscure, and "like the cur", bathetic,) gives place to the following excellent pair of lines,

> To cross between their happy star and them,
> To stand a shadow by their shining doors.

in which, balance of phrase, versification, alliteration, and the construction "to stand a shadow" are developed Tennyson, not the boy of *The Lover's Tale* of 1833.

> Hate—who lives on others' moans

is the condensed phrasing of the following passage,

> Whom woeful ailments
> Of unavailing tears and heart-deep moans
> Feed and envenom, as the milky blood
> Of hateful herbs a subtle-fanged snake.

> For me what light, what gleam on those black ways,

displaces the forced, complex, and vague image,

> For me all other hopes did sway from that
> Which hung the frailest; falling they fell too
> Crush'd link by link into the beaten earth.

> While thou a meteor of the sepulchre

takes the place of the absurd and difficult image,

> With such a costly casket in the grasp
> Of Memory.

The verses,

> The faded rhymes and scraps of ancient crones,
> Gray relics of the nurseries of the world,

epitomise the following lines of bathetic enumeration:

> Those rhymes, "The Lion and the Unicorn"
> "The Four and Twenty Black Birds," "Banbury Cross,"
> "The Gander" and "The Man of Mitylene,"
> And all the quaint old scraps of ancient crones.

In the following passage we have a typical example of the manner in which thought, language, and metre were frequently rehandled for strength and definiteness:

> The lithe limbs bowed as with a heavy weight,
> And all the senses weaken'd in all, save that
> Which

becomes

> The weight as if of age upon my limbs,
> The grasp of hopeless grief about my heart,
> And all the senses weaken'd save in that
> Which

Here, note the shift of the weak measure in the first line, strengthening the line; note the strengthening of the verse and of the moral force, by the parallel construction and rhythm of the second line (*which was added*); note the greater regularity of rhythm in the last line, which is secured by eliminating the extra-syllable in the fourth measure and by increasing the stress in the fifth, and which is augmented by alliteration.

Another passage:

> Perchance assimilated all our tastes
> And future fancies. 'Tis a beautiful
> And pleasant meditation that what e'er, etc.

In the following substitute for the foregoing, note the apparent simplicity and poetic intensity of the revised diction, and yet the greater artifice, the adroit repetition and balance:

> Made all our tastes and fancies like, perhaps,
> All—All but one; and strange to me and sweet,
> Sweet thro' strange years to know that what soe'er, etc.

Frequently, the vigor of a passage is increased by at once simplifying the language and increasing the "moral" content of the words. Such a description as the following, for example,

>   Her face
> Was starry-fair, not pale, tenderly flush'd
> As 'twere with dawn

is transformed by the substitution of a moral for a physical characterization:

>   A face
> Most starry fair, but *kindled from within*
> As 'twere with dawn.

"Kindled from within" is obviously an advance, in thought content, upon "tenderly flush'd". Note, also, that a caesural inversion is removed by the substitution. In the following comparatively slight change of a few words the poet has, at

6

a stroke, removed tautology, strengthened his rhythm, and provided a vigorous and particular image with a higher moral exponent, for a vague and conventional one, in substituting for "a valley and a gulf", the phrase, "a deep and stormy strait";

> And tho years
> Have hollowed out *a deep and stormy strait*
> Betwixt the native land of Love and me.

In a few cases the revision amends an actual confusion of imagery. There was an absurd apostrophe to the "Genius of that hour",

> Amid thy melancholy mates far-seen,
> Who walk before thee, and whose eyes are dim
> With gazing on the light and depth of thine.

Tennyson rationalized this image, physically, by changing to

> Who walk before thee, *ever turning round,*
> To gaze upon thee till their eyes are dim.

To summarize, then: the revision of the poem made for a simpler and more natural, but at the same time, more skilful and poetic, language; in some cases, for the substitution of moral instead of sensuous characterization; generally, for condensation; and occasionally, where opportunity offered, for amplification; for more rational, vivid, and original imagery; and finally, for the strengthening of the versification according to the standards of the poet's matured style. The last point deserves particular analysis and illustration, for the changes which Tennyson made in the versification of this poem point us to some of the essential elements in which his treatment of blank verse was modified with the maturing of his style.

The changes which Tennyson made in the text of *The Lover's Tale,* primarily for their effect on the verse, fall under two heads, the handling of extra-syllables, and the handling of stress. In connection with some of the examples already given, it was noted that among results of the revision

were a greater regularity of verse structure as to syllabic
number and stress, and a more studied balance of rhythms.

The syllabication of the verse was considerably changed
in the revision. A comparison of the two versions shows the
following results as to Tennyson's use of extra-syllables. In
the first canto, of exactly 800 lines, the revised form of 1879
gives 75 slurred and 24 unslurred syllables[17], 31 double and
4 triple endings, and 13 epic caesurae; to these should be
added 15 double endings and 6 epic caesurae of the "Heaven"
class. There are 6 cases of pronounced "ed". Now, in this
portion of the poem, Tennyson excised 174, and replaced them
by about 126 lines, besides making numerous verbal changes.
The 126 new lines contain only 2 of the double endings and
one triple ending, but 10 of the 13 epic-caesurae are found
here. There is no case of pronounced "ed". The 174 lines
that were excised have 17 double and 4 triple endings, but
no case of epic caesura of any sort. Also, the 174 excised lines
have 8 cases of pronounced "ed" as against 6 in the entire
portion retained in the final version. Of the interior extra-
syllables, 13 slurred and 2 unslurred belong to the 126 new
lines; while 23 slurred and 12 unslurred disappeared with
the 174 lines which were excised. The original 848 lines, it
will be seen, had 85 slurred, 34 unslurred, 46 double endings,
7 triple endings, 3 epic caesurae, 14 cases of pronounced "ed".
The revision, then, resulted in a slight reduction in the proportion of extra syllables of the unslurred class, for considerable reduction of double and triple ending, for a decided
decrease of syllabic "ed", and for the introduction of practically all the cases of epic caesura.

The table of these changes follows:

---

[17] For the distinction between "slurred" and "unslurred" syllables in
these tests, see below, p. 168, note.

EXTRA SYLLABLES IN THE LOVER'S TALE

	ll.	Slur.	Un-slur-red.	D. E.	D. E. H.	Trip.	E. C.	E. C. H.	"ed."
1833 version................	884	88	34	46	15	7	3	4	14
1879 version................	800	75	24	31	15	4	13	6	6
New parts.................	126	13	2	2	3	1	10	2	0
Excised parts..............	174	26	12	17	3	4	0	0	8

In the distribution of stress the 1833 version of *The Lover's Tale* represents a very early stage of Tennyson's blank verse structure, and the changes which he made therein give us a clue to the line which his development subsequently took. *The most striking features of the revision, so far as verse structure is concerned, are the reduction of weak first and fifth measures, the increase generally of syllabic weight in the line, the total exclusion of weak-endings, the discontinuance of recessional accent, and the reduced proportion of caesural inversion.* These are the salient points revealed by an examination of the stress characteristics of the 800 lines of the first canto and of the new and excised portions of the poem. The 800 lines of the 1879 version have 63 weak first measures, 50 weak fifth measures, and a total of 510 or 63.7 per cent[18] weak measures in all. The 126 new lines added but 6 weak first measures, 6 weak fifth measures, and a total of 75 or 59.5 per cent. weak measures in all. There were removed in revision, 30 weak first measures, 21 weak fifth measures, and a total of 164 weak measures in all. Not all of these weak measures were in the 176 lines that were completely, or virtually excised, but their proportion to that number of lines is 94.2 per cent. The revision removed, also, all occurrences of weak ending and recessional accent, 2 of the former, and 5 of the latter.

---

[18] This means of course the average number of weak measures in 100 lines, not the actual ratio of weak measures to the entire number of measures.

The proportion of beginning inversion remains practically unchanged, a somewhat larger number being added than were
excised; but of the 19 cases of caesural inversion only 3 were
added in the 126 new lines, while 11 cases disappeared with
the 176 lines excised; 3 cases of hovering accent were removed, but none were added, and there are 5 in the final
version of the poem. A tabular view of the stress distribution follows:

THE LOVER'S TALE—STRESS TABLES

	ll.	I	II	III	IV	V	Total	Total pr.ct.	W. E.	Rec.	Tri.
1879..............	800 plus	63 24	106 4	130 23	161 23	50 15	510 89	63.7	0	0	2
1833..............	848	87	110	153	184	65	599	70.6	......	......	......
New..............	126		22	15	26	6	75	59.5	0	0	1
Excised..........	174		26	38	49	21	164	94.2	2	5	2

INVERSIONS

	ll.	Beg. In.	Caes.	C. Caes.	Int.	Hov. Ac.
1879..................	800	188	19	7	9	5
1833..................	848	185	27	6	9	8
New..................	126	49	3	2	0	0
Excised	174	46	11	1	0	3

There remains one important example of Tennyson's early
blank verse, the *Œnone* of 1833. This was the only complete
blank verse poem of early composition which the poet saw
fit to reissue in the revised collection of 1842. The poem had
been begun in 1830[19] in the valley of the Cauteretz whose
scenery it describes. It was practically rewritten during the
period in which the numerous blank verse poems of the 1842
issue were in preparation, and the changes in the language

---

[19] *Memoir*, I, 55.

and versification of *Œnone* furnish a valuable index of
Tennyson's development during the period under consideration.   In the second *Œnone,* then, we shall see his blank
verse style come fairly to maturity, though even the drastic
revision to which this poem was subjected did not remove
all traces of the earlier style. The *Œnone* of 1833 richly
illustrates those characteristics of Tennyson's earlier style
which have already been noticed at some length, the fulness
and luxuriance of description marred by frequent straining
after these qualities, by tastelessness, by sweetness of sound
gained at the heavy cost of vague description or imperfect
sense and of unnatural or affected diction. And the poem
was revised with great and characteristic skill, preserving
those qualities which the poet had aimed at and even aug-
menting them, while, at the same time, the sense was
strengthened, and the expression rationalized. Many coined
and compounded substantives and epithets of varying degrees
of offensiveness to taste were excised and the same or similar
ideas were expressed in more natural and conventional terms,
with the result that the poet produces the effects he desired
of rich and luxuriant image and sound, without, as formerly,
simultaneously confusing or disenchanting the reader through
the obtrusiveness of the means by which they are produced.
*This is the main principle of Tennyson's progress by means
of revision, his consistent standardizing of language and
verse, while securing with the simpler and more conventional
means an augmentation of the very stylistic and metrical
effect at which he had originally aimed.*

The revised descriptions are frequently much more distinct
and graphic, and they sometimes gain more than they lose
even in that vague magic or charm with which the poet
sought to invest them. Let us examine the familiar description of the "vale in Ida" at the beginning of the poem. In
the first *Œnone* it is described as

> beautiful
> With emerald slopes of sunny sward, that lean
> Above the loud glenriver, which hath worn
> A path thro' steepdown granite walls below
> Mantled with flowering tendriltwine.

Here the descriptive *effort* is plainly felt. It is felt in that unrestraint in the use of epithets which impairs the emphasis of all, and in the forced character of some of them : we have *"emerald slopes"*, *"sunny* sward", *"loud* glenriver", *"steepdown granite* walls", "flowering tendriltwine"; while "glenriver", "steepdown", "tendriltwine", each strikes us successively as unusual, perhaps affected. Finally, the grammatical construction is such that the picture flows together, is perhaps confused, is not analysed and graphic to the mind's eye. The corresponding passage in the revised poem reads as follows :

On either hand

>The lawns and meadow-ledges midway down
>Hang rich in flowers, and far below them roars
>The long brook falling thro' the clov'n ravine
>In cataract after cataract to the sea.

Similarly the image and setting of "Ilion's column'd citadel", are statelier, simpler, far more memorable, in the revised description. Originally they were described as follows :

In front

>The cedarshadowy valleys open wide.
>Far-seen, high over all the God-built wall
>And many a snowycolumned range divine,
>Mounted with awful sculptures—men and Gods,
>The work of Gods—bright on the dark-blue sky
>The windy citadel of Ilion
>Shone, like the crown of Troas.

Fewer strokes, well calculated and well delivered, do far more in the following, which is the present reading :

>Behind the valley topmost Gargarus
>Stands up and takes the morning: but in front
>The gorges, opening wide apart, reveal
>Troas and Ilion's column'd citadel,
>The crown of Troas.

Such condensations throughout the poem make room for new details which are frequently inserted, as, for example, in the opening lines, the description of "the swimming vapour" which

> slopes athwart the glen
> Puts forth an arm, and creeps from pine to pine,
> And loiters, slowly drawn.

Thus is introduced at the very beginning of the poem a detail of landscape of which significant use is made later on. These amplifications are often as brief as their effect is magical in enhancing the scene or the story and filling out the rhythm as well as the sense. At the first introduction of Œnone such effects are produced by the addition of the simple phrases, "at noon" and "on the hills". This passage read, at first, as follows:

> Hither came
> Mournful Œnone, wandering forlorn
> Of Paris once her playmate. Round her neck
> Her neck all marble white and marble cold
> Floated her hair or seemed to float in rest.

This becomes in the later version:

> Hither came *at noon*
> Mournful Œnone, wandering forlorn
> Of Paris, once her playmate *on the hills*.
> *Her cheek had lost the rose*, and round her neck
> Floated her hair or seemed to float in rest.

Similar, in the gain of both naturalness and fluidity, is Œnone's description of the coming of Paris on the morning of the judgment. This read formerly:

> I sate alone: *the goldensandalled morn*
> *Rosehued the scornful hills*: I sate alone
> With down-dropt eyes.

Instead of this obvious poetising and dubious rhetoric, we have now these flowing and wonderfully suggestive lines:

> Far-off the torrent call'd me from the cleft:
> Far up the solitary morning smote
> The streaks of virgin snow. With down-dropt eyes
> I sat alone.

Thus, the poem as a whole is even richer in passages of full and luxuriant description than formerly; but many strained or overloaded passages have been pruned and brought within the bounds of taste. The description of the coming of the goddesses, for example, receives many added touches, the "crested peacock", "the crocus" that "brake like fire",

> Violet amaracus and asphodel,
> Lotus and lillies:

a much more natural phrasing than

> Lustrous with lilyflower, violeteyed
> Both white and blue, with lotetree-fruit thickset.

Instead of the line,

> Above, the overwandering ivy and vine,

we have

> And overhead the wandering ivy and vine.

"More lovelier" disappears; "vine-entwined stone" becomes "a fragment twined with vine"; and such unnecessary oddities as "fulleyed", "greengulphed", "water-rounded", and "evilwilledness" give place to more ordinary expressions with a more extraordinary effect. Sometimes epithets are transferred instead of being excised, as for example, "ambrosial" and "fragrant"; Aphrodite's hair which had been "fragrant and thick" becomes "ambrosial";[20] and by way of compensation the "golden glorious cloud", which is now simply "golden", drops "fragrant" instead of "ambrosial" dew. Paris's address to Œnone,

> As lovelier than whatever Oread haunt
> The knolls of Ida, loveliest in all grace
> Of movement and the charm of married brows.

---

[20] For the relation of this passage to *Æneid*, I, 402–405, 415–417, see Appendix A, p. 229.

is added. The first characterization of Juno,

> Then first I heard the voice of her to whom
> Coming thro' Heaven, like a light that grows
> Larger and clearer, with one mind the Gods
> Rise up for reverence,

is substituted for the less successful lines,

> First spake the imperial Olympian
> With arched eyebrow smiling sovranly
> Fulleyed Here.

In fact, there is hardly an item in the entire poem which the hand of the reviser touched that it did not, one need not say improve, but re-create.

VERSIFICATION

And revolutionary as were the changes in the language and phrasing of the poem, these are commonplace in their effect if taken without coincident observation of their adjustment to the structure of the verse. It is not to be expected that the changes which Tennyson made in versification can be completely analyzed and described in terms of technical generalization, but probably more can be accomplished in this direction than the casual reader would anticipate.

Generally speaking, the changes in versification were analogous to the changes in style; there was a tendency toward the standardizing of the metre.   The key to Tennyson's slight but magical changes in the syllabication and accent of *Œnone* may be found in the first two lines of the poem.[21] It was a minute but not insignificant flaw in the opening of the poem that it began on a weak foot.   Thereby the gentle stateliness

---

[21] 1833 : *There is a dale in Ida lovelier*
    Than any in old Ionia, beautiful
    With etc.

   1842 : There lies a vale in Ida lovelier
    Than all the valleys of Ionian hills.

of movement aimed at in the verse was, at the outset, de-
feated. The substitution of "lies" for "is" makes all the
difference in the world in starting the reader aright. The
substitution of "vale" for "dale", while it loses the disguised alliteration with the "d" in "Ida", preserves the same
vowel and marries another "v" with that which is stowed
away in the interior of "lovelier" and makes a patent alliteration with the one which is the more prominent in "valley" for receiving the corresponding stress of the next verse.

The total result óf the change is at least equal sweetness
of sound with increased regularity of stress and an effect
of balance. Again, the play of sound in the words, "Than
any in old Ionia", is in itself sufficiently pleasant and ingenious (with the four n's, the vowel music, and the two extra
syllables) but the ripple in the quiet movement of the syllables
occurs too early in the poem to be advantageous. In the change,
one of the extra syllables has been retained in the second line,
but immediately the movement of the metre is reconfirmed by
the full stress of the last measure, followed by the normal
full-stop of the verse. "Beautiful" was a mistake, giving,
as it did to the end of this line, precisely the same cadence
as the end of the first line, and that not the cadence of a
normal verse; "beautiful" precisely balanced "lovelier"
both in stress-distribution and in its relation to the end pause
of the verse.

The changes here made are, as has been said, the key to
the changes made throughout the poem. Whether consciously
or not, Tennyson in the course of his revision greatly reduced
the proportion of weak measures, and particularly of weak
fifth measures. In spite of a slight increase in the length
of the poem, the total number of weak measures was reduced
from 130 to 112, a decrease from 51 to 42 for each 100 lines.
Six tribrachs occur in place of weak measures in the '42 version. The single weak ending of 1833 disappears. The
number of weak fifth measures is decreased from 14 to 6;
there is a noticeable reduction of weak measures in the middle

of the line; in only one position do as many weak measures appear as in the earlier version,—in the fourth, there is an increase of 2.   Characteristic changes for the sake of avoiding or shifting weak stresses may be noticed in the following:

1833:   Naked they came *to the* smooth-swarded bower,
1842:   Naked they came *to that* smooth-swarded bower,

1833:   *From his* white shoulder drooped, his sunny hair,
1842:   *Droop'd from* his shoulder, but his sunny hair,

The following lines may be compared for the manner in which identical syllables are placed in the verse-structure:

1833:   *More lovelier* than all the world beside
1842:   *As lovelier* than whatever Oread haunt

Numerous lines having more than one weak measure were modified or completely excised.   Such are:

Ambrosially smelling, from his lip

First spake the imperial Olympian.

The windy citadel of Ilion.

Inversions show little change, though beginning inversion is reduced from 26 per cent to 21 per cent in the later version.

Some changes were made in the rhythm of the poem as affected by the number and position of extra-syllables; but these changes were hardly such that they can be regarded as radical.   The most noticeable shift in the placing of extra-syllables is perhaps the decrease of the double-ending and the increase of epic-caesurae, the former decreased from 6 to 3, the latter increased from *none* to 5.[22]   In addition there were 8 double endings caused by proper names and 8 of the "Heaven" class, and these proportions remain practically the same; there was, also, in the original version, one epic-caesura of the "Heaven" class which was retained.   There was, further, a slight increase of slurred extra-syllables from 18 to 24, and a slight decrease of the unslurred from 14 to 10.

---

[22] Observe that these changes are analogous to those in *The Lover's Tale.*

The effect of the syllabic changes, then, was slight, but, such as it was, tended to increase the syllabic fullness of the lines while disturbing less the normal iambic rhythm.

Changes in the pause scheme made more pronouncedly for accentuation of the typical verse structure. This was accomplished by a noticeable increase of the proportion of verses without interior pause and a corresponding increased frequency of the end pause. There was also a striking reduction of pauses after 7 and a corresponding increase of the pauses after 3. Pauses 4, 5 and 6 remain practically the same, but there is a slight increase of 2 and decrease of 8 while 1 and 9 disappear in the later version.

In every particular of syllabication, stress, and pause, then, the revision of the poem conformed the verse more nearly to the blank verse norm. The poet has by this time discovered the advantage of adhering closely to the typical structure of the verse, gaining thereby, first, the power and beauty conferred by the mere physical conformity of his language to the primitive rhythm; and second, a greater emphasis and effectiveness in those cases where variation is employed.

The stages by which Tennyson arrived at something like a constant blank verse form are now before us. In *Timbuctoo,* we have an excellent example of his verse at a stage when many of the tricks of blank verse rhythm are at his command, but before he has completely settled to an ideal of that form. In *The Lover's Tale,* another immature poem, we have seen the drastic changes to which the verse was subjected long after his ideas of the form had become thoroughly settled and established. The two versions of *Œnone* reveal his command of the form in the very process of coming to maturity. That this is so, namely, that the poet's blank verse is approaching a constant form, so far as its use for idyllic purposes is concerned, is proved by the fact that the changes made in the versification of *Œnone* between 1833 and 1842 are analogous in kind, though not in degree, with those which mark the revision of *The Lover's Tale,*—a far later, but less serious revision of a considerably earlier poem.

CHAPTER V

MATURITY: THE NEW POEMS OF 1842

Although nearly ten years of almost unbroken silence elapsed before the corrected versions of Tennyson's earlier volumes were given to the public along with the new poems of his 1842 issue, we have every reason to think of the development which these record as following closely upon the publication of the volume just reviewed. In 1834, Tennyson wrote to Spedding, "I have corrected much of my last volume."[1] Early in 1835, he took up the subject again. Having been told that Mill was going to review him, "and favourable", in the new *London Review,* he expressed a wish that some friend might persuade Mill to give up this intention, adding, "*I do not wish to be dragged before the reading public at present,* particularly on the score of my old poems, most of which I have so corrected, (particularly *Œnone*) as to make it much less imperfect."[2] These and similar allusions in the correspondence of these months together with many other facts and inferences conduce to the opinion that Tennyson no sooner saw his poems in print and temporarily beyond the reach of his revising hand than he became painfully aware of their defects. It was seeing *The Lover's Tale* in print that finally determined him to suppress it; the next time he published, and ever after, he took the precaution of having his poems before him for some time in printed form before allowing them to escape his control.

But we have other than mere mechanical reasons for placing the period of Tennyson's artistic ripening in the years immediately following the publication of the 1833

---

[1] *Memoir,* I, 141.
[2] *Memoir,* I, 145.

volume. When this volume was put through the press the poet was only in his twenty-fourth year and was yet to know that of life which should make him regard seriously, in the deep and better sense, himself, the world, and his art. That perfection which was soon to become a master passion had touched his fancy, but had not yet won him for its very own. He was the darling of a coterie. The circle of "Cantabs" to whom he was personally known, while it was intelligent, regarded him with an affectionate approbation which was inclined to dote. They took his poems on faith, perhaps read into them some of the genius which they felt in the man, and gave them the benefit of every doubt. Genius cannot afford to be thus pampered; and a plunge in the stinging bath of Lockhart's icy sarcasms, together with a sense of the wider public of which these were an earnest, had a salutary, bracing effect upon a constitution which was, happily, strong enough to react and to keep what was strongest and best in it intact.

Again, the spirit of the age could hardly fail to have a tonic effect upon a soul tenacious enough to work out its own salvation in the midst of its stirring perplexities. The years from 1830 to 1845 were years of enterprise in many directions. The new Democracy was beginning to bestir itself, to feel the spring of its untried sinews, and to thrill with expectation of triumphs yet to come; the Reform Bill followed by Chartist and Socialist agitation kept the political atmosphere active and electric. A new religious unrest was abroad; the intellectual strength of the nation, as it had not done for a century and a half, moved into line for the long struggle of which the Tractarian Movement was as a sign that went before, and of which the religious genius of Newman was the most brilliant personal manifestation. Carlyle was thundering with hoarse and stormy eloquence the call to spiritual battle. The large simplicity and noble ethic of the now venerable Wordsworth were making themselves effective among thinking men everywhere and among the Cambridge coterie peculiarly. A novel strident cry of intellectualized and strenuous passion rang from the youthful Browning, just "entering bright

halls where all would rise and shout for him.'' Great movements and ideas gathering all about and ringing names on
every hand were a source of power and a challenge to which
a strong spirit must needs find answer.

Finally, there were events in Tennyson's private experience
which shook the superstructure of his life and set him to lay
bare the rocks of its foundation. Arthur Hallam's death in
the autumn of 1833 plunged him in temporary despair, but
did not long render him inactive; rather it set him searching
for the source of life and committed him to a pursuit of perfection which, if no longer light-hearted, was too remorseless
and exacting to admit of failure. The misfortunes of his
family, the discomforting material circumstances of himself
and the dubiety of his calling, together with the apparent
hopelessness of his attachment for Emily Sellwood (''Of love
that never found his earthly close What sequel?''), darkened
but did not obscure his spirit. He emerged from all,
strengthened in the fortitude ''which looks on tempests and
is never shaken''; ''the faith which looks through Death,
the years which bring the philosophic mind''. Carlyle's
memorable crayon of him a few years later is authentic for
all this period: ''a man solitary and sad, as certain men are,
dwelling in an element of gloom, *carrying a bit of Chaos
about him, in short, which he is manufacturing into Cosmos.*''[3]

There is something perennially impressive, like the unswerv-
ing enterprise of nature, in the way a born artist proceeds
about his business through shocks and tentative failures,
correlating all that is merely personal in his life to a greater
purpose in obedience to the law that, for him, art is more
than life, the abiding than the transitory—a law higher than
himself and stronger than his personal happiness. In spite
of all temptations to despair, Tennyson was immediately at
work, manufacturing Cosmos out of Chaos, mastering for
art the currents of his life and the currents of the life about
him, never letting these master him, but turning them into
prearranged channels to ply the wheels of his poetic mill.

---

[3] Letter to Emerson, quoted *Memoir*, I, 187.

We have already seen the results of this inspired industry in the re-creation of many of the earlier poems. But new works were already in the loom. *In Memoriam*, which was to be seventeen years a-weaving, and many of the poems of the 1842 issue were in progress. As early as November, 1833, we meet with mention of the *Morte d'Arthur* in a letter from Spring Rice to Tennyson. *Ulysses*, according to Tennyson himself, was written soon after Arthur Hallam's death, and expressed his sense of "the need of going on". *Tithonus* though not published until 1860 was begun about the same time as *Ulysses*. There is an evident allusion to *The Gardener's Daughter* and a mention of *St. Simeon Stylites* in a letter from Kemble to Tennyson, November, 1833. Some of his best political poems were written during these months. Fitzgerald saw *Dora* with some of the others in MS, in 1835; *Godiva* in 1840. It is quite certain that, during this entire period, these poems and many others not mentioned, some of them never published, were continuously undergoing revision and elaboration.

The poems of this issue exhibit no radical departure in scope and plan from those of the preceding. They are distinguished only by greater solidity and unity of substance and greater restraint and evenness of workmanship. There is less encroachment upon the province of the sister arts of painting and sculpture; there are no frameworks for the introduction of miscellaneous studies like those in *The Palace of Art* and *A Dream of Fair Women*. From whatever source it may be taken, each poem is a solid unit in itself. Most of the poems are quite short; none are of great length. (There was a clearly conceived plan back of this, which is indicated by Tennyson's statement to his son at a later period: "I felt certain of one point then; if I meant to make any mark at all, it must be by shortness, for the men before me had been so diffuse, and most of the big things except *King Arthur* had been done." That the plan of a longer poem on this subject had already knocked at the door of his mind we guess from

7

the allusion to an epic of twelve books in the Prologue to
the *Morte d'Arthur;* that he dismissed the plan for the time
being is equally obvious. He gave his best powers for the
present to mobilize a small but sufficient phalanx of veteran
poems which should advance upon the redoubts of public
opinion with no chance of a repulse and no provision for
retreat.

And, as he spared no pains to deserve success, so he
disdained no honorable precautions to insure it. The reception of his poems would not be left to accident. He had
now a considerable acquaintance among men of ability and
influence. They should open the gates to popular favor.
Early in 1842 Tennyson wrote to Lushington, his brother-
in-law, ''I have not yet taken my book to Moxon. Spedding's
going to America has a little disheartened me, for some fop
will get the start of him in the 'Ed. Review' where he promised to put an article and I have had abuse enough. Moreover Spedding was just the man to do it, both as knowing
me, and writing from clear conviction.'' However, Milnes
and Sterling were at hand to take his place and ''led the
chorus of favourable reviews'';[4] Spedding was not long in
following them up with his essay in the *Edinburgh Review,*
April, 1843. The article is proof of the soundness of Tennyson's judgment; public opinion could hardly have had more
competent leadership than the discriminating, firm, and just
presentation of the Tennysonian merit in this masterly
critique, by the learned editor of Bacon. After three quarters
of a century of voluminous writing about Tennyson, it remains unsuperseded as an account of the poet's progress
in his period of most significant advance. It would be
captious to deprecate too seriously Tennyson's calculation
in regard to the reception of his poems. As he said, he had
''had abuse enough''. He had atoned for his faults in the
only way an artist can, by correcting them. Yet, though it
would have been quixotic in him to have neglected this help
to recognition, we should admire him more unstintedly if

---

[4] *Memoir,* I, 188.

he had. But, again, his behavior in this instance is interesting as an evidence that his tact was analogous to his taste. His care and his sound judgment in regard to the acceptance of his poems by the public was a corollary of the infinite trouble to which he put himself that they might be worthy of acceptance.

On the strictly literary side the most significant aspects of Tennyson's self-cultivation are, (1) his increasing allegiance to the ancient classics and (2) his ever dominant interest in the very best things of the very best writers, whether ancient or modern. For, though his acquaintance with the poets of antiquity continually increased, and though his interest in modern literature constantly broadened, he never relaxed his allegiance to our own masters, particularly to Shakspere and Milton. But already in the poems of 1833, as we have seen, direct appropriations of phrase or cadence from these sources had ceased to be frequent. In the period which followed, Tennyson's assiduous study of ancient poetry is manifested, not only by the increasing frequency, but by the different range and character of his classical adaptations in the poems he was then revising and, even more conspicuously, in the new creations of these years. In the new poems of 1842, direct reminiscences of English poetry have practically ceased, and that augmented power of imagination which first showed itself by leading the poet to remoter sources and models has now accomplished a more original and assimilative use of these. There are frequent echoes of Virgil and Horace and even more frequent reminders of Lucretius, while Theocritus and Homer are, perhaps, still more pervasive forces; but his mind has learned to keep its own tone and purpose, while continuing to live beneath their more habitual sway.[5]

These alien elements introduce no discord or confusion

---

[5] These generalizations are mainly derived from a study, in their chronological relations, of the classical evidences collected in Mustard's *Classical Echoes*, in Collins' *Illustrations*, etc. I disclaim any pretence of a systematic first-hand study of this phase of the subject.

into Tennyson's work. Rather, they harmonize with an inward strength born of sterner experience and more earnest reflection. His deepening familiarity with the classics confirms the tendency evolving from his own arduous experience as an artist and settles him the more firmly under the discipline of that *aurea mediocritas* which constitutes the classic message in art. He has acquired the classic sense, the sense of the finiteness of art in the midst of the infinity of nature. There comes a modesty and reticence of purpose which, while it limits the scope of endeavor, still finds unlimited occupation for the artist in ennobling the proficiency of his means. The art of the past has penetrated his mind, levels his opinions, instructs him in design, and tempers while it enriches his decoration. For in no particular is his discipleship more conspicuous than in the moderation with which he uses these elements. All that he learned and used from the ancients was "adapted" with such wisdom and tact to the material of his own observation, to the thought and needs of his time, to the genius of his own race and of his native language and rhythms, that they seem thoroughly original and indigenous. He bravely avoids that absorption into the world of classic culture which makes even *Lycidas* and *Thyrsis* seem esoteric, which makes the finest of Landor's *Hellenics* seem so utterly exotic and irrelevant to our needs and ways of thought, and which makes so much of Swinburne's best work (as it does some of Tennyson's later "Experiments") seem futile and unreal. He is autochthonous as Wordsworth or Burns. In only one poem, in Gray's *Elegy in a Country Churchyard*, is so instructed an art so congenially wedded to homebred scenes and thought.

And this quality of Tennyson's poetry, if we regard it merely from the standpoint of his acceptableness in his own generation, though it can hardly have been in any thoroughgoing sense calculated to this end, was probably well advised. It placed him in harmony with one of those reactions which seem to attend the fluctuations of literary taste. It was not merely that the men before him "had been so diffuse" or that all "the big things had been done". All his immediate predecessors of any size, Wordsworth, Coleridge, Scott, Byron, Shelley, even Keats, each and all had been, in one way or another, *wild* poets. Byron, in his grand and imperfect way, had experienced this reaction, and expressed it in his extravagant admiration of Pope. "We are all on a wrong tack ('Lakers' and all)", said he; "our successors will have to go back to the riding-school and the *manège* and learn to ride the great horse." Wordsworth had a moral, and Keats an instinctive, apprehension of the value of classic sanity and orderliness; but the former lacked the artistic pertinacity, and the latter the lease of years, fully to substantiate the conception. It remained for Tennyson, within the limits of his imaginative faculty, to bring the idea to fulfilment.

The same law that controlled Tennyson in the above-mentioned characteristics of his art determined his treatment of metre. Experience taught him that his forte lay in the delicate modulation of established rhythms rather than in the invention of complicated melodic systems or the discovery of new and surprising movements. The tendency toward simplification of form which marked the revision of the 1833 survivals culminates in the new poems of 1842. The basic fact in the versification of these pieces is their almost complete adherence to simple stanzaic schemes and standard metres.

The new portion of the 1842 issue contained forty titles, or thirty poems, if we consider *Morte d'Arthur* and its "prelude of disparagement" one poem, and if we regard the ten parts of *The Day Dream* as a single whole. To these must be added six new poems which were placed among the selections from the 1833 volume, though now published for the first time. Of these 36 poems, 9 are in blank verse; two are in free-syllabled ballad movements; two are anapaestic; two are trochaic; only one, *The Vision of Sin*, has any radical change of metre, and all the rhymed poems, with this exception, are in fixed strophic or couplet forms. Twenty of the poems are consistently iambic and, of these, all but two are in simple quatrain arrangements of four-stress or four-and-three-stress verses. Let us consider first this large and significant body of poems in simple strophes of iambic verse, after which the exceptional pieces may be discussed, reserving those in blank verse for final mention.

The majority of these compositions are in simple strophes built out of quatrains of combined four-stress and three-stress verses, but in scarcely any two are these elements combined in precisely the same manner. The simplest form is the plain quatrain of broken septenaries with alternate rhyme which we find in *The Talking Oak*. The same quatrain is employed in *A Farewell*, but here variation is introduced in the form of two-syllabled "b" rhymes, and interior rhyme in the third line of each quatrain. The lyricism of this little poem is emphasized by converting into a burden the second half of the quatrain. Another short poem, that "absurd trifle", *The Skipping Rope*,[6] is cross-rhymed throughout on the same rhymes. In *The Goose*, printed among the 1833 poems in the issue of 1842, we have the same quatrain with the "b" rhymes consistently two-syllabled and grotesque. In *Amphion* and *Will Waterproof's Lyrical Monologue* we have a stanza of two quatrains; in the former the "b" rhymes of both quatrains, in the latter the "b" rhymes of the second quatrain are two-syllabled, in both cases for playful effect. *St. Agnes* is in a stanza composed by merely spacing as a unit three quatrains of the same pattern. In *Sir Galahad*, again, we have a three quatrain stanza, but its scheme is more elaborate. The first quatrain is our simple cross-rhyme of four and three stress lines; the second quatrain varies this pattern by extending the second line to four stresses; and the third quatrain is composed entirely of four-stress verses, with the first verse silent as to rhyme, and interior rhyme in the third. The poem, *Of Old Sat Freedom on the Heights*, which is another of those printed in 1842, though included among the poems of 1833, is a quatrain precisely

---

[6] Collins, *Early Poems*, 309.

like the second quatrain of the *Sir Galahad* stanza. The
nine-line stanza of *Sir Lancelot and Queen Guinevere* is
modelled after that of *The Lady of Shalott* but differs from
it in the absence of the refrain element in the fifth and ninth
lines. It is mentioned at this point only because its series
of four-stress ambics is finished off by a three-stress verse.
Fitzgerald has transmitted a stanza of *The Courtship of Sir
Lancelot,* known at Cambridge when he was there, which
has the regular quatrain of four-stress verses.

A number of the poems are in quatrains of four-stress lines
and they fall roughly into two groups, those with cross-rhyme
and those with enclosed rhyme. The quatrain of *Lady Clare*
belongs to the first class; but while the prevailing movement
is iambic, there are some ballad freedoms of syllabling and
accentuation, and three-stress verses occur sporadically,
particularly as the closing verse of the quatrain. The ten
poems which make up *The Day Dream* continue the stanza
of paired quatrains, used formerly in *The Miller's Daughter,*
and in *The Sleeping Beauty,* of which *The Day Dream* is an
amplification. This arrangement is varied in the *Prologue,
Moral, L'Envoi,* and *Epilogue,* by massing the quatrains continuously. In *The Beggar Maid,* the stanza of *The Day Dream*
is modulated by introducing interior rhyme into the first
verse of the second quatrain and leaving its third verse silent.
In *Lady Clara Vere De Vere,* printed in 1842 among the 1833
poems, the second quatrain is the same as that of *The Beggar
Maid,* but there is the further modification that, in the first
quatrain, only the even verses rhyme. The lyric, *Move East-
ward Happy Earth,* is composed of three quatrains which
recall the stanza of *Mariana,* the first and third having alternate rhyme, the middle stanza, enclosed rhyme. The third
quatrain, however, is spaced as a separate stanza. It differs
from the *Mariana* arrangement in repeating the "b" rhyme
of the first quatrain for the "a" rhyme of the second.

STANZAIC TABLE (Four and Three Stress Iambic), 1842

Metre	Title	Rhyme-Scheme	Notes
4xa & **3xa ..**	*The Talking Oak*.........	a b a b...	
"	*A Farewell*...	a b $\overset{R}{\overline{a\ b}}$	"b" rhymes feminine
"	*The Goose*....	a b a b...	"b" rhymes feminine
"	*Amphion*	a b a b c d c d...........................	"b" & "d" rhymes feminine
"	*Will Water-proof*.......	a b a b c d c d...........................	"d" rhymes feminine
"	*St. Agnes*.....	a b a b c d c d e f e f...........................	
Iambic	*Sir Galahad* .	a^4 b^3 a^4 b^3 c^4 d^4 c^4 d^3 $(s)^4$ e^4 $(ff)^4$ e^4	{ (line 9 silent; line 11 interior rhyme
"	*Of Old Sat Freedom*....	a^4 b^4 a^4 b^3	
"	*Sir Lancelot and Queen Guinevere*..	a^4 a^4 a^4 a^4 b^4 c^4 c^4 c^4 b^3	
4xa	*Lady Clare*...	a b a b...	ballad variations
"	*The Day Dream*	a b a b c d c d...........................	Quatrains massed in some pieces
"	*The Beggar Maid*	a b a b (cc) d (s) d........................	{ line 5 interior rhyme; line 7 silent
"	*Lady Clara Verede Vere*	(s) a (s) a (bb) c (s) c......................	{ lines 1 and 3 silent; line 7 silent; line 5 interior rhyme
"	*Move East-Ward*, etc..	a b a b b c c b d e d e...........................	
"	*The Statesman* (1831, *Memoir*)....	a b b a	First published in the *Memoir*
"	*You Ask Me Why*........	a b b a...	
"	*Love Thou Thy Land*..	a b b a...	
"	*The Blackbird*	a b b a...	
"	*The Two Voices*	a a a...	

The quatrain of four-stress iambics with enclosed rhyme, a stanza afterward made famous by *In Memoriam*, was obviously evolved out of Tennyson's manifold permutations of the quatrain. Tennyson neither stumbled upon this arrangement nor did he adopt it from any of his predecessors. It was a natural product of his experiments.[7] He himself has declared on this point, "I had no notion till 1880 that Lord Herbert of Cherbury had written his occasional verses in the same metre. I believed myself the originator of the metre, until after *In Memoriam* came out, when some one told me that Ben Jonson and Sir Philip Sidney had used it."[8] This is Tennyson's statement. It was undoubtedly sincere, and there is little question that his memory in the matter was sound. His period of apprenticeship was over. Some of Wordsworth's loveliest lyrics, such as the "Lucy" poems, and some of Burns' songs undoubtedly weighed with him and attracted his attention to the possibilities of the simple quatrain—many of the above permutations of the quatrain can be duplicated in Burns and Wordsworth; but Tennyson was no longer imitative in these matters; he was learning more about technique from the work of his own hands than from any previous maker of verse. The fragment of nine lines which Lord Tennyson calls "the germ of *In Memoriam*"[9] is not in the stanza afterward adopted for that poem, but in the cross-rhyme quatrain. Sometime between the jotting of those lines in the last days of 1833 and the composition of the lyrics with which *In Memoriam* really began, not many months after, he had settled upon the metre in which these "occasional poems" were to be written. If the author of the Life is correct in setting the date of 1831 for the poem, *The Statesman*,[10] that is the first complete poem by Tennyson in this metre of which we have any record. The fitness of this stanza for poems of sustained dignity and thoughtful content seems to have been early appreciated by Tennyson.

[7] See, however, Chapter III, p. 43, note.
[8] *Memoir*, I, 305.
[9] *Memoir*, I, 107.
[10] *Memoir*, I, 110.

Two of the best of his political patriotic poems, ''You ask
me why tho ill at ease'' and ''Love thou thy land with love
far-brought'' were among the poems included with the 1833
pieces, though first published in 1842;[11] *The Blackbird* is
somewhat more trivial in content.

The few fragments and unpublished pieces which have
been preserved to us from these years confirm the evidence
of the 1842 collection as to the character of Tennyson's experiments at this stage. Thus, *Youth,* dated 1833 in the
Life,[12] a very considerable example of Tennyson's style at
this period, and the slight pieces, ''Along this glimmering
gallery''[13] and *Whispers,*[14] are in varieties of cross-rhyme
quatrain. By their position among the pieces of 1842, in the
later collections as well as from their quality, we may assume
that *The Letter* and *The Voyage* were of early composition.
Both are in stanzas of paired quatrains after the manner of
The Miller's Daughter, The Day Dream, etc. The lines *On
a Mourner* (''Nature so far as in her lies'') were not published until 1865, but they are referred to in a letter from
Spedding, in September, 1834.[15] Here we have a repetition
of the stanza of the poem *To—* (''My life is full of weary
days'') published in 1833, but suppressed in 1842 and republished in *Juvenilia,* 1871, *viz.,* a five-line stanza composed
by pairing the last verse of the ordinary cross-rhyme
quatrain.[16] The tiny lyric, *Requiescat,* though not published
until 1864, is referred to in the same letter, September 19,
1834.[17] The quatrain is reminiscent, in its mingling of
three, four, and five stress lines of the stanza of *The Palace
of Art.* ''Come not when I am dead,'' afterward printed

---

[11] *To* ———, *after reading a Life and Letters, Examiner,* 1849, *Dedica-
tion to the Queen,* 1851, and *To E. L. on his Travels in Greece,* 1853, all
of them afterward placed in the early portion of Tennyson's collected
editions, are composed in this stanza.
[12] *Memoir,* I, 112.
[13] *Memoir,* I, 146.
[14] *Memoir,* I, 145.
[15] *Memoir,* I, 139.
[16] See above, p. 39.
[17] *Memoir,* I, 139.

among the earlier poems, but first published in *The Keepsake,*
in 1851, is a somewhat more complex trifle in iambic movement. Finally, *The Two Voices,* which was composed not
long after Hallam's death and "was known among Tennyson's friends, under the title, 'Thoughts of a Suicide'," is
in regular four-stress iambics, rhyming in triplets. This arrangement gives a strophic unit of much greater capacity
than the ordinary couplet in this measure, while retaining
an effect of drastic condensation which, combined with its
slower movement and monotonous insistence, peculiarly fits
it to the subject-matter of the poem.[18] The fragment entitled *The Eagle,* first collected in 1851, is in the same metre.
It is clear from this rapid survey that in addition to a large
proportion of the poems of the 1842 volume, practically all
of Tennyson's experiments of this period, both those which
were permanently withheld from circulation and those which
he afterward allowed to come forth from their hiding, were
written in simple four-stress iambics, arranged, in the vast
majority of cases, in simple quatrain form.

We turn now to the few poems in exceptional movements.
Edward Gray is a simple ballad in quatrain of four-stress
free-syllabled verse, the first and third lines silent, a common
ballad movement.[19] The *Conclusion* of *The May Queen,*
naturally, was in the metre of the earlier parts, *viz.,* the full
length, free-syllabled septenary, rhymed in couplets. Two
brief lyrics, *Break, Break, Break* and *The Poet's Song,* are
anapaestic in movement and, in both, the alternation of
anapaests with substituted iambs and spondees is exceedingly
ingenious and expressive. Simple as *Break, Break, Break*
seems, its variety of rhythm is astonishing. Though the
sense of anapaestic time is never lost, scarcely two verses have
precisely the same movement. In the 16 lines there are
twelve different combinations of iambs and anapaests.   All
the possible permutations are run through, except that we
never have more than two iambs to the verse, and never two

---

[18] Mr. Gwynn does not agree with this. *Tennyson,* p. 210.
[19] See Gummere, *Ballads,* Appendix II.

in succession at the opening of a verse. Then, in the third stanza, when the possible permutations of the three-stress verse are all but exhausted, the third line is extended to four stresses, a variation which is repeated in the fourth stanza. In addition, we have the wondrous silences of the opening verse, repeated at the beginning of the last stanza; the magical spondee of the second verse contrasting with the full anapaestic opening of the corresponding line in the last stanza; the feminine ending of the third; while, except for the first line itself, the only movements employed more than once are those of the fourth verse repeated in the seventh and sixteenth, in the last, at least, for balance; and the full three anapaests of the sixth verse, repeated in the eighth and twelfth, surely for balanced effect. Note effects of balance:

I........	1	$-'\ -'\ -'$	IV......	1,-13	$-'\ -'\ -'$
	2	xx$-'\ -\ -'\ -\ -'$		14	xx$-'$ xx$-'$ $-$ $-'$
	3	xx$-$ $'$xx$-$ $'$x$-$ $'$x		15	xx$-'$ x$-'$ xx$-'$ xx$-'$
	4	x$-'$ xx$-'$ x$-'$ 4-7-16		16	x$-'$ xx$-'$ x$-'$
II	5	x$-'$ xx$-'$ xx$-'$	III	9	xx$-'$ x$'$ $-$ x$'$ $-$
	6	xx$-'$ xx$-'$ xx$-'$ 6-8-12		10	xx$-'$ x$-'$ xx$-'$
	7	x$-'$ xx$-'$ x$-'$		11	x$-'$ xx$-'$ xx$-'$ x$-'$
	8	xx$-'$ xx$-'$ xx$-'$		12	xx$-'$ xx$-'$ xx$-'$

The Poet's Song, in four-stress anapaestics shifting to four and three at the end of the first and throughout the second stanza, introduces the iamb somewhat more freely. On account of the length of the verse, there is greater scope for variety; but for that very reason the variety of this poem is less striking. The type set by the first line, two iambs followed by two anapaests, occurs frequently in the poem. Most of the lines have two iambs, two have three, and only one has none.

In the *Vision of Sin,* three distinct types of metre are used and there is a clear intention to adapt metre to substance somewhat after the fashion of *The Lotos Eaters.* The opening narrative is a series of heroic couplets, but concludes with a triplet closing in an alexandrine. The second section, describing the music and the dance, is taken up in five-stress trochaic catalectic, which alternates irregularly with full trochaic movement, sometimes extending to six stress and sometimes dropping to four, varied by occasional dactylic substitutions, and rhyming anarchically. The third section drops back to a dignified movement of regular five-stress iambic, but now the rhymes are mostly alternate or enclosed. The fourth section, the monologue, returns to trochaic movement; but now it is the regular quatrain of four-stress lines. This section has, indeed, the effect of a ballad; but the movement is exceedingly regular, and the consistent truncation and opening on an emphatic syllable seems curiously fitted to the cynical bravado and malevolent irony of the old sinner who speaks.[20] In section 5, the solemn key is resumed, and here we get a regular succession of heroic couplets as in the opening section. We may note, by way of summary, that the opening and closing sections of the poem are in the very same verse; that the iambics of section 3, on account of the difference of rhyme-arrangement, have an effect very different from that of 1 and 5. Again the trochaics of 2 and 4 have something in common owing to this movement, which sets off their recklessness and unrestraint against the dignity and repose of the iambic parts; and yet, though they have this something in common, they are also entirely distinct from each other.

The Lord of Burleigh is composed in a trochaic ballad metre[21] precisely like that of the fourth section of *The Vision of Sin*, except that the ''a'' rhymes are consistently two-syllabled; this seemingly slight variation approximates the metre very closely to that of *Locksley Hall* as will be illustrated below. Aside from the last named piece the only

---

[20] I say seems, for such theories as to the appropriateness of specific movements to specific feelings are often confuted by unexpected contradictions in practice.

[21] *The Captain*, first published in the *Selections* in 1865, was placed by Tennyson among the earlier poems, and was probably, therefore, of early mintage. It, too, is a ballad in trochaics.

other important example of trochaics, belonging to this period, is the poem ''O that 'twere possible'' published in *The Tribute* in 1837 and afterward elaborated into *Maud,* and this is trochaic only in passages.

The metre of *Locksley Hall* was a striking novelty and will call for extended notice. In formal terms, it is eight-stress catalectic trochaic, rhyming in couplets. So far as I have been able to discover, it had never been anticipated by any English poet except by Tennyson himself in a few sporadic lines of *The Lotos Eaters.* And yet, unusual as the metre seems, it is not so remote as one might at first think from the other verse schemes which Tennyson was fashioning about the same time. Many of the rhymed poems of the 1842 volume were in simple quatrains of four-stress iambics or in simple modifications of these forms. In the course of these experiments a consistent truncation to trochaic would have been perfectly natural. And if, by such a stage, the metre of *The Lord of Burleigh* had been discovered (Fitzgerald seems to have known the poem as early as 1835) and if then Tennyson had thought to leave the first and third lines silent (as indeed he did in some of his permutations of the iambic quatrain), he had but to print two lines as one (as he had already printed the septenaries of *The May Queen*), and the invention was complete. The printing of a few lines of *The Lord of Burleigh* in this manner will demonstrate how closely its rhythm resembles that of *Locksley Hall.*

All at once the color flushes her sweet face from brow to chin,
As it were with shame she blushes and her spirit changed within,
Then her countenance all over pale again as death did prove;
But he clasp'd her like a lover, and he cheered her soul with love.

Now let us compare:

Then her cheek was pale and thinner than should be for one so
    young,
And her eyes on all my motions with a mute observance hung,
And she turned her bosom shaken with a sudden storm of sighs—
All the spirit deeply dawning in the dark of hazel eyes.

The invention seems complete,[22] but its possibilities are only begun. Even more remarkable than the invention of the metre of this poem is the combined restraint and adequacy with which its possibilities are utilized. It is natural for a long metre of this kind to break up with more or less monotony, and this monotony Tennyson permits and, to a certain point, even encourages. The natural pause at the end of the verse and of the couplet is never violated, and of the 194 lines which constitute the poem, 147 have the caesural pause after the fourth foot, against 47 in which the pause falls elsewhere. The 47 unusual pauses are, however, distributed so as to keep the sense of the long rhythm in equilibrium against the tendency to break into four-stress units. In 33 of these cases the pause falls in the midst of the fourth measure, while in 6 cases it falls after the fifth, in 5 cases after the third, in 1 case within the fifth, and in 2 cases within the third foot. The normal rhythm therefore is that of the lines quoted above as analogous to that of the four-stress trochaic of *The Lord of Burleigh;* but while this rhythm is carefully preserved it is quite as carefully modulated by variations like the following:

Rolled in one anothers arms, // and silent in a last embrace.
Glares at one that nods and winks, // behind a slowly dying fire.

Here at least, where nature sickens, nothing. // Oh for some retreat
Breaths of tropic shade and palms in cluster, // knots of Paradise.

Full of sad experience, // moving toward the stillness of his rest.
Never comes the trader // never floats an European flag.

The lingering of the medial pause is also enhanced by frequent spondees, or something very like spondees, in the fourth measure of the verse. Thus, while the pause at that point tends to preserve the trochaic movement in balance against the catalectic close of the second half line, this effect is modulated by a frequent long quantity in the normally short syllable.

---

[22] For more extended discussion of the origin of this metre see Appendix B, p. 244: *Note on the Origin of the Locksley Hall Metre.*

Finally, there is a tendency in so long a metre for the measures, by alternate stress, to group themselves into "pæonic" rhythm, and while this tendency is allowed considerable swing, it is also considerably resisted, and a fine equilibrium is preserved between the trochaic, and the pæonic movement. In the following couplet, for example, the dactylic substitutions at the beginning of the first verse render a break into pæonic rhythm peculiarly easy. Note, then, how the trochaic movement is reestablished at the end of the first verse and in the second, third, and fourth measures of the second verse, after which it again glides freely into pæonic.

Màny an evéning by the wáters did we wátch the státely shíps
Ànd our spírits rúshed togéther àt the touching òf the líps.

The movement is expressed by the following diagram:

xxx-´ xxxx-´x xx-´ x-´ x-´

xx_´x_´x_´xxx_´xxx_´

The result of all these balances is a remarkably fluent and flexible rhythm, at once swift and slow, exuberant and dignified, buoyant and strong, the whole exceedingly expressive, haunting, and, one may add, widely imitated.

But at the very time that Tennyson was destined by a casual metrical exploit to stimulate his most distinguished contemporaries into further experiments in metrical novelty, he was himself setting his practice to a more conservative modulation of simple standard metres. The very metre which produced this effect was, in all probability, merely a striking off-shoot of those elaborate permutations of simple metre with which Tennyson was occupied throughout this period.

CHAPTER VI

THE BLANK VERSE POEMS OF 1842

The most signal evidence of the maturity of Tennyson's workmanship in this period was his creation of a characteristic blank verse. We have seen that during the years immediately following the publication of the *Œnone* volume his ideal of blank verse was settling to a constant. One of the first fruits of this maturity was the revised form of *Œnone*. In *Œnone* he had originated a style of verse, very different from his earlier experiments in imitation of Milton and Shakspere, and in some ways different from any that had preceded it in English poetry. In the revision of that poem and in the composition of others which were published with it in the 1842 volume he carried this style to completion.

It has been conjectured[1] that the model for Tennyson's blank verse was that of Shakspere in the *King John* period. Our studies thus far have been to little purpose, however, if they have not rendered it reasonably certain that in this period Tennyson was outgrowing external influences in such matters and creating a technique of his own. In his blank verse as elsewhere, his style, though remotely derived through his formative periods from that of others, acquires a character peculiar to himself. It is the outgrowth of his own experiments and answerable to no fixed standard save that set by his own judgment.

A perception of the effect which may be gained by a close adherence to prescribed rhythms is the grand discovery, so far as this period goes, of Tennyson as a metrical artist. The practices which we noticed in the revision of *Œnone* and

---

[1] Collins, *Early Poems*, Introduction, p. xviii, note.

8

The Lover's Tale are carried into all the blank verse of this period. Striking as are the processes of his standardization of other forms, they are unsophisticated in comparison with his application of the same principle to the subtlest of all English metres. Having set narrow limits to variation, he is prepared to develop within those limits every capability of manipulation which the prescribed form will permit. By keeping the sense of the typical rhythm powerfully dominant he sustains a rhythmic pressure from which are evolved all his most expressive cadences. The reader is kept alive to every pulse of the metre and sensitive to its slightest change. An intensive cultivation of a limited and yet sufficient range of minute variations is the secret of Tennyson's metrical charm so far as such a quality can be analyzed and measured. There is, in the most perfect equilibrium, variety and uniformity. The restriction of the more obvious and noticeable devices of variation not only keeps the primitive rhythm effective, but it raises to a high power the minutest nuances of movement and intensifies every subtlest modulation. By such restriction, the poet is at once forced and helped to a superlative delicacy of shading. Such is the helpfulness, to an artist, of a highly conventionalized and sophisticated practice of form. It remains now to analyze the blank verse of these poems so that we may see as distinctly as possible the precise technical means by which Tennyson arrived at such a result.

First of all, it should be noted that the change in the language of the poems is inseparable from the achievements of the metre. Upon the simplifying of Tennyson's language there follows a physical fact of the greatest importance from the metrical standpoint. His diction becomes still more strongly monosyllabic. To fit such a diction to a scheme of verse without violating the natural order of the words and still preserve the fulness and the fluency of the metre and the distinction of the style, is a supreme test of metrical skill. The more closely we examine Tennyson's verse the more we must admire the skillfulness with which this feat has been accomplished.

Regularity of stress is insistent. The iambic movement is jealously preserved. Inversions of all kinds are sparingly introduced; beginning and caesural inversion occur in moderation; interior inversions are practically unknown; the stressed positions, and particularly the verse-end, are emphasized by filling them with prolongable and sonorous syllables. As a result the movement is characteristically deliberate and emphatic and this quality is enhanced by the occasional introduction of spondees. This additional weight in the unstressed portion of the measure further fills out and slows the rhythm. Weak measures are carefully limited and with equal care distributed so that the mild hastenings which attend them do not impair the general effect of regularity and deliberation. Variations of syllabic number are likewise severely limited, and the extra-syllables are almost invariably of the slurrable variety; double-endings and epic-caesurae are rare.

The sense of the rhythmic norm is further strengthened by emphasis of the verse unit. The pause falls with a high degree of regularity at the verse-end and frequently fails within the verse. The end-pause is invariably masculine; the interior pause is predominantly though not excessively so. The weakened stresses are largely confined to the medial measures so that the normal rhythm is, as a rule, strongly enforced at the end of the verse, and to a less degree at its beginning. Typical movements are so balanced and modulated as to create an idiosyncratic set of rhythms without becoming disagreeably monotonous.

That this type of verse does not seem stilted and stiff is due, in part, to the shortness of the poems and to their almost lyrical intensity and condensation. It is noteworthy that in such poems as the *Morte d'Arthur* and *The Gardener's Daughter*, which are somewhat longer than the average of this group, the severity of the verse-structure is appreciably relaxed, while in the shortest poems, such as *Ulysses* and *Tithonus*, this severity reaches its extreme. Likewise, in the isometric lyrics which Tennyson later inserted in his longer blank verse poems, he almost invariably returned to the severer patterns of this period. Finally, the success of the verse is due, in no small measure, to the opulence with which all the resources of the language are lavished in devices of tone-color and sound coordination.

We may establish a hypothetical norm of blank verse structure for this group of poems by averaging together the metrical statistics for them all. This done we shall be able, by comparison with the average standard, to demonstrate the relative uniformity of Tennyson's practice, and we shall also have a basis for estimating the particular idiosyncrasies of the respective poems. I shall include in these averages the observations for *Tithonus*. We have Tennyson's assurance that this poem was written about the same time as *Ulysses*, though not published until nearly twenty years later. This gives us ten poems, aggregating 1,510 lines of blank verse, the sum total of Tennyson's output of blank verse in his new poems of 1842, with *Tithonus* added. In the following statements, unless otherwise indicated, the term "per cent" means in each one-hundred lines.

The regularity of stress is indicated by the following statistics. There are, in the entire 1,510 lines, 151 cases of beginning inversion, or an average of precisely 10 per cent. Caesural inversion occurs 15 times, or a little less than 1 per cent. The counter-caesural inversion occurs 3 times. There are 2 cases of recessional accent.

There are 736 weak measures, an average of 48.7 per cent. They are distributed as follows: the first measure 77 or 5 per cent, the second, 119, or 7.8 per cent; the third, 174, or 11.5 per cent; the fourth, 302, or 20 per cent; the fifth, 64, or 4 per cent. The points to be noted here are the infrequency of stress-failure in the first and last positions of the verse and its relatively great frequency in the fourth, which is nearly twice that of the next in order, the third.

Spondees are less frequent than stress failure, but still are present in sufficient numbers to counterbalance, in part, the hastening effect of the latter. The total number of spondaic substitutions is 411, an average of 27.2 per cent. These are distributed in a manner noticeably different from the arrangement of stress failures. Spondees occur as follows: in the first position there are 116, or 7.6 per cent; in the second, 141, or 9.37 per cent; in the third, 76 or 5 per cent; in the fourth, 31, or 2 per cent; in the fifth, 47, or 3.1 per cent. Note that conversely with the weak measures, they are least frequent in the fourth and of relatively high frequency in the second and first positions. But in the fifth they are, like the weak measure, relatively rare.

Trisyllabic substitutions are very sparingly introduced; particularly is the grouping of numerous light syllables together avoided. There are only 19 tribrachs in the fifteen hundred and odd lines, a little more than 1 per cent. Slurrable syllables are occasionally introduced. Usually they are of the most gliding vowel sort. There are, all told, 88, or 5.8 per cent. This does not include two sporadic cases of double ending, and 12 epic-caesurae. The syllable-counting is close; obviously, the license of metrical equivalence is not abused.

PAUSE

The emphasis of the verse-unit may be set forth in terms of the pause distribution. Run-on lines average 27.2 per cent or, conversely stated, 72.8 per cent of the lines are end-stopped. The interior pause is negligible in 33 per cent of the lines. But the fluency in certain of the lines is offset by the occurrence of more than one pause in others, so that we get a total of 1,276 interior pauses or an average of 84.5 per 100 lines. Now if we add together the percentages of interior pauses and end-stops we shall be able to indicate in statistical terms the average frequency of pause. Our result is 157.3 per cent. From this we derive the ratio of pause to measure, namely 1:3.18, which may be taken for the *exponent of fluency*. Of the total 1,276 rhetorical pauses within the verse, 758 are masculine, that is, 59.4 per cent of them fall after a stressed syllable. In 332 cases, the pause falls at the close of the second measure; that is 21.9 per cent follow the fourth syllable. The others in order of frequency are as follows: after the sixth syllable, 14.6 per cent; the seventh, 11.1 per cent; the fifth, 10.3 per cent; the third, 9.2 per cent; the eighth, 7.5 per cent; the second, 6 per cent; the first, 1.9 per cent; the ninth, 1.7 per cent.

These averages provide us with a set of standards for estimating the metrical characteristics of the various poems of the volume and we may now proceed with our discussion of the individual poems. It will be our study to discover and set forth in as definite a manner as possible the devices by which, with comparatively small latitude for deviation from the typical pattern of the verse, the poet modified the rhythm of his verse so as to adapt it to a number of poems of considerable diversity in theme and key, and gave to each a more or less characteristic music of its own. An explicit classification of the poems would be alluring, but it would, perhaps, decoy us into exaggerations and beget hair-splitting and the over-emphasis of insignificant minutiae.

There is, nevertheless, a certain contrast between what may be called *free* and *severe,* or, perhaps, *idyllic* and *heroic,* types of verse. The first employs to a greater degree the feminine devices of rhythm. By means of the feminine caesura, by a less monosyllabic diction and the linking of measures, by a varied distribution of weak measures, and a relatively free use of enjambement and extra syllables, the pauses are minimized and a movement not rapid but more continuous is produced, which may be fairly characterized as feminine. Such verse, when successful, is noticeable for its fluency and sweetness. It usually accompanies considerable ornateness and redundancy of style. Its defects are lack of incisiveness, and vigor; it tends to run into voluptuousness or even prettiness. Perhaps the best representative of this type is *The Gardener's Daughter*.

The *heroic* verse is the accompaniment of more robust sentiment and language. The diction is more noticeably monosyllabic. The pulse of the verse is more determined; both the ictus and the pauses are more pronounced; the movement is varied more by shifts of stress and pause, and less by changes of syllabic number. The masculine caesura prevails more noticeably, the close of the measure more frequently coincides with the end of word or word group, and the pauses are thereby accentuated. Weak measures are massed in the medial positions, and the iambic rhythm has clear sway at the beginning and end of the verse. There is much balance and massing of movements and time-intervals. The result is an increase of dignity and solidity in the verse structure. The deep-chested vowels linger on the ear. The slow, massive, regular and balanced periods give an effect of thoughtfulness and deliberation, of restrained and noble passion. The opening and closing passages of the *Morte d'Arthur* furnish admirable illustrations of this type of metre.

But the poem which combines these elements most conspicuously is *Ulysses*. This poem must have been in process at the very time when Tennyson was giving those reforming touches to his *Œnone*, which were to translate it into so signal an illustration of his development in technique. Like *Œnone*, *Ulysses* represents Tennyson's application of his imagination to classical materials, in this case, apparently, with a suggestion from Dante. Like *Œnone*, it represents a free reach of the imagination toward a subject-matter remote from immediate interests and surroundings. But both its external materials and its underlying thought are much more robust than anything in *Œnone*, and are more closely woven into one texture than is the case with the earlier poem. This too is indicative of the progress of his mind and art. In *Œnone*, the moral ideas are like the descriptions, more or less embroidered upon the groundwork of the poem. But in *Ulysses* they seem an inevitable part of the structure of the poem. Indeed, there are very few of Tennyson's works in which his imagination has so completely fused a noble idea and the materials which embody it. And there are few in which such ideas and materials have been so adequately fitted with words and music. In this sum-total of effect, the versification is of great importance.

Much of the vigorous and yet continent power of *Ulysses*, what John Addington Symonds called its "calm majesty", is due to its "heroic" rhythm. No other poem of Tennyson has more of this quality, and no other poem is more "heroic" in versification. The metre is masculine and austere. The iambic movement is severely maintained. The chief modulations are beginning inversions which slightly exceed the average frequency, 10 in 72 lines, or 13 per cent. These have an energetic effect. Weak measures are slightly below the average frequency, 33 in all, or 45 per cent; they are massed in the medial positions, 15, nearly half, in the fourth measure; 10 in the third; 5 in the second; 2, in the fifth, and 1 in the first. Spondees slightly exceed the average frequency, 22 in all, and these are massed in the earlier measures, 9 in the first position, 6 in the second, 5 in the third, 1 in the fourth and 1 in the fifth; a total of 30 per cent. There is 1 tribrach, and no other variation in syllabic number.

The verses without interior pause are a couple of points above average frequency, 35 per cent. The same is true of run-on lines, 31 per cent. But these characteristics are, in part, off-set by a slightly higher ratio of interior pause—86 per cent. Still, the exponent of fluency is a shade above the average, *viz.*, 3.24. Masculine pause strongly predominates, whether we consider rhetorical or metrical caesurae; of the former 66 per cent, of the latter 64 per cent are masculine. The rhetorical pauses are distributed with much variety as follows: after the fourth syllable 15; the sixth, 14; the fifth, 10; the seventh, 8; the eighth, 7; the second, 5; the third, 3.

If the metrical pauses were enumerated a somewhat different distribution would appear.

These somewhat tedious details and perhaps over-ingenious balances serve to make definite what is meant when we say that the verse of *Ulysses* is extraordinarily regular and solidly syllabled and yet not lacking in fluency. Perhaps it should be added that the last named quality is enhanced by resting the stresses upon ringing and well-vowelled monosyllables, and by the judicious distribution of such feminine elements of rhythm as are admitted. The total effect needs no further praise or even characterization; but we can afford to indulge ourselves in a brief illustration which embraces most of the characteristics enumerated above:

> The lights begin to twinkle from the rocks:
> The long day wanes: the slow moon climbs: the deep
> Moans round with many voices. Come, my friends,
> 'Tis not too late to seek a newer world.
> Push off, and sitting well in order smite
> The sounding furrows; for my purpose holds
> To sail beyond the sunset, and the baths
> Of all the western stars, until I die.

Tithonus is a singularly perfect specimen of Tennyson's mature artistry. We have the poet's authority that it was written about the same time as *Ulysses*,[2] and it may well be considered in comparison with that poem. It is on precisely the same scale, and is a similar feat of the imagination. Though less animated and less interesting for many reasons, it is more characteristic of Tennyson, and even more perfectly executed, than *Ulysses*. In its seventy-five lines of condensed and polished verse there is not a false or superfluous syllable. We must turn to Collins' *Ode to Evening* to find "the gradual dusky veil" of perfectly modulated speech as softly and harmoniously folded to its imagery as here. That the chief impression is made by the images themselves there need be no doubt. The decaying woods, the vapours, the "white-haired shadow roaming like a dream", twilights, far-folded mists, dim fields, "wrinkled feet on glimmering thresh-

---

[2] *Memoir*, II, 9.

olds'', crimsoning portals, empty courts, soft airs fanning
the clouds apart, starlight on tremulous eyes that fill with
tears, rose shadows, strange songs far off and long ago,
whispers, and ''ever silent spaces of the East'', do their work;
we sense the silent gradual spread of dawn.   Here is genuine
imaginative sympathy with ancient myth; and here is landscape as impressionistically toned to one mood as in a Whistler
nocturne.   But the rhythm moves in unison with these im-
pressions, ''like perfect music unto perfect words'', and bears
its due part in the total effect.

Superficially, *Tithonus* is in the same type of verse as
Ulysses, but by delicate shading of sound and rhythm, an entirely different result has been produced.   In *Ulysses*, the
syllables march to the ear ''with dint of armed heels;'' here
they steal and tremble forward as softly as ''the old myster-
ious glimmer'' itself.   As in *Ulysses* the movement is slow
and regular; but it is varied in a different manner.   Inversions are fewer; there are but 7 beginning inversions, an
average of 9 per cent, and there is 1 caesural inversion.
Weak measures are slightly more abundant, 48 per cent, and
the failure of the stress in the fourth measure amounts to a
characteristic of the rhythm.   One-half of the weak measures,
18, fall in this place; there are 9 in the third position, 4 in the
fifth, and 3 and 2 in the first and second, respectively.   There
are 21 spondees or 28 per cent, and the frequency of these in
the second measure constitutes another characteristic of the
rhythm.   The second position, with 9, is followed by the first
with 6; the third has 4, and the fourth and fifth, 1 each.
There is less than average frequency of run-on, 26 per cent.
But one of the most striking characteristics of the rhythm is
the extraordinary number of lines without interior pause, 35,
or 46 per cent.   So that while the proportion of end-stops is
unusually great there is still an unusually high exponent of
fluency, 3.37.   The commonest sense pause within the line is
after the fourth syllable, 14; the third follows with 10; then
follows the seventh, with 8; the sixth with 6; the eighth with
4; the second and fifth with 3 each, and the ninth and first

with 2 and 1, respectively. Note that, in addition to the large number of lines with only end pause, there is an unusual freedom in the distribution of the other pauses, as indicated by the breaking down of the usual order of frequency, particularly the very small proportion of pauses after the fifth and sixth and the larger proportion after the third and seventh. The ratio of even pauses is 56 per cent, which is slightly below standard average and 10 per cent below *Ulysses*. This index of a feminine rhythm is more than confirmed by a computation of the metrical caesurae. These prove to be 56 per cent feminine and give a further emphasis to the fourth and seventh positions, each with 23 per cent; the fifth, sixth and third follow at a considerable interval with 14 per cent each. Finally the poem exceeds any other of this group in the proportion of extra-syllables. There are ten of these and one tribrach, an average of 14 per cent, but all are of the most slurrable vowel or liquid kind and produce only the faintest ripple in the quiet current of the verse.

If we review these statistics, we shall note that they indicate a series of characteristic features. The typical iambic movement is carefully set in the first verse:

The woods decay, the woods decay and fall.

Then sets in a dominant feminine rhythm frequently rippled by extra vowels, and often flowing on continuously to an end stop; regularity of iambic movement in the first two measures of the verse, frequent slowing by spondees in these positions and pause after the fourth syllables; frequent hastenings in the middle measure and doubly frequent hastening in the fourth, often a slight check after the seventh syllable and then a hastening on to the fall and full pause at the end of the next and last foot of the verse. This is the dominant movement but not the only one. In passages like the following,

A white-haired shadow roaming like a dream
The ever-silent spaces of the East,
Far-folded mists, and gleaming halls of morn.

> Once more the old mysterious glimmer steals
> From thy pure brows, and from thy shoulders pure
> And bosom beating with a heart renewed.

the soft-syllabled stream, checked and hurried and checked again, dips on and on with an ever varied sameness of rhythm to the final fall and cease. That such a music is suited to the substance and atmosphere of the poem it is almost idle to remark.

Love and Duty has some characteristic cadences of its own which may be fairly set forth in terms of its metrical differentia. In this poem Tennyson departs somewhat from his usual key. Whether, as seems likely, the poem represents an occasion in the poet's own experience, or whether it is chiefly imaginary and was only remotely suggested by his relation with Emily Sellwood, it is perhaps futile, and, in view of Tennyson's silence on the subject, would be impertinent, to inquire. Certain it is, however, that we have here a presentment of passion quite distinct from anything else in this series. That haze of memory or distance with which Tennyson invested all of his subjects in this series and that elaboration of descriptive and sentimental accessories in which he enveloped and involved his characters and action are here relatively absent; the actions and passions are more directly presented, are brought more boldly into the foreground; there is a cry of strenuous and personal passion very different from the tone of dreamy and musical reverie which pervades the idyllic pieces. In this poem, the language of powerful passion is fitted to the normal pattern of the verse. In Shakspere's, Chapman's and Milton's blank verse, under such circumstances, the verse norm frequently staggers and gives way to the irregular emphasis and syllabling of impassioned speech. Tennyson solidly adheres to all the salient outlines of the verse structure, and only the subtler modulations are employed, with accumulative effect, to simulate the broken rhythms of passion. Five beginning inversions and one caesural inversion in 98 lines are the only violations of the stress scheme, and there are but three extra-syllables. But fullness in syllabic weight is perhaps the distinctive charac-

teristic of the verse. *Love and Duty* has a smaller proportion
of weak measures than any other poem in this group, 31 per
cent; which is 17.7 points below the average for the group. It
leads all the others in the frequency of spondees, 41 per cent,
or 13.8 above the average. The weak measures are more than
usually massed in the fourth position, 17 out of 31. The
spondees are even more strikingly massed in the first and
second measures, 12 and 19, respectively, out of the total, 41.
The pauses are distributed with free variety and the *full stop*
is frequently within the verse; 56 per cent, somewhat less
than the usual predominance, are masculine; and there is a
strong predominance of the fourth, 29 per cent. The proportion of lines without interior pause, 31 per cent, is slightly
below, the proportion of run-on lines, 33 per cent, slightly
above, average. There is one monosyllabic preposition, "by",
in the final position, but this receives so strong a rhetorical
ictus that it cannot be regarded as a weak-ending. Thus the
most striking characteristics of the rhythm, taking the poem
as a whole, are syllabic emphasis, regularity of stress, and a
broken scheme of determined pauses. But this last idiosyncrasy is constantly resolved by a return to the full integrity
of the verse unit, so that the total findings for the poem show
no revolutionary discrepancies from the averages for the
group. The broken cadence is struck at the outset:

> Of love that never found his earthly close
> What sequel? Streaming eyes and breaking hearts?
> Or all the same as if he had not been?
> Not so.

Here are the disjointed movement, the broken syntax, the
short, abrupt, exclamatory phrases of passionate speech.
Then follows a hurry through several verses without end pause,
some of them without interior pause.

> Shall Error in the round of time
> Still father truth? O shall the braggart shout
> For some blind glimpse of freedom work itself
> Thro' madness, hated by the wise, to law
> System and empire? Sin itself be found

The cloudy porch oft opening on the Sun?
And only he, this wonder, dead, become
Mere highway dust? or year by year alone
Sit brooding in the ruins of a life,
Nightmare of youth, the spectre of himself.

Such passages merge into movements whose fierce emphatic syllables are freighted with passion, as

Then not to dare to see!   When thy low voice
Faltering, would break its syllables, to keep
My own full-tuned, hold passion in a leash
And not leap forth and fall about thy neck.

The following tense syllabling is tremulous with emotional life:

                        The trance gave way
To those caresses, when a hundred times
In that last kiss, which never was the last,
Farewell, like endless welcome, lived and died.

Till now the dark was worn and overhead
The lights of sunset and of sunrise mix'd
In that brief night; the summer night, that paused
Among her stars to hear us; stars that hung
Love-charm'd to listen: All the wheels of Time
Spun round in station, but the end had come.

Finally, the tense emphatic movement is all but resolved into the full-toned Tennysonian iambic, in the long after-swell, still heaved into waves of rhythm by the scattered spondees, fewer now and softer,

And leave thee freer till thou wake refresh'd
Then when the first low matin-chirp hath grown
Full quire, and morning driv'n her plow of pearl
Far furrowing into light the mounded rack
Beyond the fair green field and eastern sea.

Thus the normal iambic verse has been moulded by delicate variations of quantity and pause into the rhythms of unwonted passion, and then by delicate gradations resolved back once more, in sympathy with the imagery and the feeling, into the main idyllic music.

Another subtle differentiation of the blank verse structure is found in *Dora*. The verse peculiarities of this poem indicate in a telling manner the close relation which exists between the ornate language of Tennyson and the characteristic sonorities and rhythms of his verse.

The problem of style which was before Tennyson in the writing of *Dora* is well stated in his own note[3], " 'Dora' being the tale of a nobly simple country girl, had to be told in the simplest possible poetical language, and therefore was one of the poems which gave most trouble." As we are told elsewhere,[4] "Spedding used humorously to say that this was the poem which Wordsworth always intended to have written." In fact, Wordsworth himself once said to Tennyson, "I have been endeavoring all my life to write a pastoral like your 'Dora' and have not succeeded."[5] We have only to compare Tennyson's manner in this poem "so Hebraic in its stern and unadorned simplicity",[6] with the padded descriptions and over-wrought sentimentality of Miss Mitford's telling of the tale in her *Dora Creswell*, from which its main outlines were taken, to appreciate the contrast between a condensed and suggestive poetical masterpiece and a mediocre prose sketch. And yet, successful as *Dora* is, it is not unqualifiedly so. Its simplicity of style is visibly labored. It is clearly not in Tennyson's native vein. Such simplicity as he achieved in this poem he achieved by a *tour de force* of self-suppression. One note of style is sufficient to indicate how foreign is the workmanship of *Dora* to the native handicraft of the author of *The Gardener's Daughter*. In *The Gardener's Daughter* there are over one hundred and fifty qualitative epithets; in *Dora*, which is nearly as long, there are four. It matters little that the effort which could produce such a result was conscious on the poet's part; but it matters a great deal that he has not succeeded in concealing that effort from the consciousness of the reader. In trying to

---

[3] *Memoir*, I, 196.
[4] Eversley ed. Vol. I, p. 392.
[5] *Memoir*, I, 265.
[6] Aubrey de Vere, *Memoir*, I, Appendix, p. 501.

steer as close as possible to the shores of prose, he has scraped bottom even if he has not run aground.

Dora, then, is not merely austere in style; it approximates the manner of prose. It is not surprising that, as the language approaches the language of prose, there should be a corresponding approximation to the rhythms of prose. It is instructive to observe just what peculiarities of versification attend his adherence to the idioms of prose speech. As in the other poems which have been analyzed, there is no considerable relaxation of the general outlines of verse structure. The fundamental iámbic movment is not roughly disturbed, and the syllabic scheme remains practically intact. The change in the quality of the verse is effected chiefly by the management of weak measures, spondees, syllabic quantity, and pause distribution. In the 168 lines of the poem, there are but 6 beginning, and 2 caesural inversions. There are, however, counter-caesural inversion and one wrenched stress in the last measure of the verse coupled with a double ending, the dramatically expressive "Look to it."

But the important variation is in the use of weak measures; even after making due allowance for the extraordinary stress which is laid upon parts of speech that in a less simple language would receive less stress, we have still an excessively high frequency of weak measures. There are 106 weak-measures, 63 per cent, which is about 15 per cent above the average for the group and more than double the frequency in *Love and Duty.* And this failure of stresses is uncompensated by spondaic substitutions. There are but 26 spondees, or 15 per cent,—hardly more than a third of the proportion in *Love and Duty,* and a little more than half the average proportion for the group. Nor are these divergences from the normal stress distributed in the ordinary manner; the usual predominance of stress failures in the medial measures of the verse is not maintained, there being 21 in the first measure, 20 in the second, 23 in the third, 37 in the fourth, and 5 in the fifth. Thus, although in all of the first four measures there is more than the average proportion of stress failures, the number in the fifth measure is below average, and the usual ratio among the first four is not preserved. In the fourth, we have 22 per cent, which is two points above average; but the 12 per cent of the first is two and one half times the usual proportion, and the ratio to the fourth is more than 1 to 2, whereas in *Love and Duty*, it is 1 to 8.5; the second and third are about 4 and 3 points, respectively, above average frequency.

The relation of these phenomena to Tennyson's usual practice in blank verse is clearly established by a comparison with Wordsworth. The likeness of Tennyson's style in this poem to that of Wordsworth, particularly to that of Wordsworth's similar poem of homely life, *Michael*, has frequently been noticed; but the similarity in versification has not been pointed out. In *Dora*, Tennyson much more closely approximates Wordsworth's practice in regard to weak measures than in any other poem of this group. Wordsworth, following out his precept in regard to fitting the language of real life to metre, is much freer in his management of stress than is Tennyson. Inversions and extra-syllables are more freely introduced; but far more important than either in determining the character of his verse is his practice in regard to stress failures. Even in *Dora* there is no such license in regard to the frequency, distribution, and character of the weak measures as is prevalent in Wordsworth's blank verse.

The first 100 lines of *Michael* may be taken as sufficiently representative. We find a total of 95 weak measures and 2 tribrachs against a total of 63 per cent in *Dora*. And their distribution is as much freer than that in *Dora,* as that in *Dora* is freer than is usual with Tennyson. The distribution of stress failures in these 100 lines of *Michael* is as follows: in the first measure, 21, in the second 20, in the third 20, in the fourth 26, in the fifth 8. In *Dora* they run, per 100 lines, in the first 12, in the second 11, in the third 13, in the fourth 22, in the fifth 2.9. Obviously the older poet has used far less circumspection, if any, in the distribution of weak measures. Nor do these comparisons indicate com-

9

pletely the difference .between Tennyson's practice and Wordsworth's. In Tennyson's verse the weak measures are due to the occurrence in the stressed position of monosyllabic prepositions, conjunctives, unemphatic auxiliaries, copulatives and pronouns, and the secondary stresses of polysyllables: but almost never does he permit the verse stress to fall upon articles or possessive pronouns. In the few cases where this is permitted, the weak-measure is almost invariably followed by a spondee, and is either at the beginning of the verse or immediately after the caesural pause, so that inversion can take place and the ictus falls upon the preposition or conjunctive which precedes the article. The second condition is usually present in Wordsworth but the first is not observed. The following are examples of Tennyson's practice:

> Ere yet they blind the stars, *and the wild team.*
> > *Tithonus.*
> *By the long wash* of Australasian seas.
> > *The Brook.*
> *And the sun fell*, and all the land was dark.
> > *Dora.*

In Tennyson's verse, not only does the compensating spondee fall immediately after such weak measures, but the adjacent measures are usually pronouncedly iambic, so that the regular movement is only momentarily lost sight of. Further, Tennyson only rarely permits more than one stress failure in any single verse, and practically never in two successive measures; whereas all these occurrences are frequent in Wordsworth. In *Michael*, for example, we meet such lines as the following,

> *For the* delight *of a* few natural hearts.
>
> *And with* yet fonder feel*ings, for* the sake
>
> *That the* green vall*eys, and* the streams and rocks
>
> A plea*surable* feel*ing of* blind love
>
> *That they were as* a prov*erb in* the vale
>
> So many in*cidents upon* his mind.

Now, allowing that in a blank verse of this sort the rhythm of pure speech is somewhat modified by the incidence of the verse ictus upon its unemphatic particles, it is clear that the verse must suffer a corresponding relaxation of its specific character as distinguished from prose; its characteristic regularity and sonority of rhythm is thus reduced to something approximating the more colorless rhythms of prose. Byron, whose own blank verse was too loosely patterned to permit us the belief that he was scoring this particular vice of Wordsworth's versification, has nevertheless epigrammatically phrased the matter in the couplet which pillories the chief of the "Lakers" as a bard,

> Who both by precept and example shows
> That prose is verse, and verse is only prose.

It should be observed, however, that the lowered tone which this type of versification imposes upon Wordsworth's writing had from his standpoint its peculiar stylistic value, and when his purpose served, he could gather his syllables into as noble rhythms as are to be found in any but the very greatest English blank verse.

> For I have learned
> To look on Nature not *as in* the hour
> Of thoughtless youth, but hearing oftentimes
> The still sad mu*sic of* human*ity*
> Nor harsh, nor grat*ing*, *though* of ample power
> To cha*sten and* subdue. *And I* have felt
> A pre*sence that* disturbs *me with* the joy
> Of ele*va*ted thoughts, a sense sublime
> Of something far more deep*ly* *in*terfused
> Whose dwel*ling is* the light of setting suns
> *And the* round o*cean, and* the living air,
> *And the* blue sky, *and in* the mind of man,
> A mo*tion and* a spirit which impels
> All thinking things, all ob*jects of* all thought
> And rolls through all things.

In such passages he wings a flight, with singular beauty and force of contrast, above the pedestrian plane of his ordinary way of travel. Modulations which were mainly instinctive in Wordsworth, in Tennyson realize the extreme of sophistication.

The remaining peculiarities of the verse of *Dora* are less striking, but their effect is augmentative. There are 9 extra syllables, 1 tribrach, 1 double ending, 2 epic caesurae. This is a conservative variation of syllabic number, but the variations are mainly massed in particular passages and are almost always dramatically expressive. The pauses are somewhat differently distributed than elsewhere. A larger number than usual are feminine, only 52 per cent are after the even syllables, as against the general average of 59.4 per cent and the 66 per cent of *Ulysses*. Perhaps this enhances somewhat the peculiar rhythms of the poem,—an effect which is made the more characteristic in that the monosyllabic diction precludes any considerable occurrence of the ordinary feminine rhythm. Moreover, the absolute frequency of such pauses is greater than appears from our form of statement because of the relatively small number of lines without interior pause, 25 per cent. Thus, the pauses after the fifth syllable are expressed by 16 per cent, as against the average, 10.3 per cent. As the third, 13 per cent, is considerably above average, and all the other stops except the fourth, 25 per cent, are more or less below average, it follows that the stops are pretty well massed in the middle of the verse. Add that the proportion of run-on lines, 25 per cent, is considerably below average, and it becomes clear that the position of the pauses tends to maintain that sense of the normal verse structure which other characteristics tend to relax. This is another and a striking example of Tennyson's power of keeping variety and uniformity in equilibrium; so that when for expressive purposes the verse scheme is relaxed in some one particular, it is the more rigidly enforced in some other. Finally, the combined frequency of end stops and interior pauses gives us an unusually low exponent of fluency, 3.07. This is the statistical way of saying that Tennyson's usual fluidity has yielded to a stern concision of statement which is reflected in the movements of the rhythm.

The characteristics of style and verse in this poem are seen at their best in the following passage:

> So saying, he took the boy, that cried aloud
> And struggled hard. The wreath of flowers fell
> At Dora's feet. She bow'd upon her hands,
> And the boy's cry came to her from the field,[7]
> More and more distant. She bow'd down her head,
> Remembering the day when first she came,
> And all the things that had been. She bow'd down
> And wept in secret; and the reapers reaped
> And the sun fell, and all the land was dark.

Here are the concise phrasing, the determined pauses, the failures and adroit shifts of stress, the compensating spondees, and the resolution to the full normal rise and fall of syllables, the suspension and final satisfying return of the rhythmic norm. Thus, though *Dora* has certain characteristics in common with *Michael* and similar poems of Wordsworth, it is, taken altogether, as far as possible from the diffuse manner of that poet. What we have here is not an imitation of Wordsworth's versification, but a reproduction by Tennyson of some of its characteristics for the adaptation of his own kind of verse to similar uses.

In connection with *The Gardener's Daughter* we have some glimpses of Tennyson at work which give us a more or less intimate knowledge of his attitude toward his creations. Tennyson himself said: "The centre of the poem, that passage describing the girl must be full and rich. The poem is so, to a fault, especially the descriptions of nature, for the lover is an artist, but this being so, the central passage must hold its place." That is, the poem as a whole being highly ornate, the "central passage" must not be less so, for it must be in keeping with the remainder. We may compare with this statement, Poe's assertion that having written the climacteric stanza of *The Raven*, he would have purposely weakened any

---

[7] Cf. the phrasing and the stress upon "to" with
"The winds come *to* me from the fields of Sleep."
Wordsworth: *Intimations.*

preceding passage rather than permit it to outshine the portion he was "writing up to."

We have it on Tennyson's authority[8] that the passage following the phrase, "Her beauty grew", which in the first edition, ran

> till drawn in narrowing arcs
> The southing Autumn touch'd with sallower gleams
> The granges on the fallows.

was perhaps omitted because Fitzgerald had said that the autumn landscape was taken from a background of Titian. Churton Collins has observed that, "if this was the reason he must have been in an unusually scrupulous mood."[9] And indeed, it seems more likely that the poet may have been induced to substitute for this bit of description, admirable though it is, the human narrative interest which now fills its place, because he realized that the poem was too profuse in descriptions of nature. Few other changes were made in the published texts of the poem. From his privately printed text of 1842, the poet "drove an ugly sibilant away", substituting "her" for "his"[10] in the passage "Stole from her sister Sorrow." The heroine was left in the ludicrous situation of "lisping" her consent until 1850, when "faltering"[11] was substituted.

Before its publication the poem was carefully labored. Aubrey de Vere tells[12] of finding Tennyson one day in Spedding's rooms. "He shewed me the Ms. and said, 'The corrections jostled with each other, and the poem seemed out of gear. Spedding has just now remarked that it wants nothing but that this passage, forty lines, should be omitted. He is right.' It was omitted." The passage omitted may have been *The Antechamber*, an unpublished poem of 52 lines,

---

[8] *Memoir*, I, 198.
[9] Collins, *Early Poems*, 157.
[10] *Early Poems*, p. 158.
[11] *Ibid.*, 157.
[12] *Memoir*, I, Appendix, p. 501.

which was originally intended as a prologue, but which, Lord Tennyson explains, his father "wished never to be printed in front of 'The Gardener's Daughter' because this is already full enough."[13] The fragment is of some interest as the only discarded study of the period which remains to us.

As printed in the Life [14], this fragment has some features which may well have made the poet feel that it was "out of gear" with the rest of the poem. It will be sufficient to notice that the versification seems somewhat wooden in comparison with the finished poem of which it was originally a part, and has characteristics which suggest that Tennyson's ear could hardly have been satisfied with its cadences. It has, for example, more than the ordinary amount of inversion, 18 per cent beginning, 6 per cent caesural inversion. The weak measures amount to 64 per cent, a greater frequency than obtains in any poem of the 1842 group, though *Dora* comes near it; and these are not distributed in the usual proportion, running 6 per cent in the first position, 14 per cent in the second, 22 per cent in the third, 12 per cent in the fourth, and 10 per cent in the fifth. The spondee distribution is about normal, 24 per cent in all. The pause distribution is exceedingly abnormal and is perhaps the most striking indication of unsatisfactory execution from Tennyson's standpoint. The pauses are 83 per cent masculine, a predominance quite unapproached in any complete poem of the series. There is no pause after the third syllable, only 1 after the seventh, and only 5 after the fifth. The lines without interior pause are of the same frequency as in *The Gardener's Daughter,* 36 per cent; but the run-on lines only half as frequent, 18 per cent. Finally there are two cases of extra-syllable which violate Tennyson's usual practice in this period and would probably have been eradicated had the poem been finished for publication. We should be ill-advised to lay serious stress upon these findings, and yet it is worth noting that aberrations of practice are found in a discarded study which do not appear in any published poem, and which

[13] *Memoir,* I, 198.
[14] *Memoir,* I, 199.

differentiate it widely from the poem that it was originally intended to accompany.

The Gardener's Daughter may be taken to represent the logical acme of Tennyson's idyllic method. Like most of this group the poem is a monologue by one of the characters in the action. Tennyson has chosen his character and his point of departure with due regard to the purposes of his art. As he himself has pointed out, there is some significance in the fact that the speaker is an artist. This condition of composition gives the poet an opportunity to indulge his love of picturesque settings and poses and his taste for lavish paintings of natural scenery. The artist is now an old man and he tells his story musingly, garrulously, and with many divagations. And not only is his story enveloped in the haze of distance; it is veiled by that reticence which the poet evidently considered appropriate in the portrayal of the passions. Nothing could be clearer than the phrasing of this principle of his art, toward the close of the poem. After some two hundred lines of elaborately embellished narration, leading up to the culmination of his wooing, the narrator is made to say,

> "Would you learn at full
> How passion rose thro' circumstantial grades
> Beyond all grades develop'd? and indeed
> I had not staid so long to tell you all,
> But while I mused came Memory with sad eyes,
> Holding the folded annals of my youth;
> And while I mused, Love with knit brows went by
> And with a flying finger swept my lips,
> And spoke, *'Be wise: not easily forgiven*
> *Are those, who, setting wide the doors, that bar*
> *The secret bridal chambers of the heart*
> *Let in the day.'* "

In other words, it takes me eleven lines of elaborate and charming blank verse to tell you that I'm not going to tell you anything. "Yet might I tell", the narrator nevertheless continues, "of meetings, of farewells," and he mentions, certain

> whispers, like the whispers of the leaves,
> That tremble round a nightingale

and certain "sighs", "vows", "kisses", which are characterized with the same elaborateness and the same vagueness, and finally Memory gets free only when, by a turn of association, she looses herself upon the background of the passionate scenes which have been hinted,

> as above
> The heavens between their fairy fleeces pale
> Sow'd all their mystic gulfs with fleeting stars;
> Or while the balmy glooming, crescent-lit,
> Spread the light haze along the river-shores,
> And in the hollows; or as once we met
> Unheedful, tho' beneath a whispering rain
> Night slid down one long stream of sighing wind
> And in her bosom bore the baby, Sleep.

If one chose to be impatient for a story, he might object that here is much time and labor spent in telling us that two youthful lovers once went to sleep in the rain. And to crown all, what do we get? The old man raises a curtain and shows us a portrait!

But such criticism would be myopic and unfair; for those "heavens" that "Sow'd all their mystic gulfs with fleeting stars" are no ordinary heavens, they are the mystic skies that emparadise two lovers. The rich scenes of nature which are woven in with the thin skein of the story in this poem are not mere objective descriptions; they tell us all we need to know, or at least all the poet wishes us to be told; for they are the scenes among which these dreamland lovers moved in the hey-day of their romance, scenes still transfused with the colors of their fancy, lovingly selected by Memory, and musingly retouched and toned by tender retrospect. If, as is doubtless true, Tennyson has carried to a faulty extreme, here, his method of subordinating the characters, the actions, and the passions to the background, the accessories, and the sentiments of his story, the poem is all the more suggestive as a specimen of his idyllic manner.

The versification of *The Gardener's Daughter* need not detain us long. The poem is a very just example of Tennyson's versification, and the statistics of its phenomena are in many cases so close to the average for the group that a characterization of the group may almost apply directly to the individual. It is, however, considerably freer than the average as to inversion: there are 40 beginning inversions in 250 lines, or 16 per cent, and there are 6 caesural inversions. Weak measures are distributed practically in the average proportions; there are 4 per cent in the first position; 7+ per cent in the second; 10.8 per cent in the third; 21.6 per cent in the fourth; 5.6 per cent in the fifth, a total, therefore, of 49.6 per cent which is less than 1 per cent above average. The same is true of spondees with a total of 26+ per cent which is about 1 per cent below average. Both weak measures and spondees are slightly above average frequency in the fifth measure. Rhetorical pauses are slightly more feminine than average, 56 per cent even; there is a slight excess of average frequency after the seventh and ninth syllables. Metrical caesurae are 52 per cent feminine. Run-on lines are considerably above average frequency, 36 per cent. Lines without interior pause are slightly more numerous than usual, also 36 per cent. The exponent of fluency is high, 3.34 per cent. In syllabication as in inversions the verse is relatively free. There are 18 extra-syllables, 7 tribrachs, and 3 epic-caesurae, a total of 11 per cent against the average of 5.8 per cent, and higher than in any other poem except *Tithonus*. These freedoms, together with the feminine pauses, the plentiful inversions, and the full quota of weak measures give a slight *insouciance* to the rhythm which is in keeping with the tone of the poem.

But the full-syllabled Tennysonian iambic is well preserved; the diction is extraordinarily rich in liquids and vowels, and the poem is as a whole one of Tennyson's finest examples of verbal melody. Such passages as those quoted above, especially such lines as, ''Holding the folded annals, of my youth'', the full-syllabled and yet fluid line,

Night slid down one long stream of sighing wind,

and others oft-quoted, such as,

> The windy clanging of the minster clock,
>
> The lime a summer home of murmurous wings,
>
> A league of grass, washed by a slow broad stream,
>
> The mellow ouzel fluted in the elm.
>
> Thro' crowded, lilac-ambush trimly pruned,
>
> The twinkling laurel scatter'd silver lights,
>
> Stole all the golden gloss and wavering
> Lovingly lower, trembled on her waist
>
> Till every daisy slept, and Love's white star
> Beam'd thro' the thicken'd cedar in the dusk
>
> And all that night I heard the watchman peal
> The sliding season: all that night I heard
> The heavy clocks knolling the drowsy hours.

these and numberless passages of similar character, many of them, it will be noted, mainly feminine in rhythm, are striking examples of that marshalling of syllables in which Tennyson seemed to have enlarged the expressive, as well as the melodious and rhythmical, capabilities of the language. But to this phase of his art, full justice has long ago been done.

Tennyson never met a theme more consonant with his genius and never struck a more successful balance between the austere and the decorative elements of his art than in his first heroic study from the Arthurian legend. His choice of a theme was inspired and his execution was no less so, when he produced the *Morte d'Arthur*. Fitzgerald was undoubtedly right in preferring it to anything else that Tennyson ever did. One of Tennyson's most conscientious critics has well said, that it is "as near perfection as any work of this kind could be",[15] and what Rogers said of *Locksley Hall*, he might more justly have said of this poem, "Shakspere could not have done it better." And yet it is "no whit like

---

[15] Churton Collins, *Early Poems*, p. 142.

Shakspere." Indeed, the critics have been nonplussed to say what it is like. Some have objected to the poet's own epithet, "Homeric", and have pointed out its Virgilian characteristics; and Milton has as clear a title as any of these to an interest in its inspiration. But the fact is that it is like none of these. It is sheer Tennyson, and Tennyson in the plentitude of both his strength and his charm, with the faintest trace of his defects. It is as though he had combined here the vigor and freshness of *Ulysses* with the ineffable glamour of *Tithonus*. It is evidence of the inherent vitality of his conception that it remained alive while his life lasted and endured expansion into the larger scheme of *The Idylls of the King*.

When Tennyson appropriated to his use "an old world story", he secured for himself one of the greatest advantages which an artist can enjoy. He not only enjoyed the advantage of reconsecrating to art a subject which had been seasoned to its uses by the long lapse of time, but he was doubly fortunate in the circumstance that it still remained singularly unhackneyed. It would be perilous to conjecture how far the immense vogue of the Arthurian story throughout the second half of the nineteenth century, together with the whole artistic and academic interest in Celtic antiquity, took its rise from this poem. Undoubtedly, there were other currents of influence and, as early as Ossian and Warton's *Grave of King Arthur*, these had come full flow into the romantic stream; but no one did so much to popularize this interest and widen its later influence as Tennyson with his *Morte d'Arthur*. From Spenser and Milton down, the English poets had coyed with this subject; but the good stars met in our horoscope when Tennyson and the Arthurian legend came into conjunction.

His literary problem here was the converse of that in *Dora*. The two curiously unlike poems have this in common, that in each Tennyson was working over into poetic form a definite prose original, a condition which is not present elsewhere in this series. In *Dora* the poet's problem was to condense a diffuse modern story, strip it of irrelevancies and tawdriness,

modify its incidents to suit his own purpose, and confer upon
it the austerity and lasting beauty of poetic form; in executing this design he proceeded to an extreme of bareness
and concision. In the other case, it was his function at once
to condense and to embellish. He himself said of Malory's
Morte d'Arthur that it had "very fine things in it, but all
strung together without art."[16] From Malory's pithy and
yet rambling account, he selected some of these "fine things",
digested them into an organized whole and embellished them
with some of the ornaments of sophisticated style. In addition, he set them to his own music and breathed round them
the aura of his own refined contemplation and delight.

Hence the subject came to Tennyson not only trailing its
peculiar glory of romantic associations, but bearing with it
elements of expression which left their traces upon his
embodiment of the legend and transformed his idyllic manner
to something rather different from anything else in the poems
of this volume. From Malory he admitted a moderate number
of archaisms of diction and idiom which he compounded with
graceful pseudo-archaisms of his own into a language not altogether unlike that of his earlier experiments, but more
judiciously tempered and answerable to taste. Such are the
expressions, "as thou art *lief and dear*", "*lightly* bring thee
word", "aftertimes", "place of tombs", the "*dint* of armed
heels". In some cases, he employs a phraseology of this kind
which is not in Malory. For example, Excalibur is referred
to as "him", whereas, in Malory, the ordinary pronoun is
used.

But these are mere bits of romantic color. On the whole,
surprisingly little is taken from Malory, or left as the poet
found it. The workmanship is in Tennyson's own composite manner with less indebtedness to Theocritus than in
the other idyls, but with strong infusions of Homer, Virgil,
Lucretius, and Milton. Nature touches which are mere hints
in Malory are expanded, after Tennyson's manner, into an
elaborate background. Mere hints like the references to the

---

[16] *Memoir*, I, 194.

richness of the sword are expanded into detailed descriptions.
Sir Bedivere's perplexity as he stands,

> This way and that dividing the swift mind,

is described in language which Tennyson, for once, delights
us by frankly calling "A *translation* of Virgil."[17]

Incidents are transformed and reinterpreted. Malory's
circumstantial, but few and simple, details of how Sir Bedivere
"went to the sword and lightly took it up and went to the
waterside, and then he bound the girdle about the hilt and
then he threw the sword as far into the water as he might,"
are amplified into a series of pictures, embellished with a
Miltonic simile and concluded with a leisurely epic summary,
as follows:

> Then quickly rose Sir Bedivere, and ran
> And, leaping down the ridges lightly, plunged
> Among the bulrush-beds, and clutch'd the sword,
> And strongly wheel'd and threw it. The great brand
> Made lightnings in the splendour of the moon,
> And flashing round and round, and whirl'd in an arch,
> Shot like a streamer of the northern morn
> Seen where the moving isles of winter shock
> By night, with noises of the northern sea.
> So flash'd and fell the brand Excalibur.

The curt speeches are elaborated into sententious commentaries. Sir Bedivere's "Oh, my Lord Arthur, what shall
become of me now ye go from me and leave me here alone
among mine enemies?" is expanded into a dozen lines which
not only express this sentiment but present a succinct history
of the Round Table and comment upon its significance. And
Arthur's reply, "Comfort thyself, and do as well as thou
mayest, for in me is no trust to trust in.—And if thou never
hear more of me, pray for my soul," becomes

> The old order changeth yielding place to new,
> And God fulfills himself in many ways,
> Lest one good custom should corrupt the world.

---

[17] Eversley ed., Vol. I, p. 387.

Comfort thyself: what comfort is in me?
I have lived my life, and that which I have done
May He within himself make pure! But thou
If thou shouldst never see my face again,
Pray for my soul.

Whereupon follow nine verses concerning the efficacy of prayer. Then the sentence which filled the hiatus in the last quotation from Malory, "For I will unto the vale of Avilion to heal me of my grievous wound," is enlarged into nine verses containing Arthur's description of "the island valley of Avilion", a description which Tennyson himself has authorized us to think of as derived both from the *Odyssey* and from Lucretius, with perhaps an epithet from Pindar.[18]

And yet, notwithstanding these seeming amplifications, nothing could be more false than to imply that there is anything diffuse about Tennyson's plan. He has not in reality enlarged upon Malory, but has thrown the materials into another arrangement. As compared with the rambling and prolix method of the original, Tennyson's manner of treatment is really an economy of space. He has, in fact, extracted the quintessence of his original and infused it into an art work of totally different form and scope.

And something analogous is true of the heroic manner of the poem. The real wonder of the *Morte d'Arthur* is the slightness of its bulk compared with what it accomplishes. Tennyson has not so much reproduced the heroic style as reduced it to its lowest terms. It is this which is really novel and really wonderful in his achievement. He has not merely mimicked the effects of heroic poetry; he has produced something like it which is new and on a different scale. He has reproduced "the grand style" in miniature. He has moderated it: he has moderated the old absurdities; he has rejected much of the old machinery; but he has retained an exquisite transparency of the old effect. The "grand style" has often been burlesqued; but Tennyson has not travestied the "grand style"; he has passed it through the strainer of his own taste and fancy; he has idyllicised it.

---

[18] Eversley ed., Vol. I, p. 389.

These balances and moderations are reflected in the versification. The combined stateliness and ease, the united strength and luxury of rhythm are tallied in the mechanism of the verse. There is less restraint and regularity than in *Ulysses;* the syllabling is not close and emphatic like that in *Love and Duty;* at the same time, there is little of the obvious *morbidezza* which we find in *Tithonus,* and *The Gardener's Daughter.* The relaxations in the metre are more in the direction of *Dora,* in the interests of naturalness and dramatic realism of speech, rather than of musical floriation. But the musical background so to speak, is resonantly heroic. The rhythm is set at the outset in the splendid full-syllabled roll of the opening lines which Tennyson in his grand voice

> Read, mouthing out his hollow oes and aes
> Deep-chested music,—
>
> So all day long the noise of battle rolled
> Among the mountains by the winter sea.

In the verse of this poem, complete shifts of stress are only moderately employed; beginning inversion is 15 per cent, and there are 4 cases of caesural, 1 of counter-caesural inversion. But the verse is peculiarly rich in those subtler modulations of the time which come from the skilful distribution of weak measures and spondees; there are 55 per cent weak-measures and 31 per cent spondees. The stress failures are, therefore, more numerous than in any poem except *Dora;* and spondees are more frequent only in *Love and Duty,* though *Ulysses* comes near. *Dora,* however, has a notably small proportion of spondees, and *Love and Duty* of weak-measures; so that neither furnishes a parallel for the prevailing cadences of the *Morte.* The weak stresses are distributed in about the normal proportions, 13 in the first measure, 22 in the second, 37 in the third, 57 in the fourth, 23 in the fifth. The only thing exceptional in the distribution is the excess of stress failure in the fifth measure as compared with the first; this is to be accounted for by the fondness of Tennyson, in this poem, for ending his verse wth polysyllables, especially with proper names (Bedivere, Excalibur, etc.), thus procuring a peculiar lingering emphasis upon the last syllable which enhances the sonority and dignity of the word. Further, the stresses more frequently fall on an article than is usual with Tennyson. There are four cases, for example, in which the stress falls upon the particle "a":

> That stood *on a* dark strait of barren land;
>
> Brightening the skirts *of a* long cloud, ran forth
>
> That nour*ish a* blind life within the brain.
>
> But now farewell. I am go*ing a* long way.

Notice that in every case where the stress fails in this manner the compensating spondee immediately follows, and not only does the language take on a peculiar intonation on account of the emphasis of the article through the incidence of the verse, but a time-emphasis is conferred upon the monosyllabic adjective which absorbs the interval that would normally be occupied by the preceding syllable. It is probably no accident, that in two cases out of the four, the monosyllable which receives this time-emphasis is the word "long". When the compensating spondee is delayed one measure we get a still different effect, as in the following,

> And looking wist*fully* with *wide blue eyes.*

The converse effect of weak measures in the midst of a full-syllabled passage is well exemplified in the following. Notice the energetic effect of the harsh emphatic syllables and then the resolution to a lighter and more fluid movement, accompanied by a more liquid diction.

> Dry clash'd his harness in the icy caves
> And barren chasms, and all to left and right
> The bare black cliff clang'd round him, as he based
> His feet on juts of slippery crag that rang
> Sharp-smitten with the dint of armed heels—
> And on a sudden, lo! the level lake
> And the long glories of the winter moon.

10

A notable passage in which the modulation of the rhythm is produced almost entirely by spondees is the following:

> And in the moon athwart the place of tombs,
> Where lay the mighty bones of ancient men,
> *Old knights*, and over them the *sea-wind sang*
> *Shrill, chill*, with flakes of foam. He stepping down
> By *zig-zag paths*, and juts of pointed rock,
> Came on the shining levels of the lake.

Tennyson pushes his practice in regard to weak measures still farther, admitting two failures of stress in the same verse more frequently than elsewhere. In these cases the weak-stresses usually alternate with full-stress measures, as in the last line of the first extract above, where the first and third stresses are weak:

> *And the* long glo*ries of* the winter moon.

But more frequently, the stresses fail in the second and fourth, as:

> Made light*nings in* the splen*dour of* the moon.

> Laid wid*ow'd of* the pow*er in* his eye.

In such cases, or when two weak measures fall together, or when these conditions are combined with inversion or extra-syllables, we get a hurried or logacedic movement, as in the line,

> Ah mis*erable and* unkind, untrue,

where the weak second and third give us a hurry through the middle of the line which is dramatically effective. A similar example is the following:

> Mut*tering and* mur*muring at* his ear, "Quick, quick!
> I fear *it is* too late *and I* shall die."

In the first line there is but one weak measure, the third, but the inversion and extra-syllables help to create the hurried movement. Such movements are sparingly employed and are invariably checked by spondees and directly resolved back into the full iambic rhythm. But the fact remains that the *Morte d'Arthur* is richer in such movements than any other poem of the series.

How then is the stateliness of the verse preserved? What satisfies that demand for regularity and the sense of restraint which confer dignity upon the rhythm? Partly the constant recurrence of the iambic movement; but peculiarly, the regular disposition of pause: 80 per cent of the lines are end-stopped; 36 per cent have no interior pause; rhetorical caesurae are 61 per cent masculine, and metrical caesurae about the same, 60 per cent. The pause at the fourth syllable has a strong predominance, though there is a normal variety of distribution. The pause scheme is as follows:

1	2	3	4	5	6	7	8	9	10
/	/	/	/	/	/	/	/	/	/
1	18	17	52	28	38	29	13	1	216

There are, in 272 lines of the *Morte d'Arthur* proper, only 197 interior pauses, or 72 per cent. In spite of the infrequency of enjambement, therefore, we have an exponent of fluency, 3.29 which is a shade above that of *Ulysses*. The syllabling is relatively free, 19 extra-syllables, 3 tribrachs, 2 epic-caesurae, a freedom exceeded only in *Tithonus* and *The Gardener's Daughter*. Freedoms in syllabling and stress modulation, then, are skilfully balanced by careful maintenance of the verse unit and regularity in the disposition of pause; expressiveness and fluency on the one hand, in equilibrium with regularity and restraint on the other. The result is a verse which its maker never excelled for combined nobility and sweetness.

In spite of the sophistication implied in the foregoing analysis, the poem has the crowning grace of studied perfection, it does not seem studied at all. Everything is in such perfect keeping: ideas, language, rhythm,—all seem so precisely what they should be, that, in spite of the fact that they are groomed and finished to the nail, they seem quite unconscious, inevitable. The language is noble but never pretentious; the rhythm is expressive, but never self-consciously dramatic; both are frequently of haunting beauty, but this seems to befall quite by chance; in short, there is no visible straining after effect of any kind. This is what we mean by perfection; and here, if anywhere, Tennyson has attained perfection.

There remain four poems of this series which may be dismissed with briefer comment. *Godiva* and *St. Simeon Stylites* belong with the legendary pieces; *Walking to the Mail* and *Audley Court* are contemporary pastorals.

Godiva was written after a visit to Coventry, the home of the legend, in 1840. It is executed with the sureness of a practiced hand. The modern setting, the story, and the comment are dispatched swiftly, and yet with no trace of scurry. The poem has the qualities of Tennyson's solid assured workmanship, not inspired or inspiring, but natural, adequate, satisfactory. Four lines give the modern circumstances and connect the poem with Coventry. A few more carry us from the present to the time of the legend and the story is in progress. Narrative slips into dialogue, dialogue into narrative again, and narrative into description which is so managed as to reflect the experience of the heroine, and almost before we know it, the story is before us, introduced, backgrounded, and told, in 80 lines. The verse is compact, expressive, self-contained. As is usual in the shorter pieces it is exceedingly regular. The 1 caesural and 5 beginning inversions are all used for expressive effect. Weak measures and spondees are mingled with Tennyson's usual art, 47.5 per cent of the former, 32.5 per cent of the latter. They are distributed as follows:

	I	II	III	IV	V	Total
Weak measures	2	7	7	21	1	38
Spondees	5	10	7	1	3	26

He finds room in this slight sketch for most of his favorite modulations. There is the usual skillful alternation of broken and fluent movements, though the proportion of the former is greater than usual, as proved by the low index of fluency,

3.07. Run-on lines are six points above average, 33.75 per cent. Lines without interior stop are 4 or 5 points below average, 28.75 per cent. The proportion of interior pauses is high, 96 per cent, arranged as follows:

1	2	3	4	5	6	7	8	9
2	5	8	26	7	10	7	10	2

The even pauses strongly predominate, 66 per cent, and there is a strong predominance of the pause at four. But in spite of these facts and in spite of the brevity of the poem, the pauses are distributed with animated variety to the other positions, especially to the positions near the beginning and end of the verse. There are only 3 extra-syllables and 1 tribrach; but there are 2 epic caesurae, which are skilfully introduced, particularly that in the following passage:

> He answer'd "Ride you naked thro the town
> And I repeal *it*;" // *and* nodding as in scorn,
> He parted, with great strides among his dogs.

These characteristics of the verse unite with the condensed rhetoric and certain idiomatic touches in the diction to give the poem an air of pleasant *brusquerie* which is not quite usual with Tennyson.

In *St. Simeon Stylites* the element of character is brought more nakedly into the foreground than in any other poem of this group. Tennyson has not Browning's thrilling gift for shadowing character to its penetralia and surprising it into sudden damning witness against itself. He rather constructs than examines character, and he dwells on accessories which are picturesque rather than evidential. Still, in *St. Simeon Stylites,* he comes closer to that species of character poem which Browning called the ''dramatic monologue'' than elsewhere in the early series. One thinks readily of studies in Browning which are similar in conception and aim. The poem is Tennyson's exposure of religious paranoia, its essential folly and hideousness. It is perhaps his best literary expression of the vein of robust and sardonic humor which many anecdotes and characterizations prove him to have possessed. According to Fitzgerald's notes ''This is one of the Poems A. T. would read with grotesque Grimness, especially at such passages as 'Coughs, Aches, Stitches, etc.,' laughing aloud at times.''[19]

The dramatic character of the poem is well reflected in the verse, not by any striking irregularity, but by crowding the rhythm with syllables, so that it seems to hammer emphasis from them. The passage alluded to by Fitzgerald is a good example of this:

> Let this avail, just, dreadful, mighty God,
> This not be all in vain, that thrice ten years,
> Thrice multiplied by superhuman pangs,
> In hungers and in thirsts, fevers and cold,
> In coughs, aches, stitches, ulcerous throes and cramps,
> A sign betwixt the meadow and the cloud,
> Patient on this tall pillar I have borne
> Rain, wind, frost, heat, hail, damp, and sleet, and snow.

Notice that in spite of the extreme of close syllabling in the above passage, this is never carried too far; but the verses which have this quality to the highest degree are constantly alternated with verses of lighter movement, so that the contrast with the normal rhythm never loses its power of emphasis. As a result of this care in preserving the rhythmic norm, the statistical description of the poem as a whole shows no glaring discrepancies with the normal average.

In the 221 lines there are 20 beginning inversions and 4 inversions at the interior pause, the first a little below, the other somewhat above, average frequency. There is one counter caesural inversion, one recessional, and one hovering accent. The 44 per cent weak-measures and 26 per cent spondees are distributed as follows:

	I	II	III	IV	V	Total
Weak measures	15	15	20	38	10	98
Spondees	17	21	13	2	6	59

The weak measures, in particular, are more evenly distributed than usual to the various positions of the verse, but these

19 Eversley ed., Vol. I, p. 394.

proportions would be somewhat changed and the total number of weak measures significantly reduced with the ironical incidence of the verse upon the personal pronoun "I" left out of the reckoning, as perhaps it ought to be. The verse-end is firmly emphasized; only 21 per cent of the verses run-on. The proportion of lines without interior pause precisely coincides with the general average, 33 per cent. These pause characteristics, taken together with the high frequency of interior pause, 90 per cent, gives us the lowest exponent of fluency in the group, 2.95. The extra-syllables, though only 12 in number, are mostly used for dramatic effect and so as to add to the syllabic crowding of the lines. Practically all of these characteristics of the verse are due to the fact that it is fitted to a language of acrid and humorous energy; it would have been impossible for Tennyson to secure the quaint ironical emphasis of this poem without the assistance of a well-managed verse.

Walking to the Mail and *Audley Court* are Tennyson's two experiments in the amœbean pastoral. In the first, two friends, John and James, chat together upon a country by-way on their way to the Mail; there is a bit of local gossip; one of them tells, humoristically, a folk-tale of the country-side about a haunted house; there is a little chatter concerning the farmer's wife, a brief screed of politics, a tale of a college prank, involving a sow and her farrow, a slender preachment, and the trifle ends with the mention of the approaching four-in-hand "three pie-balds and a roan". The poem is chiefly interesting in that it shows Tennyson's emptiness when he tarries in mere realism. It trails the dust of triviality and platitude. "The weakest Wordsworthian line", for the credit of which Tennyson and Fitzgerald contended,

A Mr. Wilkinson, a clergyman

is hardly more serenely barren than the opening and closing passages of this poem. By a just malice of the angered Muse, the poem was visited for years with a ridiculous misprint near its close, "But put your best *'boot'* forward", etc. It fell an easy victim to Calverley's genius for parody.

The poem is, however, closely carpentered. The result is not unlike that of an exquisite piece of furniture fashioned out of ill-colored deal ends. Tennyson's studied artisanship seems a trifle absurd applied to such materials. Perhaps the secret of our discontent is, that we resent the garment of poetry upon a lay-figure of prose. At any rate we must swallow our disgust and learn what we can about the methods of the artist. Tennyson did a little fussing with this job at a later time and the manner of it is slightly instructive. The poem as it was published in 1842 contained 98 lines. Later some ten lines were added, and three verses (one of them containing a vulgarity quite singular in Tennyson) were excised. The changes, therefore, were slight; but such as they were, they were significant. The metrical characteristics of the 1842 text were as follows. There were 4 beginning, and 2 caesural inversions, and 1 counter-caesural inversion. There were 45 per cent weak measures, 19 per cent spondees, distributed as follows:

	I	II	III	IV	V	Total
Weak measures	4	9	8	21	1	45
Spondees	5	3	6	2	3	19

The pause distribution was as follows:

1	2	3	4	5	6	7	8	9
/	/	/	/	/	/	/	/	/
1	8	8	27	5	23	10	5	2

Fifty out of 89 pauses are after the fourth and sixth syllables, and the proportion of masculine pauses is 73 per cent, or 7 per cent higher than in any other poem of this group. The frequency of run-on lines was 25 per cent, and of lines without interior pause 34 per cent. There were 3 extra-syllables, and 1 tribrach; no other variations of the metre. This is a very masculine and systematic verse. It lacks the lightness and variety of syllabling and pause which would fit it to informal dialogue and is responsible for much of the stodginess which we instinctively feel in this poem. Though the changes which Tennyson afterward made were slight, they tended to relieve this condition. The stress scheme remains practically unaltered, but by adding ten lines, and deleting three, there was a gain of 2 beginning inversions, hovering accent was introduced, the proportion of masculine pauses was reduced to 67 per cent, the number of run-on lines was increased by 6, the lines without interior pause were decreased by 3, and the syllabling was considerably modified in the addition of 1 tribrach, 1 double-ending, and 3 epic-caesurae.   Let us illustrate. The opening lines stood:

> I'm glad I walk'd. How fresh the country looks!
> Is yonder planting where this byway joins
> The turnpike?

The present reading:

> *John.* I'm glad I walked. How fresh the meadows look
> Above the river, *and, but* a month ago,
> The whole hill-side was redder than a fox.
> Is yon plantation, etc.

Does the following change, not made until 1851, owe something to Browning's manner, by this time well-known?

Excised: *James.* You saw the man but yesterday:
> He picked the pebble from your horse's foot.
> His house was haunted by a jolly ghost,
> That rummaged like a rat.

Added: *James.* You saw the man on Monday, *was it?*
> There by the humpback'd willow; half stands up
> And bristles; half has fall'n and made a bridge
> And there he caught the younker tickling trout—
> Caught in *flagrante*—what's the Latin word?—
> *Delicto;* but his house, for so they say,
> Was haunted with a jolly ghost, that shook
> The curtains, whined in lobbies, tapt at doors,
> And rummag'd like a rat.

It will be seen not only that these changes and their like tended to relieve the bareness of the original inconsequences by addition of detail, but that they introduce a freer type of metre more adapted to the subject-matter than that which has been described above. The changes were not sufficiently thorough-going to save the poem and perhaps the only mistake made was that of trying to save it.

Audley Court, on the other hand, is delightful from end to
end.   Instead of the pure dialogue which Tennyson attempted
in the piece we have just noticed, he uses here his most fortunate method of narrative-description.   The backgrounding is
only less rich than that of *The Gardener's Daughter,* but not
like that, over-elaborate; there is not a detail to wish away.
The plan of the poem like that of *The Gardener's Daughter,*
and many of the incidents and descriptive passages, together
with the qualities of diction and of metre, are directly suggested by Theocritus, particularly Idyl VII.[20]   But the landscape of the poem was directly suggested by Abbey Park at
Torquay where the remarkable closing description of the poem
was written.   "Torquay was in old days the loveliest sea
village in England."[21]   Here, in a full garden landscape, the
sea in the distance,

> while Audley feast
> Humm'd like a hive all round the narrow quay,

two English youths take their basket supper.   The lunch is
described, the talk sketched but not given: then song replies to song in amœbean fashion; and then, in the twilight
hush, they saunter home,

> beneath a moon that, just
> In crescent, dimly rained about the leaf
> Twilights of airy silver, till we reach'd
> The limit of the hills; and as we sank
> From rock to rock upon the gloomy quay,
> The town was hush'd beneath us: lower down
> The bay was oily-calm: the harbour buoy,
> Sole star of phosphorescence in the calm,
> With one green sparkle ever and anon
> Dipt by itself, and we were glad at heart.

There is scarcely a hint of incident or description that cannot
be fairly paralleled in Theocritus, and yet the whole is vitally
Englished, to the minutest efficient of color, sound or sentiment.   The diction has the idiomatic relish of Tennyson at

---

[20] See Stedman, *Victorian Poets,* pp. 229–231.
 Also, Mustard, *Classical Echoes,* pp. 33–34.
[21] *Memoir,* I, 240.

his indescribable happiest, and the description is penetrated with his happiest magic.

In metre, as in materials and rhetoric, the poem is the perfection of Tennyson's ornate yet terse idyllic style. In the 86 lines of the 1842 text there are 8 beginning inversions and no other complete shifts of stress. Weak measures are 45 per cent, and spondees 24 per cent; each therefore about three points below average. They are distributed as follows:

	I	II	III	IV	V	Total
Weak measures	2	7	14	16	0	39
Spondees	11	5	4	0	1	21

Run-on lines are 29 per cent, lines without interior pause 24 per cent. Interior pauses are 51.9 per cent masculine, their total frequency 89 per cent, and the index of fluency 3.11. There are 4 extra-syllables. But all of these indications would be somewhat modified if we excluded the observations for the two songs.

These songs are Tennyson's first experiment in the "isometric song" and anticipated his later "blank verse lyrics" in *The Princess, The Golden Year*, etc. This feature of the poem, like many others, was suggested by the practice of Theocritus. Each song has its peculiar cadences which differentiate it from its companion. The first, a song of denial, is cast in four blank verse strophes of four verses, each set off by refrain and rhetorical parallelisms. The whole is metrically systematic, the pause masculine, and mostly after the second measure, the lines end-stopped, with one run-on in each strophe, and the only other variation an occasional verse without interior rhetorical pause. The second lyric, a delicate love song, is in four blank verse triplets, each marked at the beginning by the exhortative "sleep" and at the close by the close of the sentence; the pause scheme is feminine, the lines all end-stopped and these movements are varied only by two masculine pauses and one run-on near the close, while the refrain is omitted at the beginning of the last strophe and the whole is rounded by the return of the opening verse.

Sleep, Ellen Aubrey, sleep and dream of me.

By such arts, metrical and rhetorical, are the lyrical outlines defined from the body of the description in which they lie, like "lark and leveret", "Imbedded and injellied".

The entire poem is no less delicately proportioned and articulated than these tiny masterpieces. Two lines which were inserted in its closing period, in 1857 and 1872, respectively,

A rolling stone of here and everywhere

and

Sole star of phosphorescence in the calm.

(the second, according to Tennyson, the germ of the poem) took their places not more for the sake of the characterizing and descriptive touches they add than for their effect upon the suspense of the rhythm. We have only to contrast this poem with *Walking to the Mail* to see what Tennyson cannot do, and what he can do better than anybody else.

The manner in which Tennyson had set about manufacturing Cosmos out of Chaos, is characteristic. Deliberately, without haste and without rest, he went to work to fashion the garment of immortality. The symbols of his suffering are everywhere: in the chastened diction, in the simplicity and unwearying subtlety of the metre, in the deeper morality and soundness of his interpretation of life. The prettinesses and the silly finery have largely been stripped away. His eyes are on life; but it is not mere life that he gives us. He has not made the mistake of substituting mere fact for truth. He spreads the shimmering veil of beauty over all. The harsh and acrid lines of reality are subdued and tranquillized and brought within the realms of dream and art. It matters little whether his materials are drawn from the romance or legend of the past or from the England that lay before his own eyes; when the Tennyson of this period is at his best the result is the same. Arthur speaking from the barge, Ulysses haranguing his followers before setting out beyond the sunset and the baths of all the western stars, St. Simeon haranguing from his pillar, Godiva in the streets of medieval

Coventry, Dora or the Gardener's Daughter in the fields or gardens of contemporary England, Will Waterproof in a contemporary tavern, himself in the throes of Love and Duty or the Vision of Sin, all alike are

> Rolled on each other, rounded, smoothed and brought
> Into the gulfs of sleep.

Ideas and images float in the music of the verse as in a crystal fluid, and the garment of transparent words clothes but does not hide them. All has the imponderable quality, the charm, the unreality, the dimness and yet freshness, the strangeness and yet familiarity, the instantaneousness and the permanence, the remoteness, with the incredible nearness and clearness of the world of dreams.

In short, each subject is treated in a poetical manner, the peculiar poetical manner of Tennyson. Even when his subjects were drawn from the heat of the controversies that were waging all about him, as in his political poems, or the exegetical passages of *In Memoriam,* there is no hint of journalistic shallowness or polemical rancour; his singing robes are on, his song is "high and aloof, safe from the wolf's black jaw and the dull ass's hoof"; he breathes a *largior æther* than that of contemporary politics or polemics. In the cases where he descended to personalities, as later in the well-provoked attack upon Bulwer, earlier in the lines *To Christopher North,* he was not worthy of himself; the poems betray a petty and a scolding spirit. Essentially the artist, he could not with impunity dabble in colors other than those which were native to his brush.

This uniformity of tone in Tennyson's best work, his subdual of all things to one medium, is held by some to argue a lack of original power and genuine poetic vitality. Men regret that his undoubted force of personality did not wreak itself more unreservedly in art. He is accused of tameness, of want of passion, want of salient thoughtfulness; he is said to lack realistic force of detail, lyric swiftness, dramatic fire, and is unfavorably compared with Browning. To all this there is only one answer. These are not the qualities of

Tennyson. We are dealing here with an artist who paints in the colors and under a light peculiar to himself: to those who do not like the colors and the light there is nothing more to be said; they who prefer the flesh paints and the dazzling foreground must look elsewhere.

It is true that in most of the qualities enumerated above, Tennyson is inferior to Browning and to many other poets. He is even inferior to himself. That is to say, his best poems, —best because most perfect and most intrinsically his,—are frequently surpassed in these qualities by passages in less successful poems of his own. It is even true, and this is more paradoxical still, that his own peculiar quality of profound and musical reverie is nowhere present in this volume in the same degree as in some of the earlier and less perfect poems. Perhaps the Tennysonian note is nowhere as plangent as in certain of the best poems in the 1833 volume, and even in one or two of the *Poems, Chiefly Lyrical.* Lovers of Tennyson must be content to miss forever, from his later, perfecter work, that luxury of divine excess, so sweet the sense faints picturing it, which drenches until it drowns the meaning of the earlier poems. Some will feel that those glories of fervent youth, faulty though they were, augured a mightier and more thrilling fulfillment than is vouchsafed in the comparatively timid perfection of the maturer artist. They will question whether Tennyson did not pay for the evenness of execution too dearly out of the robuster constituents of his art. We can not forbid the reflection that Keats, so like Tennyson in many of his characteristics, was not like him in this. Keats never found time, in his brief span, to expunge the imperfections of *Endymion* and refashion it into a more rational and satisfactory poem. Plans more imperative besieged his fancy and left him no time or energy to patch up the errors of immaturity. It may be doubted whether any gift of leisure and long life could have tempted Keats to set aside new plans for old. Browning's creed, *"quod scripsi, scripsi,"* was his, phrased by a different temperament and framed in other circumstances. Such comparisons furnish no sufficient standard for measuring Tennyson; but they throw light upon the utterly different quality and extent of his inspiration as a poet.

There is no doubt that, in all departments, Tennyson's art attains its norm in the 1842 poems. In his response to all his sources of inspiration, in his choice of materials, this is the standard Tennyson. In diversity and in limitation of poetic key, in the design and scope of individual poems, in style and versification, it is the standard Tennyson. He departed frequently from this standard afterward; sometimes he departed brilliantly; but always, at his peril. *In Memoriam* is no exception, for it was synchronous with these poems in conception and mostly synchronous with them in composition. Moreover, its true effect is less that of a large design executed in masterly fashion, than it is the effect of a series of small poems exquisitely modulated in one key. He surprises us with a larger and more complex plan in *The Princess,* but the perfect things in it are the songs, one idyl, and the episodic descriptions; he surprises us with novel passion and lyric fire in *Maud,* but the drama and characterizations fail to win us; he adopts the idyllic style with wonderful cleverness to the larger scheme of the *Idylls of the King;* but we are not convinced; he bends himself with skill and strength to humorous and realistic ballad, to the philosophical lyric, to historical drama; but everywhere we accept his success as tentative if not dubious; we make comparisons; he is present on sufferance. In the 1842 poems, his success is not tentative, he is not present on sufferance, he acknowledges no master; we make no comparisons; the success is absolute; within the limits assigned, the work is final, perfect.

CHAPTER VII

THE PRINCESS

There is substantial agreement among critics as to the absolute excellence of most of the poems which we have just passed in review. It is when we come to the later and longer works, produced, most of them, after recognition was won and fortune had begun to smile, that the assay of Tennyson's poetry begets confusion among critics and splits his readers into camps, as it begot factions in his own day. Fitzgerald's querulous complaints in regard to the later direction of his friend's development are well known. "The last, as I think, of old Alfred's best", he said with that delicate regret, alluding to the tearing up of the old "butcher's book" in Spedding's rooms for the printer of the 1842 issues. And again, "Alfred is the same fine fellow as of old, uttering by far the finest *Prose* sayings of anyone." This, Mr. Saintsbury dubs "the fallacy of companionship," and he is undoubtedly on the right track when he admits that, "in the case of the class of poets to which Tennyson belongs, there does come a time when the rest of the products of their genius is so to speak *applied*,"—this after the very true statement that "with the 1842 book came practically the completion of Tennyson in the sense of the indication of his powers."[1] But it is doubtful if Mr. Saintsbury presses quite in the right direction, or disposes of all the difficulties of the case when he says, "The tree had blossomed; it had almost, to keep up the metaphor, set; but by far the greater part of the fruit was yet to ripen, and very much of it was to be of quality not inferior, of quantity far greater than any that had yet been given."[2] It was not a question of quantity but of scope. Spedding seems to have come nearer to the heart of the matter when, at the

---

[1] *History of Nineteenth Century Literature*, p. 259.
[2] *Ibid.*, p. 261.

close of his fine appreciation in the Edinburgh Review,[3] he called upon the poet for the application of his powers to some larger plan which should utilize all the resources of his genius.

With the reception of the 1842 volumes Tennyson became in a sense public property and the property of the ages, and the men of his time felt that they had a right to call upon him not alone for "something so written to aftertimes as they should not willingly let it die",—that was already accomplished,—but for 'some memorial of the era and of his genius which should be, in scope and power, worthy of them both.   In this, there is no doubt that they were somewhat disappointed, and unquestionably the achievements of Tennyson after the 1842 collection, splendid though some of them may be, leave us finally with a sense of something like disappointment.

When Tennyson's creative genius came to its point of most perfect efficiency, during the season from 1834 to 1842, he was passing from his twenty-fifth to his thirty-third year. During the eight years which followed, he gave the world precisely one poem of large scope, *The Princess*, which as the first long poem of his maturity will call for somewhat detailed comment.   Both in conception and workmanship, *The Princess* marks a transition in Tennyson's methods.   To a

---

[3] Spedding, *Ed. Rev.*, April, 1843, (V. 77, p. 390) says: "We cannot conclude without reminding Mr. Tennyson, that highly as we value the Poems which he has produced, we cannot accept them as a satisfactory account of the gifts which they show that he possesses; any more than we could take a painter's collection of studies for a picture in place of the picture itself.   Powers are displayed in these volumes, adequate, if we do not deceive ourselves, to the production of a great work, at least we should find it difficult to say which of the requisite powers is wanting.   But they are displayed in fragments and snatches, having no connection, and therefore deriving no light or fresh interest the one from the other.   By this their effective value is incalculably diminished.   .   .   .   If Mr. Tennyson can find a subject large enough to take the entire impress of his mind, and energy persevering enough to work it faithfully out as one whole, we are convinced that he may produce a work, which, though occupying no larger space than the contents of these volumes, shall as much exceed them in value, as a series of quantities multiplied into each other exceeds in value the same series simply added together."

11

considerable degree, as has been shown, the character of Tennyson's early poems was conditioned by the fact of shortness. Each poem presented some single mood or theme or some fragment of romance, character, or English life; each had a basis of unity and completeness in itself. In only a few cases had there been any prominence of the didactic element. There was usually an underlying ethic, but this was usually implicit or hinted rather than openly expressed. Seldom had there been any disturbing incongruities of matter, though no doubt the *Morte d'Arthur* would be just as effective without its modern setting. Even here, there had been a trace of the misgiving which was later to undermine the whole palace of art and crumble it about the poet's ears. The apologies which introduce and conclude the story of Arthur, and which, Fitzgerald explains, were "to excuse the telling of an old world tale", together with the poet's plea,

> Perhaps some modern touches here and there
> Redeem'd it from the charge of nothingness.

indicate his unwillingness to rest his case upon a pure work of art without some assurance to his audience of a modern and ethical bearing in his story. In the wavering search for a "moral" at the close of *The Day Dream*, we sense a similar nervousness, and a lack of utter conviction in his own declaration, that

> liberal applications lie
> In Art like Nature, dearest friend;
> And 'twere to cramp its use, if I
> Should hook it to some useful end.

In two subordinate particulars Tennyson continued in *The Princess* his earlier manner of work. First, he continued to draw largely for expression and embellishment upon his classical store. Few of his poems are so rich in reminiscences of classical poetry. Second, he continued, in connection with *The Princess*, his habit of "puttering" with his poems after they had left his hand. The poem was published in 1847, and a second edition was called for the following year. This edition was practically a reprint of the first. But before

the third edition of 1850, the poem underwent a sweeping
revision, and the six songs between the cantos were introduced.
The passages describing the "weird seizures" of the Prince
were added in the fourth edition of 1851, with all the changes
which these involved. And considerable additions and alterations were made in the fifth edition of 1853. But these
changes, with many minor ones made later, though some of
them tended to palliate the underlying fallacy of its conception, were not successful in overcoming it.

The Princess was the first of those somewhat pretentious
tours de force in which Tennyson sought, not always with
complete success, to unite "the transient with the abiding."
The old romance, the old glamour and color and music, in
and for themselves, seem to have lost his confidence and, from
this time on, we find him continually mingling, with even the
sheerest products of his imagination and his lyrical faculty,
moral conceptions and didactic observations, schemes and
systems of a more or less pedantic and prosaic sort. Sociology,
war, and politics in *Maud*, modernism and moral allegory in
the *Idylls of the King*, woman's rights, pro and con, in *The
Princess*, jostle and embarrass and disenchant those images
which should be instinct only with romance, chivalry, and
human passion. The message is not to be despised; but it
is delivered at a heavy cost to the artistic unity and
atmosphere of the poems. Whether Tennyson gained more
than he lost by the transaction is a question that I shall not
undertake to answer. This thing is evident, that the poet
made concessions to those who accused the earlier pieces of
lacking "depth", "meaning", and "metaphysical subtlety".
Perhaps, the growing reputation of Browning for these very
qualities which Tennyson was said to lack may have had some
influence on the latter. On this point Fitzgerald was always
playfully twitting him; and the "paltry poet" may have
been bent on showing that Robert Browning was not the only
modern bard who could "think".

Most important of all was undoubtedly his own intellectual
development, his absorption, stage by stage, of the rapidly
progressing scientific thought of the day, which he reflected

in *Locksley Hall,* then in *The Princess* and *In Memoriam,*
and in many poems of his later age, such as *De Profundis,*
the second *Locksley Hall, Vastness, God and the Universe.*
With this was combined a widening study of philosophy and,
finally, his growing and deepening interest in all the political,
religious, and humanitarian questions and enterprises of
his time.   That Tennyson ever ceased to give close attention
to matters of form, particularly to niceties of verse-construc-
tion, it would be idle to contend, in the face of the experiments in metre which interested him almost to his dying day
In *The Princess,* so costly is the elaboration of parts, so
dainty and so ornate the finishing of details, that the unwary
critic is apt to be misled into thinking that these have occupied the chief attention of the poet, and may fail to see
in the poem any departure from his former methods.   But
it is quite plain that the theme and the stuff of his poetry
came to occupy him somewhat at the expense of its architec-
tonics, its technical detail, and its atmosphere.   By 1869, he
who once bade fair to be a very king among the Pre-Raphae-
lites was in a mood to hail ''Art for Art's sake'' as ''truest
Lord of Hell''.[4]

Whatever the cause, the change took place, and it was at
this time that some of the most devoted of Tennyson's old
admirers, without abating their personal loyalty, parted
company from him, artistically.   The delicate ear of Fitzgerald, who with all his ''crotchets'' was often an exquisite
critic, was one of the first to detect the subtle rift in the poet's
lute.   Fitzgerald wrote to Hallam Tennyson in 1876, ''I am
considered a great heretic because, like Carlyle, I gave up
all hope of him after *The Princess*''.[5]   It does not come
within our scope to enter very far into the discussion which
grows out of this and like dissatisfied grumblings of Fitzgerald and Carlyle, who felt, at times, that Tennyson wasted
his resources on unremunerative themes and was not fulfilling
the poetical promise of his youth.   Yet it is not quite fair

---

[4] *Memoir,* II, 92.
[5] *Memoir,* I, 253.   See also Fitzgerald's preference for the *Morte* and
The Lady of Shalott. Memoir, II, 95 : 153.

to dismiss this criticism offhand as many critics do, as one of "Fitz's crotchets", nor push it aside, even with so enjoyable a bit of irony as that of Hallam Tennyson, who quietly comments, "Nothing, either by Thackeray or by my father, met with Fitzgerald's approbation unless he had first seen it in manuscript."[6] It must be conceded to "crotchety Fitz" that *The Princess* inaugurated a series of lengthy poems, more or less diffuse and incongruous in plan and more or less unequal in execution, if tried by a high standard, by a standard so high, even, as the best poems of Tennyson's early volumes.

Fitzgerald's sweeping condemnation of the songs of *The Princess* is not, however, sound. In some of these and in stray passages, here and there, one feels again "the glory and the dream" of the old inspiration. Here and there, particularly in *Maud*, are notes of a more poignant poetical feeling than had been heard in the early verses; here and there in *The Princess* and in *The Idylls* are sections of verse as exquisitely handled in detail, as magical in suggestive power as any to be found in the early volumes and even more commanding in accent. In many cases these passages rather lose than gain, however, by their position in the larger plan and by their association with other and frequently incongruous subjects. There are long lapses to a more prosy level; long sections where the verse, though it cannot be called rough or slipshod, yet gives unmistakable evidence that it was produced in quantity.

The chief fault in the conception of *The Princess* is obvious; but the obviousness of the objection can hardly be said to diminish its cogency. The poem fails to coordinate its naturally incongruous elements into a consistent whole; or, rather, it lacks decision and sharpness in its transition from comic to heroic and back again; it is seldom frankly one or the other, and hence the reader is often left in an uncomfortable uncertainty as to the exact intention of a passage. This must be the result of indecision or confusion

<hr>

[6] *Memoir*, I, 453.

of purpose on the part of the poet himself, and such a result
can hardly be called artistic. If one compare its mock-heroics
with those of *The Rape of the Lock* or its transitions with
those of *Don Juan* he realizes at once how much the poem
loses by lack of such distinctness as they possess. The poem
opens in a vein of travesty, but it fails to make much of an
impression in that character, for Tennyson was seldom brilliant as a humorist, in verse, whatever he may have been in
real life. One thinks, by way of contrast, of what Byron's
daring or the malice of Swift would have accomplished with
the incident of the female disguise which, in the circumspect
handling of Tennyson, barely elicits a smile. On the other
hand, many of the passages of real beauty, the description
of the tournament, the tender touches of love-story, the bits
of landscape, that splendid necklace of lyrics, how much more
telling they might have been in a more favorable environment. So the verses lose the force that their cleverness
deserves, being

> Too comic for the solemn things they are,
> Too solemn for the comic touches in them.

In the conclusion of the poem itself Tennyson virtually con-
fesses failure when he seems attempting to forestall criticism
by stating the difficulties of the framework and then says:

> I moved as in a strange diagonal
> And maybe neither pleased myself nor them.

These general characteristics of *The Princess* help us to account for the special development of his blank verse structure
which Tennyson carried out in this poem. In the first place,
it must be borne in mind that the verse, like the story,
"moves as in a strange diagonal", that certain portions of
the "medley" differ from others in versification just as they
do in other matters of style and general artistic aim. "It
is true," Tennyson said, quite late in life, "that some of the
blank verse in this poem is among the best I ever wrote."[7]

---

[7] *Memoir*, I. 251.

This estimate we may accept, with exactly the limitations Tennyson placed upon it. Throughout the poem are patches of exceptionally fine verse, verse as fine as Tennyson ever wrote, and, in general, these passages are not much different from the best verse of the 1842 volume. The verse of the poem as a whole, however, shows a considerable change in the poet's practice. A discriminating reader will feel at once that the verse of this poem is different from that of any of the earlier poems; but it requires more than a casual examination to reveal just what the variations are which produce the novel effect.

The predominating tone is that of light, often bantering, narrative and conversation, now and again slipping into heroic ardors of sentiment and more or less abandoned splendors of description and imagery. So far as they are dependent on the verse, these transitions are effected by carrying on the narrative in a style of verse which considerably extends the licenses of the "free idyllic" type, as seen in *The Gardener's Daughter,* and then changing to more heroic forms of verse for short passages; sometimes the effect is produced by a severe recurrence to the norm; at others, by a telling use of well-chosen variations, such as extra syllable, inversion, and enjambement; at the same time, in the passages where special effects are aimed at, the sound-correlation is most studied and careful. As Tennyson himself once pointed out, he takes as much pains to eliminate certain sound-sequences as he does to incorporate others; and he seldom allows us to feel that the thing has been overdone.

It is especially in the employment of extra syllables, that *The Princess* differs from the preceding compositions in blank verse. Now, the proportion of extra-syllables varies, somewhat, in different portions of *The Princess;*[3] but the entire poem of somewhat over thirty-one hundred lines shows an average of 20.16 per cent. This, though a great increase upon the proportion of such occurrences, 5.8 per cent, in

[3] That is, section by section.

the 1842 poems, is hardly sufficient to account for the sense we have of a greater license in *The Princess;* to account for this sense we have to examine more closely the character of the extra-syllables employed. All extra syllables are, to a greater or less degree, ''slurred'', in that there is a tendency to subordinate them to the laws of metrical equivalence; but they differ widely as to the amount of disturbance produced by them in the normal iambic movement of the verse, and if this effect is to be recorded with accuracy, some classification is necessary. The extra-metric occurrences which produce epic-caesura and double-ending, of course, fall into distinct classes and are quite ''unslurred.'' The extra-syllables which occur in interior positions, however, exhibit very many degrees of ''slurrability''; but it is not practicable to arrange them into more than two classes, since the result would be too complicated for intelligible comparison. We may therefore distinguish two classes of extra-syllables; the first we shall call ''slurred'', and the second, for sake of brevity, may be called ''unslurred''. In the ensuing examination of the extra-syllables of *The Princess* comparison is made between the number of extra-metric and ''unslurred'' extra-syllables on the one hand and of ''slurred'' extra syllables on the other.[9]

With the extra-syllables thus classified, it is possible to point out the difference between the practice of this license

---

[9] It has not been possible to lay down hard and fast rules for the distinction of "slurred" and "unslurred" syllables; but I have restricted myself by a few uniform rules: (1) In all cases where the two syllables of an arsis are separated by a word division they have been regarded as "unslurred". There is frequently of course the possibility of "elision", but it is my firm opinion that the effect on the eye should be taken into consideration as well as the effect on the ear, and that "elision" very seldom occurs in good modern verse. If a verse is properly read the extra-syllable is never actually "elided" but merely pronounced more lightly and rapidly. Therefore, in cases like the following:

(a) *"To a livelier* land; and so by tilth and grange."
(b) *"When the man* wants weight the woman takes it up."

I have preferred to class the syllables "to a" as "unslurred" with the syllables "when the" rather than to class them as "slurred" with the last two syllables of "livelier".

(2) In cases where syllables of the same word constitute the arsis they are regarded as "slurred" if two vowels are in juxtaposition, or if the vowels are separated by the consonants, *l, r, m, or n.*

in Tennyson's "idyllic" type of verse and in what may be
called his "epic" type of verse, that type employed in *The
Princess* and in most of *The Idylls of the King*. If we take
for the comparison one of the freest of the early idyls, the
Morte d'Arthur, we note a total percentage of 20.2 in *The
Princess* to 8 per cent in the *Morte d'Arthur*.

Although such general statements are somewhat difficult
to prove, it may be confidently asserted that, in *The Princess*,
these licenses affect particularly the verse of the light and
conversational portions of the poem. Striking cases could
be found in which the verse is thus altered for specific and
organic effect in certain descriptive passages and in some
of the more poetical and highly wrought passages; but, on
the whole, they chiefly occur in the lighter and more bantering
parts of the poem. The use of double-endings is almost exclusively reserved for the dialogue. Attention is called,
however, to the large .percentages, 22.66 and 25.4, in
the Introduction and Conclusion; also, to the fact that the
smallest percentage, 15.87, occurs in Section I, which is
largely descriptive; 4 of the 8 double endings and the only
epic-caesura, in this section, occur in the forty lines of Gama's
speech.[10] The following lines are illustrative:

---

(3) I have regarded as making epic caesurae and double-endings, the
words which are frequently used in final positions, *shower, flower, tower,
bower, Heaven, even, given, forgiven, seven,* and *fallen,* but have not so
regarded *hour, fire, desire,* etc. Words of the first class are frequently
used as dissyllables by Tennyson as they are by Milton. I will append
a few characteristic examples of Tennyson's use of these licenses, in
The Princess.
1. Of epic-caesura:
  Of thunder shower, she floated to us, and said,
  Came to the ruins. High arch'd and ivy claspt,
2. Of double-endings:
  Grant me your son, to nurse, to wait upon him.
  From whence the royal mind familiar with her.
3. Of "unslurred" extra-syllables:
  A *palace in* our own land, where you shall reign,
  Better have died and split our bones *in the* flood.
4. Of "slurred" extra-syllables:
  Myriads of *rivulets hurrying* through the lawn,
  The moan of doves in *immemorial* elms
  And *murmuring* of innumerable bees.
[10] Section I, 120-60.

                          I said no,
Yet *being an* easy man gave it and there
All wild to found an University
For maidens, on the spur she fled; and more
We know not,—only this: they see no man,
Not *even her* brother Arac, nor the twins
Her brethren, tho' they love her, look *upon her*
As on a kind of paragon; and I,
Pardon me *saying it*, were much........

....

Section III contains a larger proportion than any other
of double endings; there are, in 337 lines, 17, or 4.87 per
cent. Now, this section has an unusual amount of dialogue;
and examination shows not only that 40 lines of Cyril's somewhat flippant account of his visit to Blanche contains 6 of
these, but that every one of the 17 double endings occurs in
dialogue. In Section VI, 12 of the 13 double endings occur
in dialogue, as do both of the triple endings (or alexandrines).[11] Also, the epic-caesura and the double arsis before
the caesura oftener fall in conversational passages. The epic-
caesura often marks the end of a speech and resumption of
the narrative, a usage which may be regarded as analogous
to that of the drama, where a change of speakers is frequently
accompanied by the same peculiarity of the verse. Examples
follow:

"Poor weakling even as they are." / Passionate tears
Followed.   (VI, 291–2.)

"But I must go; I dare not *tarry*." *And* light
As flies the shadow of a bird she fled.
                                   (III, 79–80.)

Examples of double arsis before the caesura are:

O fair and strong and terrible! / Lioness
                                   (VI, 147.)

Then she, "let someone sing to us. / Lightlier move
The minutes fledged with music."
                                   (IV, 18–19.)

---

[11] Some may prefer to regard such lines as alexandrines, but I am
confident that is not their character.

Of double and triple ending:

> But Love and Nature, these are two more *terrible*.
> (VI, 149.)
> I scarce am fit for your great plans; yet *speak to me*,
> Say one soft word and let me part *forgiven*.
> (VI, 201-2.)

Two of the verses might be read as alexandrines; but it is evident, from dramatic fitness, that the poet expected them to be read with triple endings; the verses of Psyche are particularly expressive when read in this way. "*Speak* to me," ('—xx) is, evidently, the reading intended. Enough has been pointed out to show the uniformity of Tennyson's usage in these particulars and to indicate his probable consciousness of how his effects were produced; further details of this sort would be superfluous.[12]

Still more striking confirmation of the poet's alertness to all these minute variations of his verse comes to light in an examination of the changes wrought by him in his revision of the poem. Besides making many important additions to the poem in the several revisions of 1848, '50, '51, and '53, Tennyson made many verbal alterations for the express purpose apparently of removing extra-syllables. Altogether 69 cases of this license were removed in the revision of the poem, but the more remarkable fact is, that, of these changes, nearly one-half, 30, were for the removal of the epic-caesura. From Section IV, which, as it stands, contains 15 cases of epic-caesura, 15 cases were removed in the revision. Since the total number of epic-caesurae which the poem contains in its final form, is only 58, one sees how considerable, and probably conscious a change the poet made in the proportion of licenses of this sort. The freedom implied in these figures is not quite so great as that which Milton allowed himself in the verse of *Paradise Lost*, and, like Milton, Tennyson in his

---

[12] Some years ago, in examining the blank verse of Milton's *Paradise Regained*, I discovered that he had, precisely in this manner, limited his use of double ending to the speeches, and that it is partly due to the greater amount of dialogue in *Paradise Regained* that it exceeds *Paradise Lost* in the allowance of this variation.

more lofty passages usually comes back to the regular number
of syllables and gains a distinct effect by his close adherence
to the normal syllabication.[13]   Milton, however, in this as
in other respects, was able to vary the typical movement of
the line, without violating its nobility, to a degree quite beyond the scope of less consummate masters of blank verse.

There can be no doubt that Tennyson's verse, whatever it
may have gained in flexibilty, lost seriously in compactness
and strength by his increasing license in the use of extra-
syllables.   That he was aware of this seems to be indicated
by his treatment of them in the revision of *The Princess*.

If we turn, now, to the handling of pause, we find, as we
might anticipate, that the poet has varied his usage to suit
the varying purposes of the verse.   Passages of distinctly
masculine character occur, sometimes, merely for the sake
of that variety which is indispensable in a poem of considerable length, sometimes for expressive purposes.   We should,
however, expect the verse of the poem, as a whole, to favor the
feminine pause, and this it does.   I have not thought it worth
while to gather statistics on this point, for the entire poem;
but the study of long and representative portions of the poem
reveals   an   unquestioned   predominance   of   the   feminine
caesura.   The Prologue (239 lines) with its rather colloquial
narrative and bantering conversation, has 56.5 per cent
feminine pause.   A similar predominance appears in Section
I   (245 lines)—narrative   with   some   conversation—   *viz.*,
55.33 per cent feminine caesura.   Section II, 301–400, is
almost entirely conversational and is light in tone; 60 per
cent of its pauses are feminine.   If on the other hand, we
examine the last 100 lines of Section V, which contain the
ringing description of the tournament, we find 53 per cent
of the pauses masculine.

In regard to the use of enjambement, one of two things
is true: either Tennyson achieved it by an effort, or he reserved it for effective use in his more highly wrought passages.
I incline to the latter view.   Undoubtedly, those passages

---

[13] *E. g., Paradise Lost*, I, 285, et seq.; note the full syllabication of "cir-
cumference", "ammiral", "Heaven".

which Tennyson himself regarded as most successful[14] are noteworthy for the proportion of lines which run-on. Furthermore, although usually severe in syllabication, these passages make free use of spondees and of beginning, caesural, and interior inversion. Comparison of a section of verse in the pedestrian portions of the poem with one from a more highly wrought portion will make this point clear. Thus the Prologue, which is in a comparatively low key, has 22 per cent run-on, 11.5 per cent beginning inversion, 1 caesural, and 1 interior, inversion. If, now, we turn to Section V, we find 17 per cent of beginning inversion, 9 cases of caesural inversion, and 3 interior inversions; while the run-on rises from 27 per cent in lines 1–200, to 32 per cent in lines 201–300; 37 per cent in lines 301–400; 37 per cent in lines 401–500; of the 20 lines describing the opening of the tournament, 14 run-on, and the entire section has an average of 33.75 of run-on-lines.   Section VII, again, has 14 per cent beginning inversion, 7 cases of caesural inversion and 2 cases of interior inversion.   To a remarkable degree the proportion of these licenses is an index of a heightened style.   Among the passages which are remarkable for the telling variation of pause and accent, it may be profitable to instance a few.

> And then to bed, / where half in doze / I seemed
> To float about a glimmering night / and watch
> A full sea / glazed with ruffled moonlight / swell
> On some dark shore / just seen that it was rich.
>   I, 242–6.
> She ended here / and beckoned us: / the rest
> Parted; / and, glowing full-faced welcome, / she
> Began to address us / and was moving on
> In gratulation, / till as when a boat
> Tacks / and the slackened sail flaps / all her voice
> Faltering and fluttering in her throat / she cried.
>   II, 156–70.
> Not peace she looked, / the Head; / but rising up /
> Robed in the long night / of her deep hair, / so
> To the open window moved, / remaining there /

---

[14] See *Memoir*, I. Ch. XII; II. Ch. IV.

> Fixt like a beacon tower / above the waves
> Of tempest, / when the crimson rolling eye
> Glares ruin / and the wild birds / on the light
> Dash themselves dead.   / She stretch'd her arms / and called
> Across the tumult, / and the tumult fell.
>
> IV, 469–77.

Also, V, 5–11; 152–58; 240–46; *regular,* 460–71, then variation, 472–494; for regular simple rhythm, VII, 20–30; then variation, 30–40; 208–13; Conclusion, 109–15.

> Approach and fear not; / breathe upon my brows;
> In that fine air I tremble, / all the past
> Melts mistlike into this bright hour / and this
> Is morn to more, / and all the rich to come
> Reels, / as the golden autumn woodland / reels
> Athwart the smoke of burning weeds. /
>
> VII, 332–37.

Many of these passages exemplify in addition to the variations of pause and stress, the marvelous sound-correlations for which *The Princess* is noteworthy.

Nothing in Tennyson's handling of blank verse more clearly shows his confident control of that form than the success with which he differentiates it for lyrical purposes in the isometric songs of *The Princess.*   He himself once remarked[15] that the majority of people had not observed that these songs were in blank verse, and it will be found that this fact sometimes escapes the attention even of skilled and careful readers. The experiment of introducing a poem of lyrical character into a blank verse composition and differentiating it therefrom without deviating from the typical scheme of the verse (suggested by the practice of Theocritus), had been successfully made by Tennyson in a shorter poem composed about the same time, *viz., The Golden Year,*[16] and as we have seen, had been employed in *Audley Court* as early as 1838. In *The Princess* he employs the device no fewer than five times; in fact it should be observed that, not only is the poet successful

---

[15] *Memoir,* I, 253.

[16] At this time (1847) *The Golden Year* was added to the *Poems.*   *Memoir,* I, 247.

in distinguishing these lyrics from the environing portions of the narrative by the differentiation of the blank verse in which they are written, but he adheres uniformly to the isometric scheme in all these poems and thereby accurately differentiates them from the six intercalary songs which were added in the third edition. The latter are supposed to be sung, not by characters of the story proper, but by the women who figure in the *Prologue* and *Conclusion*, and these songs are all written in rhymed lyric measures like those of the 1842 volume, or in delicate modulations thereof.

We are concerned particularly with the blank verse lyrics, "Tears, idle tears," "O Swallow, swallow," "Our enemies have fallen," "Now sleeps the crimson petal," and "Come down O maid." The first three are represented as songs; the fourth, although read from a book, is clearly a lyric; while the last is called an idyl, and differs somewhat from the others in its verse characteristics. All of these poems except the third are distinguished from their environment by the greater severity with which they adhere to the typical form, particularly in the syllabling, and, with the exception of the third and the last, of end pause. All make use of repetition and parallelism, most of them employ refrain, and all make elaborate use of every device of sound coordination except the discarded structural rhyme.

The twenty lines of *Tears, Idle Tears* are divided by the end-refrain, "the days that are no more", into four equal strophic periods, each having a certain unity in imagery and thought. The pause scheme is very simple and strongly masculine in character; all the lines (with one possible exception) are end-stopt; only three are without interior pause; two have the pause after the third measure; while twelve have the pause after the second measure; this last, combined with the usual amount of beginning inversion (there are seven cases in twenty lines, of which five coincide with the pause after the fourth) determines the cadence of this poem. In two cases there is secondary pause after the first measure, —a balanced effect in the fifth lines of the second and third strophes which affects the cadence of the corresponding portion of the fourth strophe, "O Death in Life." The chief consonant correlation in the poem is that of *d,* which runs through the entire lyric in a remarkable way, becoming more and more frequent, ushering in the last strophe with fine effect, "Dear as remembered kisses after death", correlating with a great number of *t's* and giving a distinctive emphasis to the "days" of the refrain. Next in importance is *s;* also we have "Fresh as the first", "fancy feigned", "we love below", etc. All in all, the lyric unity of the poem is so thoroughly maintained by the balance of pause and the correlation of its consonant elements that we need not be surprised at the truth of Tennyson's words,[17] "Few know that it is a blank verse lyric."

The next lyric of this class, the *Swallow Song,* was originally written in rhyme, and two cases of rhyme still remain though they are not structural: "O Swallow, *swallow,* if I could *follow,*" and "Fly *to her,* and pipe and *woo her.*" The chief lyric element in the form of this poem, however, is repetition, particularly the repetition of the words and phrases, "swallow", "flying", "fly to her", and "tell her". The poem is profuse in alliteration; the consonant chiefly played upon is *l,* though *f, s,* and *t* are also considerably used. The pause scheme is strikingly in contrast with that of the preceding lyric and is thoroughly in harmony with the lighter and more vivacious mood of the poem. In the twenty-four lines there are only four masculine pauses, all the remaining lines have either feminine or epic caesura, while six have secondary and two have tertiary pauses, all feminine or epic in character; the cases where extra-syllable produces the epic caesura are six in number. Three of the lines run on. The contrast of its movement with that of *Tears, Idle Tears,* requires no further comment.

A jubilation of a more heroic and dignified order is expressed in the song chanted by Ida after the success of her brothers in tournament; its twenty-six lines are marked off into five strophes by means of the beginning refrain, "Our enemies have fallen, have fallen." The word "fallen" is

---

[17] *Memoir,* I, 253.

used ten times in twenty-six lines, each time in the place of
a monosyllable; this gives a fierce energy to the lines and,
technically speaking, produces in every case but one, an
epic-caesura. If we count "power" a dissyllable, there are
in all ten epic-caesurae in twenty-six lines. Further, a
peculiar effect of length and weight is produced by the occurrence of a great many of the pauses near the end of
the line. There is one pause after the third syllable, and
there are three after the fourth; but these all follow run-
on-lines. Four pauses occur after the fifth, and two after
the sixth, syllable. In seven cases the pause divides the fourth
measure and in nine it follows the fourth measure; but observe, further, that five of these nine are epic-caesurae; notice
further that, with two exceptions, all the twelve measures
divided by feminine caesuræ are weak measures; that one of
these exceptions is a counter-caesural inversion,—"They
mark'd it with the red *cross to* the fall;" further, there are
four secondary caesurae after the third measure, all epic;
and finally, there are three cases of extra-syllable in addition
to those which produce epic-caesurae. These are the technical
characteristics by which the massively galloping periods of
this "blank verse lyric" are made to attain a combined
dignity and vehemence of movement as far from the pensive
pause and sigh of *Tears, Idle Tears* as they are from the
fluttering "cheep and twitter" of *The Swallow Song*.

   The fourth poem, "Now sleeps the crimson petal," is most
noteworthy for its careful balance of pauses and for its use
of well correlated repetitions and alliterations. The word
"now" is used thematically, being repeated in the first verse
and used to introduce the balanced parts of two or four
verses, each of which has its own unity of thought and imagery
and ends with the word "me". The pauses are arranged in
groups. The first four verses have feminine caesuræ, the
fifth and seventh balance with each other and with the first,
all having pause after the seventh syllable; lines six and
eight balance with each other. Thus far all are end-stopt,
but now there is a slight change of cadence; the ninth verse

pauses after the eighth syllable and runs on, the next pause falling after the fifth syllable of line ten. This is balanced by the pause and run-on in thirteen and fourteen, whereas eleven and twelve return to the cadence of the earlier lines with pauses after the fifth and seventh syllables, respectively. *Notice that this balance of pause is attended by an organic balance of the ideas expressed.* Note further, that all except two or three of the feminine pauses fall in the midst of weak measures; notice the balance of stress-elements in the first measures of lines one, two, three, five, seven, nine, eleven, twelve and thirteen, which let their accent fall upon mono-syllabic words, most of them guilty of inverting the prose order,—a device to which Tennyson once declared his hostility.[18] To an unusual degree the whole poem is laced together by repetition and alliteration. In addition to the ones already mentioned, we have repetition of "waken", line 4; "like a ghost", 5 and 6; "lies", 6 and 7; "fold", 11 and 13; "slip", 12 and 13; "bosom", 12 and 14. The chief correlations of consonants are, w, seven times lines 1–4; p, four times lines 1–4; f, five times in 3 and 4; g three times in 5 and 6; and we have assonance, added, in "slides", "silent", "shining", lines 9–10. Finally, there are but two very light extra-syllables and there is no case of metrical inversion. The product of all these devices is a chaste and quiet poem, in absolutely regular blank verse, of thoroughly lyrical quality.

At the risk of being tedious, I shall make this study complete by mentioning the characteristics of the fifth and last of these isometric poems. "Come down, O Maid, from yonder mountain height" is a tiny idyl of thirty lines. It is not like the other poems divided into strophes, nor is there any structural or balanced division of it into parts: though distinct from its surroundings, it is less different than the lyrics which have been analyzed. It is in much the same verse as the idyls of the 1842 volume, though we find somewhat more repetition. The pauses are various and mixed; one-third of the lines run-on. There are no extra-syllables

---

[18] *Memoir*, II, 523. "I hate inversions."

save in the last few verses, where they are introduced with marvelous imitative results.   The only inversions, also, are the two beginning inversions near the close, which have therefore a strong effect.   Alliteration is plentiful though not profuse, and the vowel music is of unusual beauty.   Observe the passage:

> The children call, and I
> Thy shepherd pipe, and sweet is every sound,
> Sweeter thy voice, but every sound is sweet.

It has seemed worth while to discuss in detail the technical characteristics of these isometric poems, because nothing in Tennyson's practice more clearly reveals his subtle control of blank verse and his consciousness of its various possibilities, than the success with which he makes each one of these gems of song differ from the other and, at the same time, makes them all stand out in clear, lyrical relief from the narrative context.

The Princess reveals Tennyson in full mastery of those gifts of description, of that mature verse-craft, which characterized the finest work of the 1842 volumes.   Such relaxations of the verse as occur are deliberate and were invited by the nature of the subject matter.   But the tendency of his revision to reduce the licenses of the verse indicate how easily a relaxed discipline slips into excess and requires careful checking even by a consummate workman.   Perhaps the relaxation of the verse in its mechanical characteristics indicates an inclination of the poet at once to slip to a lower level of poetic feeling, and to reach after easier modes of varying the rhythm and increasing the expressiveness of his metre than was permitted by the classic restraint of his earlier poems.

In later years Tennyson was accustomed to speak of *The Princess* in a regretful way.   ''He talked of 'The Princess','' Locker-Lampson reports, ''with something of regret, of its fine blank verse and the many good things in it, 'but', said he, 'though truly original, it is after all, only a medley.' ''

And the modern reader, seeing the wealth of gorgeous imagery, the fund of poetic energy and mature verse-craft lavished upon so ungrateful a prodigal of the imagination, echoes, with something of a sigh, ''It is only a medley, after all.''

CHAPTER VIII

IN MEMORIAM AND MAUD

While *The Princess* was passing through its successive editions and revisions, Tennyson was gathering together and striving to coordinate into a systematic whole the *Elegies* upon which he had been engaged from time to time since the death of Hallam in 1833. These appeared under the title *In Memoriam*, in June, 1850, the month of his marriage; and a few months later he succeeded Wordsworth as Poet-Laureate. This was a remarkable and significant conjunction of events. Their conjunction was not fortuitous, but the product of that fine judgment with which Tennyson tempered all the conduct of his life as he did the application of his talent. In only one or two cases in English history has there been so timely an award of public honor to an artist as in the conferring of the laureateship upon Tennyson. From his own point of view it fell in with the fact that recognition was won; it confirmed and promoted the prosperity which was already at hand, and which had conditioned his marriage. The publication of *In Memoriam* signalized in every way the profit of his apprenticeship to life and art, and the richness of his triumph. Taken all together these events meant that his period of struggle and long waiting was over, that he had lived and loved, and that life had borne its fruit.

In Memoriam must ever be regarded as the main harvest of Tennyson's most precious poetical season. In substance and in workmanship it has of all his poems the most consistent claim to be regarded as a masterpiece of scale. The poem has been so often and so ably analysed that there is no need for us here to examine its contents more than incidentally, or essay any addition to former statements as to what it attempts and accomplishes.

The character of the pieces of which the poem is composed is well indicated by the title "Elegies" or "fragments of an Elegy" by which they were long known to the poet's friends. Tennyson's own statement in regard to the origin of the poems is well known: "I did not write them with any view to weaving them into a whole, or for publication, until I found that I had written so many." That such an origin should have left some effect upon the whole when the various pieces were combined into one poem was almost inevitable, and, as I have elsewhere said, "its true effect is less that of a large design executed in masterly fashion, than it is the effect of a series of poems exquisitely modulated in one key." And yet, the series of poems does produce upon the reader a remarkable totality of impression. There is a singleness of purpose which makes itself strongly felt in a reading of the entire poem. It is a poem of argument, and it is a record of experience; but both themes are more than knit, they are indissolubly fused together, or rather, it is a duet of the reason and the imagination, and where one voice fails the other takes it up. Perhaps the progress of the argument is not always perfectly satisfactory to the logical faculty, but where that fails, "the heart stands up and answers, 'I have felt'", and the progress does continue. Above all it has the power of a record of experience, the history of a soul which out of the shattering of its life's happiness gathers up the fragments of its faith and builds them together in a new and nobler temple. Step by step we rise from out the encircling gloom to a serener air, to gaze on a purposeful universe with an ever-growing consciousness of the sufficiency of the soul's strength and the soul's faith for all which it confronts; an ever enlarging perception of "the glory of the sum of things will flash along the chords and go", until at last, out of the wreck and the perplexity, a voice is lifted up to one that hears, and out of the dust to one that with us works, "a cry above the conquered years."

In Memoriam is one of the most consoling creations that ever came from human hands. There is a lift in its closing sections which raises the spirit to a serenity seldom achieved

by any art except that of architecture. Instead of the
solemnity of Wordsworth's loftier pieces or the winsomeness
of his lyrics there is a noble seriousness more gracious than
either, for, to Wordsworth's resolution and high conception
of human fortitude, Tennyson adds a humanity and "all-
comprehensive tenderness" beside which the poet to whom he
owed so much seems strenuous and hard. And there is a
hush of spirituality in parts of *In Memoriam*, a "beauty of
holiness", upon which the confident "Good cheer" of Browning jars with a boisterous and almost rowdy worldliness.
Truly, this poem never approaches that blaze of transfigura-
tion which almost blinds us in the *Paradiso* and in Milton's
Invocation to Light; but any regret for such a lack is stilled
by the exquisite and sincere humility of the poet's own simple
rejoinder when Aubrey de Vere suggested that some time he
might "give to the whole work its third part, or Paradise:"
"I have written what I have felt and known; and I will
never write anything else."

Tennyson's long practice in the rudiments of his art culminates in the workmanship of *In Memoriam*. Its limitations
in general design are the irrefragable limitations of his genius.
Its perfection of parts within the whole is the result of his
instinct for beauty and adequacy of expression, controlled
by his delicate perception of the tact between art and truth,
chastened and consummated by indefatigable constancy to
the arduous discipline in details through which art acquires
efficiency.

Although the individual poems are not by any means equal
in interest nor all of them equally flawless in shape and
finish of parts, the poet has maintained an astonishing evenness and high average of excellence. Tennyson's delight in
excellence in this scale is attested by many records of his
taste and opinions. His unbounded admiration for Burns is
in point. Rawnsley has reported him late in life as seating
himself on a rock and abandoning himself with unqualified
enjoyment to the rendition of Burns' "Go fetch to me a pint
of wine".[1] Half a century earlier, he exclaimed to Aubrey

---

[1] Rawnsley, *Recollections*.

de Vere: "Read the exquisite songs of Burns. *In shape
each of them has the perfection of the berry; in light the
radiance of the dew-drop*".[2] Late in life he said to his son,
"It is only the perfect work that will last. A small boat
built on good lines will float farther down the stream of time
than a big raft." This valuation of design on a small scale
is comparable to his valuation of device in nature, and he himself often noted the analogy. "Every short poem," he once
remarked to Aubrey de Vere, "should have a definite shape
like the curve, sometimes a single sometimes a double one,
assumed by a severed tress or the rind of an apple when
flung on the floor."[3] Walking in the fields once with
Rawnsley he stopped and picked a flower and pointing to the
brilliant red painting in the hollow of the cup, commented:
"Does not this look like the hand of a Great *Artificer,* one with
a desire to decorate?" Perhaps his finest treatment of this
idea of design in nature is in the passage about the shell in
Maud:

> Frail, but a work divine,
> Made so fairily well
> With delicate spire and whorl,
> How exquisitely minute,
> A miracle of design.

and perhaps we are justified in following the application one
step farther and quoting in apposition his last reflection,

> Small, but a work divine,
> Frail, but of force to withstand,
> Year upon year, the shock
> Of cataract seas that snap
> The three decker's oaken spine
> Athwart the ledges of rock.

Tennyson's design on a small scale reaches its highest
perfection in the poems of *In Memoriam*. The lyric sequence
has much the character of a sequence of sonnets, and there
is little doubt that the old sonnet sequences, especially the

---

[2] *Memoir*, I, 211.
[3] *Memoir*, I. Appendix, p. 507.

sonnets of Shakspere, helped suggest to his mind the conception of a long elegiac poem made up of shorter flights. To the influence of Shakspere, should be added possibly that of Petrarch; and for detail and tone something is owing also to Horace and to Catullus.

In the construction of the individual poems out of the stanza which he had adopted Tennyson was able to get something analogous to the effect of the sonnet and yet different from it. As we have seen, his early experiments with the sonnet showed little aptitude or sympathy for the form. He continued to regard it as too stereotyped and, so far as he liked it at all, preferred the Shaksperean to the Petrarchan model. In the use of the stanza adopted for *In Memoriam*, he had the advantage of treating the stanza as a structural unit which he could build into wholes of like, though not necessarily of stereotyped, design. Thus, his favorite pattern is that of four stanzas with various interior balances of which the favorite is that of two against two. Of the 131 poems which make up the body of *In Memoriam*, 49 are of the four stanza type and if some of the longer poems be examined, they will be found to show a structural arrangement based on the same pattern. Thus xcv, "At night we lingered on the lawn," one of the finest of the longer poems, falls readily into four sections of four stanzas each. Many of the most beautifully shaded curves, to adapt Tennyson's idea, are found in the five-stanza poems which come next in number, 27 of the poems being of that pattern; good examples are the series of ten poems IX–XVIII. The poems of three stanzas number 22; those of six stanzas, 14; those of seven, 7; those of eight, 4; while there are single poems of 9, 10, 11, 12, 13, 14, 16 and 30 stanzas respectively. It is perhaps worth noting that practically all of the longer poems are in the transitional third section of the poem, and are chiefly narrative and retrospective in theme. The longest of all, LXXXV, which has 30 stanzas, is peculiarly transitional in character and is a résumé of progress to that point. In addition there is the Proem, with 11, and the Epilogue, which is a continuous poem of 36 stanzas.

The stanza of *In Memoriam* has been the subject of much study and comment.   That it was developed by Tennyson in the course of his experiments with the quatrain and was not derived from any predecessor has been pointed out in a preceding chapter.[4]   The salient characteristic of the stanza is its rhyme arrangement.   The apparently simple device of exterior-interior arrangement has an astonishing effect upon its dominant cadence, making the stanzaic unity much more emphatic than that of the ordinary alternate arrangement. The enclosed lines group together as a couplet; the rhyme of the third line thus seems to be hurried in, and this ac-centuates the delay of the fourth rhyme syllable, which falls with a dimmed and mournful echo of the first, giving the entire rhyme music the effect of being conceived in a minor key, harmonizing admirably with the tone of combined sadness and austerity.   The integrity of the stanza is strongly pre-served, and the poet depends for variety largely upon move-ments within the stanzaic limits.

In the variation of the individual verse, again, great re-straint prevails.   There is precision and regularity both in stress and syllabication.   There are few inversions, and even weakened stresses are very sparingly used.   In the last particular the practice is comparable to that of his blank verse. It is the penultimate stress of the line which is most fre-quently weak, and the weak stresses most frequently occur at this position in the third line of the stanza.   Extra-syllables are exceedingly rare and the rhymes are invariably mono-syllabic.

Obviously, then, the chief device relied upon for modify-ing the movements of the metre is the shift of pause within the stanza.   Here again, great restraint is used and the modula-tions are of the subtlest.   The pause falls with much regu-larity at the close of the verse.   The run-on most frequently occurs between the third and fourth lines of the stanza; this, with the frequency of interior pause late in the third verse, gives a characteristic hurry on the second of the enclosed

---

[4] Above, Chap. V, p. 105. Cf., however, Chap. III, p. 43, note.

rhymes and is one of the striking peculiarities of the metre. Thus as the rhyme of the fourth verse is diminished by remoteness from its mate, that of the third line is frequently diminished by the movement of the sense,[5] a striking subtlety of correspondence which has much to do with the quality of the stanza as Tennyson uses it.

But the most remarkable characteristic of the verse, and that which more than any other prevents its monotony from becoming monotonous, is the naturalness and ease with which it is fitted with words. As regards diction one hardly knows which to admire first, the simplicity, and inevitableness, of the words, or their beauty and adequacy. And their arrangement is effected so as to leave practically no evidence of deferences to metre. In this characteristic excellence of the metrification and syntax, Coventry Patmore credited Tennyson with having attained "The style which has been attained by the recent poets only in short songs and crack passages."[6] And he added that this style "must henceforward be that of all verse having any chance of permanence."

In this poem Tennyson carried to its highest level that principle of perfection which had controlled him in his period of development, – the delicate modulation of metre and style, within carefully restricted limits. By these adjustments of style and metre, as well as by his adjustment of intellectual values such as the issue between science and religion, Tennyson recommended himself to a surprisingly large and varied audience. And whatever loss the poem may sustain by the failure of its intellectual substance to satisfy the needs of future generations, it is upon this achievement in a far higher degree than upon any other of his extensive undertakings that his reputation must stand.

In Memoriam was almost "the last of the old vintage". Immediately after his elevation to the laureateship and his

---

[5] Examples of this peculiarity are the following:
    a. "I the divided half of *such*
        A friendship as had mastered Time."
    b. "I loved thee, spirit, and love, nor *can*
        The soul of Shakspeare love thee more."
[6] *Ed. Rev.*, 1855.

arrival at assured success and prosperity Tennyson betrayed a tendency toward looser forms of composition and a shriller tone of commentary upon contemporary life and issues. This tendency had shown itself to a certain degree in *The Princess,* but had been strongly held in check by a pertinacious sense of form. *In Memoriam* had followed, and this poem had derived from the golden period in which a large share of its best was written a conservatism and orderliness which preserved to Tennyson his happiest perfection of manner and carried him to his highest achievement in controlled expression. His next important volume displays a curious congeries of elements, some of which contrast strongly with the sustained regularity and elevation of *In Memoriam.*

Maud, and other Poems (1855) contained, besides the piece named in the title, seven miscellaneous poems. Four of the poems are reminiscent of his earlier manner. *The Brook* is a charming idyll in blank verse of the pre-*Princess* variety, and the song of the brook incorporated into it is in quatrains like those of the 1842 volume. The poem called *The Letters* has been described in connection with poems of the same form in the earlier collection.[7] Both of these poems were doubtless of early composition. *The Daisy* presents a further modulation of the quatrain. Tennyson refers to it as "in a metre which I invented, representing in some measure the grandest of metres, the Horatian Alcaic."[8] The quatrain is composed of iambic four-stress verses, the first, second, and fourth rhyming together and the third verse silent, with feminine ending, while the third measure of the fourth verse is consistently anapaestic. Another poem of familiar address, that *To the Rev. F. D. Maurice,* is in precisely the same stanza except that it has been brought nearer to the *Alcaic* by the additional feature of systematic beginning inversion in the fourth verse. *Will* is a comparatively insignificant poem in irregular metre.

The *Ode on the Death of the Duke of Wellington,* which had been written and published three years before,[9] signalises his

---

[7] See above, Ch. V, p. 106.

[8] *Memoir,* I, 341.

[9] First Ed., 1852.

appearance in the official character of a national poet, and is the first of a series of occasional pieces which, though evidently written *con amore,* were the product of something other than innermost conviction and necessity and seem to have been constructed rather than composed.   In the *Ode* for the first time in a long while, Tennyson loosed himself upon a thoroughly irregular scheme of metre, and while he holds his rhythms well in hand, the poem is not comparable in distinction of movement to those poems in which he had applied his musical gift to the modulation of systematic metres, such as his 1842 blank verse and quatrains and the quatrains of *In Memoriam.*   In *The Charge of the Light Brigade,* again, an incident of current history inspired him, and while the poem is a striking one and has continued to enjoy, as it enjoyed at the time, a wide popularity, it is like many of Tennyson's poems of action, rather vehement than vigorous, and does not in the least show him at the top of his powers. And the same may be said of the several war poems which he contributed about this time to the newspapers.[10]   If Tennyson was not deceived in thinking that the metre of the famous *Charge* was suggested entirely by the newspaper phrase, ''someone had blundered,'' it is a remarkable coincidence that he should have hit upon a dactylic movement so like that of Drayton's *To the Cambro-Britons* for a poem of so similar content and spirit.

But *Maud* itself exhibits Tennyson's most striking departures from his previous methods.   It is not surprising that many of his followers were nonplussed and irritated by this sudden sally into the realm of raw passion and into contemporary politics.   In the poet of *In Memoriam,* who had apparently settled to a conservative compromise in all matters of opinion and belief and raised himself to an elegant aloofness and classicism of manner, this was indeed a disconcerting break beyond the pale and into what seemed to them a de-

---

[10] *Britons Guard Your Own,* in *The Examiner,* Jan. 31, 1852; *For the Penny-Wise,* in *Fraser's,* February, 1852; *The Third of February, 1852,* in *The Examiner,* Feb. 7, 1852; *Hands all Round,* in *The Examiner,* Feb. 7, 1852.

basing competition with the Spasmodic School.   In attempting
to provide a dramatic investiture for some exquisite stanzas,
which had been published in *The Tribute* eighteen years before,
the poet involves himself in a sensational novel of contemporary manners and passion, and the delineation of a hero
who, first with hysteria and then with madness, hurls himself
into cynical invectives against the commercial and social
practices of the age.   Viewed crudely as a story, the poem
presents a violent and not very original melodrama.   The
hero develops a romantic love affair, kills his sweetheart's
brother in a duel, is precipitated into madness by the subsequent death of his mistress, and emerges as a passionate
advocate of the Crimean War.

Tennyson chose to call *Maud* a "mono-drama".   It is at
least equally well described as a metrical novel, told in short
flashes or flights of autobiographic soliloquy, the characters
and incidents stripped to essentials, the soliloquy ever and
again intensifying to sheer lyric, that is to the portrayal of
reflections and moods rather than the narrative of events.
Whether considered as novel or drama, the elements in *Maud*
which begot detestation are easily discovered.   Once the
novelistic element is made prominent in a poem, its characters
and incidents invite scrutiny, and these elements in Tennyson's writing, where he is thrown upon his own invention,
seldom abide this test with much credit.   Where he is at his
best, as we have seen, his emphasis is elsewhere; usually it is
on background and accessories, not on the action.   His star-
crossed lovers are seldom edifying spectacles; they do not
very well endure comparison for example with Browning's
manlier heroes.   The hero of *Maud* is at the outset a morbid,
self-centered, rancorous malcontent; by his own confession he
is "personal, splenetic, base," and Tennyson's note on the
poem which describes him as "the heir of madness, an egotist
with the makings of a cynic" does not set him before us in a
pleasant character.   Tennyson's predilection for "second
rate sensitive" personages like those in *Locksley Hall*, and
Lady Clara Vere de Vere, suggests the presence of "the
least little touch of spleen" in himself.   We have only to

compare his characters in this sort with those of the Elizabethans, or even with the Pierre of Otway, or with Byron's
vigorous rebels, to feel their leading defect, their sorry lack of
distinction.   And Tennyson enters with too much gusto into
their railings to permit us the belief that he was totally out
of sympathy with them.   It was not, after all, mere stupidity
on the part of the critics of *Maud* that they imputed the sentiments of its hero to his creator.

And in *Maud,* from the very nature of its method, everything is coloured by the passions and prejudices of the hero.
The characters and interests of the story are depicted from
his point of view.   Even the landscape is all flooded over
with the hues of his hectic and hysterical fancy.   The *Edinburgh* critic (Coventry Patmore) was fairly justified in his
surmise that the character was assumed by the poet as an
excuse for pitching the tone of the poetry in "a key of extravagant sensibility."

Tennyson had, indeed, a profounder purpose.   He chose a
hero of this sort in order that he might represent him as
"raised to sanity by a pure and holy love."   And there is,
to be sure, nothing so fine in Tennyson, and there are few
things as fine anywhere, as those sections of *Maud* in which the
hero is raised to incandescence by the glow of passion, until,
all the dross of selfishness purged away, his spirit becomes
pure music and chimes as it were with the music of the spheres.
But this purpose is not sustained; tragedy follows, and much
of the old rancour returns.   If Tennyson meant the regen-
eration through maiden love to prelude the still higher un-
selfishness sketched at the end, in which the hero "should
feel with his native land", be "one with his kind" and
"embrace the purpose of God and the doom assigned", he
did not pursue his purpose with sufficient vigor to the end.
The poem closes with something like abruptness.   The theme
is perplexed with secondary and merely temporal issues; it
is not developed on an adequate scale or plane.   In spite of
the fine roll of rhetoric and rhythm, we come dangerously
near bathos at the last.

In style and rhythm, *Maud* is as complete a departure from

Tennyson's accomplished manner, as it is in substance and tone. As Patmore remarked in his penetrating review of the poem, "It is only after a very complete mastery has been obtained in the lower excellence of his art, that the poet can trust himself thus completely to the direction of his feelings and his instinct of rhythm." That the time had come for trusting himself and for striking out new and bolder rhythms together with a more direct and fierce presentation of life was evidently the poet's opinion. After the completion of *In Memoriam,* he seems to have felt an inclination to throw aside the pacing harness of systematic metres in which he had learned to move so smoothly. His first reaches toward a free metric we have seen in the blank verse of *The Princess.* In the polished and reticent accents of *In Memoriam* was the summation of his earlier inspirations. In *Maud* and the patriotic poems of the same period he struck out after new and fresher material, after new and unhampered rhythms. But in this he reckoned to a certain degree without his genius. The new freedom contributed much to the unprecedented verve and fire of *Maud,* but it also contributed to the un-evenness and uncertainty of touch which one feels in it, to its lack of distinction.

It is interesting and possibly significant that Tennyson should have departed in this fashion from his matured methods while working over a poem which he had composed before he standardized his verse form. Though the *Stanzas* upon which *Maud* was based were not printed until 1837, they had been written as early as 1833.[11] The earlier stanzas correspond roughly to Section IV, Part II of *Maud.* They are composed of three-stress and four-stress verses. The three-stress verses are mainly iambic in movement, while large sections of the four-stress verse are trochaic-catalectic. There is no actual stanzaic structure; the rhyme-distribution is irreg-ular, and there is considerable irregularity in syllabication; the general effect is that of utter metrical freedom.

Considerable portions of *Maud* are similar in metre to the

---

[11] "A Ms. copy of them, written in 1833, is still extant." J. W. Wise, *A Bibliography of Tennyson,* I, 305.

original stanzas. Up to a certain point the poem was apparently "written backwards." Tennyson has told us that Sir John Simeon, who greatly admired the *Stanzas*, said to him that they required a preceding poem to explain them. Having written the explanatory poem he found that the explanation needed explaining, and so on, the poem growing on his hands.

As the poem stands, the three-stress verse strongly predominates. Some of the poems, as Part I, Sections XI, XII, and XVII, are composed exclusively of three-stress lines. In most of the poems this movement is varied by an occasional extension to four-stresses, and more rarely, to five, while in a few sporadic cases the stresses drop to two. In only a few cases does the four-stress movement seem the dominant one. The concluding section is composed entirely of free-syllabled five-stress verses, and in Part I, Section XVIII ("I have led her home"), one of the finest things in the poem and in Tennyson, five-stress iambic metre is dominant. Sections I, II, III and IV of Part I are six-stress throughout. The six-stress free-syllabled metre of the opening sections was apparently evolved after the composition of the poem was considerably advanced and may have been suggested by passages of three-stress verse in which the rhyme failed and which were therefore essentially six-stress in character. Such a passage as the following:

> She came to the village church
> And sat by a pillar alone;
> An angel watching an urn
> Wept over her, carved in stone.

may easily have given the notion of the longer line. It was characteristic of Tennyson that he adopted this long rolling metre for the opening sections of the poem, leaving himself free to continue in a similar movement, but with a modified effect, by dropping to a three-stress unit in the later and more lyrical portions.

In syllabication there is great freedom; the stress falls anywhere at the caprice of the poet's desire for emphasis; the

13

only regulation is that exquisite sense of time which induces him to a certain regularity in the number of beats to the line, which are usually three or felt as variants of three, and to a limitation of the number of the unstressed syllables between beats, which never exceeds two. Throughout, we have but to "read it as prose" and as Tennyson said of *Boädicea*, "the metre will come right." The rhyme is distributed with the same freedom; in only five instances is a stanzaic scheme observed throughout a section; he does not hesitate to leave a line without its rhyme-mate; frequently the rhymed syllables are set close for emphasis; at other times the rhyme is purposely weakened by their remoteness from each other.

The result of all these freedoms, controlled by Tennyson's disciplined rhythmic sense, is a compass and variety of movements seldom equalled in English verse. At times the syllables will slip into fluent iambic rhythm, sometimes a trochaic or dactylic movement seems the natural one, but most frequently a free and easy anapaestic motion prevails. The one thing constant is the sense of a finely controlled series of beats, so that we have, with a freedom of movement almost commensurate with that of prose, a persistent sense of metre and an emphasis which is that of poetical and not of prose rhythms.

It is not strange that *Maud* was always a favorite poem with Tennyson himself. Nowhere else in his work is there such abandon to instinct, such utter freedom of expression, such reliance upon dramatic impulse and the sheer bone and sinew of poetry. There is language in every key, and rhythm at every pace; the syllables hurry, pause or swoon with passion, now loud, now low; talk, gabble, declaim or sing, whisper or scream, at his will. And yet superb as these abandons are, transcendent as some passages undoubtedly are, we miss the specific beauty of the Tennysonian art. The excellent orderliness, the sense of proportion and design, the sense of power in reserve, the sense of a voice poured forth without straining which attends us in his earlier work is missing here. Some of the notes are ill-practiced and shrill, and some of them are false. The result is distrust and uneasiness, an instinct that all is not well. We feel that he has been carried beyond his compass, has ''o'er-stepped the modesty of nature.''

CHAPTER IX

TENNYSON'S LATER WORK

We have seen that, during one period of his development, Tennyson conformed his style and especially his use of metre to a certain standard of regularity. Under this discipline, he produced the poems which established his reputation in 1842 and which confirmed it eight years later, when *In Memoriam* was published. It seems safe to declare that this was his best period. And, in the light of his subsequent development, it seems reasonable to infer that the limitations to which he submitted himself in this "best period" were contributory to the artistic success which accompanied them. When, toward the end of this period, Tennyson undertook to widen the scope of his art and increase its variety and its intimacy with contemporary life, he appreciably relaxed the strictness which had regulated his style. This greater freedom, as we have seen, is reflected in his metrical practice. Thus, he introduced a much freer treatment of blank verse in *The Princess* and adopted still freer and more varied types of rhythm in *Maud*. It is the purpose of this chapter to pursue a little farther the examination of Tennyson's departures from the practices of his "classic" period.

There still remained to Tennyson nearly forty years of vigorous life, during which poetry continued to be his most serious occupation. The result was a mass of writing which, in volume, greatly exceeds that we have examined, but which, though sincere in workmanship and often of considerable excellence, is generally inferior in interest to the earlier pieces. A detailed description and metrical analysis of this large body of work does not fall within the scope of a volume whose subject is the "formation" of Tennyson's style; but it is believed that a short survey of Tennyson's later development will not be found irrelevant to the present study. The notices of the later poems contained in this chapter are relatively brief, and illustrative rather than complete. While the chronology of the later works and the history of their publication will be borne in mind, they will be classified, for this discussion, according to metrical form, from which their general aim and manner is never completely dissociated. From this point of view, the bulk of the later poems fall into five groups of unequal extent and importance: (1) a blank verse group in which the chief items are *The Idylls of the King* and the Dramas; (2) a group of poems to which Tennyson sometimes gave the name Ballads; (3) a group of poems in the *Locksley Hall* metre and similar forms; (4) poems in classical metres; (5) poems in quatrain form.

After the publication of *Maud* and after the excitement caused by its stormy reception had subsided, Tennyson began the new series of studies from the Arthurian legend which grew to be his most voluminous single work. If we except the *Morte d'Arthur,* which had taken shape as early as 1833, *The Idylls of the King* occupied him at three separate periods. The first period extended from February 1856, when the poem now known as *Merlin and Vivien* was begun, until June, 1859, when the four parts then entitled, *Enid, Vivien, Guinevere,* and *Elaine,* were published. The second period was about ten years later, extending from 1868 to 1872. *The Holy Grail, The Coming of Arthur, Pelleas and Ettarre,* and *The Passing of Arthur* were published together in 1869. *The Last Tournament* appeared exactly two years later, and, in the meantime, *Gareth and Lynnette* had nearly reached completion and was published the following July (1872). Thirteen years later Tennyson made his last addition to the series, *Balin and Balan* (1885).

During the last twenty years of Tennyson's life, the *Idylls* received more attention from his admirers than any other department of his work and inspired a large body of commentary. In this respect they are equalled by no other work of Tennyson and rivalled only by *In Memoriam.* This group of poems constitutes, of course, his most substantial claim to estimation as a poet of magnitude. But it is doubtful if many of his judicious admirers would be willing that Tennyson's position among English poets should be determined on the basis of this achievement. Except the dramas, there is no department of his work in which his limitations tell so heavily against a first rate result. Like the dramas and like a large part of his later work, the material chosen for the *Idylls* calls for the exercise of dramatic faculty, and Tennyson's special genius was essentially non-dramatic. This is not to say that he was without more than average narrative skill; but there is a long step between average skill and special genius, and Tennyson's real genius lay elsewhere than in the portrayal of character and action. In the *Morte d'Arthur* he had chosen from Malory an incident of exceedingly limited action, but an incident strikingly picturesque and full of lyrical suggestion. He thus left himself free to elaborate the background and accessories with his peculiar power of leisurely and harmonious description, while from his overflowing sense of the beauty of the legend he poured through the whole the special music of his own plangent lyrical reverie. The same was true, in an even greater degree, of *The Lady of Shalott*. In most of the stories adopted for the later *Idylls*, Tennyson committed himself to wider and more complicated plans of action and a more varied clash of characters. For the treatment of such subjects, he was less adequately gifted. One scarcely suppresses the impractical wish that, instead of spending his energy on the relatively thankless task which he set himself in *The Princess*, he might have given those golden years to the execution of the epic, in the manner of *Morte d'Arthur*, at which he hints in the Prologue to that piece. That he could have overcome his inherent limitations at this time or at any other, we have no reason to suppose; but there is some ground for surmising that an Arthurian epic executed at that time might have become a more satisfactory unit than the group of poems which we possess in the *Idylls*.

It is clear, however, that Tennyson lacked the conviction for such an enterprise. Otherwise he would scarcely have been prevented, "by John Sterling's review in the *Quarterly*,"[1] from executing his early plan, or had the idea "knocked out of him" by the reviews.[2]   One of the fundamental defects of the *Idylls*, indeed, is the absence of a central, compelling idea from the design as a whole.   Various plans for a long poem based on the Arthurian legend were entertained by Tennyson and partly worked out at different times, but none of them took a powerful hold on his imagination and, in the end, he seems to have drifted into, rather than projected, the plan according to which the several poems were eventually arranged.   The first installment of the *Idylls, Enid, Vivien, Guinevere, and Elaine*, when first printed, in "Trial Edition," bore the title *The True and the False*.   The relationship among them then prominent in Tennyson's mind was, evidently, the contrast of feminine characters,—between the true maiden and the true wife, Elaine and Enid, on the one hand, and the harlot and the unfaithful queen, Vivien and Guinevere, on the other.   That the relation of these feminine types to the ideals of the Table Round and the part the evil women were to play in its final dissolution was already seen, is true.   This is made clear in the king's speech at the end of *Guinevere*.   But the departure of the king at the end of this poem was long thought of by Tennyson as the conclusion of the series and he doubted whether it would be possible for him to find a more effective ending.   And, when urged to complete the epic "he would protest that it was next to impossible now to put the thing properly together, because he had taken up a fragmentary mode of treatment."[3] These and similar evidences of Tennyson's half-heartedness in regard to the general design of the *Idylls* forbid us to think of it as having taken a powerful hold upon his mind.   The best of the *Idylls* and what is best in them sprang from isolated inspirations and not from the working out of a central idea of which they were the organic expression.

The presence of a more or less external design reacted un-

---

[1] *Idylls of the King*, Eversley Ed., p. 436.
[2] Letter of Sir James Knowles, *Ibid.*, p. 489.
[3] Letter from Knowles, *Ibid.*, p. 489.

favorably in some respects upon the individual pieces. In
some cases it complicated the narrative form; in some it accentuated the note of didacticism. In the later version of
Merlin and Vivien, for instance, considerable passages are
added which are of doubtful value to the individual story,
but which tend to bring it into line with the general purpose of the series. The didactic trend of thought which increased as Tennyson proceeded was probably responsible for
his having wrecked the beautiful legend of Tristram and
Isolt in *The Last Tournament.* Here the romance of Tristram
is broken through by episodes from the Lancelot-Guinevere
story and unhappily degraded in order that it may take its
place in the epic of the Round Table's degeneration and
dissolution. In order to fit it for this position in the general
narrative, the story of Tristram and Isolt is robbed of its
ennobling touches and becomes a mere appanage of the larger
scheme, yet fails to serve the general design with sufficient
directness and tragic power to justify the vulgarization of
a world story.

The necessity of interrelating the several stories in the
general design increased in each the perfunctory element
which is bound to invade any narrative of considerable length,
and assisted in the vitiation of the style in which the *Idylls*
were composed. The cross references by which the several
pieces were knit together encouraged a habit of mechanical
repetition which grew on Tennyson as he proceeded and ag-
gravated the sense of self-consciousness, or mannerism, which
frequently annoys us in his later writing. When a happy
phrase has arisen inevitably in some memorable passage
with which it is associated in the reader's mind, it is painful
to find it serving a perfunctory purpose elsewhere. We are
not rejoiced, at the close of *The Coming of Arthur,* to find
the king plundering the "old *Morte*" of one of its finest
lines,

> The old order changeth, yielding place to new.

And after, in the opening lines of *The Passing of Arthur,*
"the bold Sir Bedivere" begins his story among "new faces,

other minds'', there is a distinct subtraction from our sense of his spontaneity, when a little later he says to King Arthur:

> And the days darken round me, and the years,
> Among new men, strange faces, other minds.

It may be said that this is too conscious on the part of the critic. It certainly is too conscious on the part of the poet.

These strictures upon the repetitions of the *Idylls* are not, of course, strictures upon the use of repetition, as such, but upon the manner of its use. Ruskin once objected to the ''evidence of art'' that he noticed in the *Idylls*. To this Lord Tennyson replies that they were not artfully written, having been finished, *Guinevere* and *Elaine,* each of them, in a few weeks and hardly corrected at all. These apparently contradictory opinions are, perhaps, not irreconcilable. May not the defect of the *Idylls* which Ruskin noticed be due, in part, to the very fact which Lord Tennyson pleaded in rebuttal? It is one of the commonplaces of criticism that the artist's final stroke is in removing the ''evidence of art''. This Tennyson did to an unusual degree in the earlier poems; in fact, this was one of the chief secrets of his success in revision. It is in the longer and hastier though more practiced work that the calculation of effect betrays itself. This is not a way of saying that Tennyson became careless; Tennyson was never technically careless; but he did become in some respects more bold, and he became more diffuse. He never ceased to be conscientious, and he became if anything more jealous of his reputation. The numerous ''trial editions'', the long delays before publication, the minute corrections in and after ''the press'', are evidence of these facts. The later and longer poems hardly could have been, however, and certainly were not, considered with the nine years' anxious care which wrought the perfection of their predecessors. Naturally, he worked more rapidly. He had acquired by study and practice an easy control of the machinery of expression and greater independence in its use. But increased facility made possible the rapid execution of more diffuse plans, and the larger

scale on which he worked was a temptation to try new experiments in expression and, even more frequently, to slip
into stereotyped application of old devices. In short there
is more facile workmanship in the later *Idylls* with less inspiration and less self-criticism,—a perilous condition for
the artist.

The negative criticism contained in the foregoing paragraphs is not intended to diminish admiration for the many
beauties of Tennyson's *Idylls of the King*, but to explain in
some measure the more qualified pleasure they give as compared with the earlier work, and to set in relief the peculiar
perfection of the earlier art. The substance of our unfavor-
able criticism of the *Idylls* is, then, that the appeal of the
component parts is more injured than enhanced by their
association in the general design, and that the artfulness
with which they are composed too frequently betrays itself.

The self-consciousness of Tennyson's style in the *Idylls*
can be marked with much definiteness in his treatment of
metre. In returning to the subject which he had earlier
broached in the *Morte d'Arthur*, he had, naturally enough,
resorted again to blank verse, from which he had been somewhat estranged during the time he had been at work upon
In Memoriam and *Maud*. There is evidence both external
and internal that he gave careful thought to his practice in
the verse of the *Idylls*. We have his statement that "the
blank verse throughout each of the twelve *Idylls* varies according to the subject."[4] It is, of course, a verse much less
uniform in style, much less restricted as to its variations than
that of the *Morte d'Arthur*, or indeed than that of any of
the 1842 blank verse poems. Because of the greater length
of these narratives and because of the lowered intensity of
large sections of them, the verse on the whole seeks after
lightness, grace, and variety, rather than the sonority or
rich fulness of verbal music, which characterized the 1842
poems. Between the separate *Idylls* there are considerable
contrasts of practice, and, as Tennyson's phrase suggests,

---

[4] Eversley Ed., p. 453.

there is more or less variation "throughout each." The verse fluctuates, then, between a regularity approaching, in passages, that of the 1842 poems, and a general freedom of movement approximating and sometimes exceeding that of *The Princess*. Most of the devices which Tennyson employed to give sprightliness and variety to the metre have been seen in *The Princess;* but some of these were more fully developed or were employed more frequently and more systematically in the *Idylls*. The practices which are characteristic of the *Idylls* have to do especially with the use of extra syllables, with the treatment of weak measures, and with the relation of both to inversions, to interior pause, and to the verse end. These practices will be illustrated by the presentation of a few metrical statistics and a few examples.

The most obvious variation of movement in this type of verse is that produced by the introduction of extra-syllables. On the average, extra-syllables are more abundant than in *The Princess*. This applies to the number of extra-syllables, regardless of their character; on the other hand, a much smaller proportion of them are of the "unslurred" kind. To such an extent is this true that, in the statistics that will be given, no distinction is made between "slurred" and "unslurred" extra-syllables. It may be well to remind ourselves that the average frequency of extra-syllables in the blank verse poems of 1842 was 5.8 per cent, while the average for all of *The Princess* was 20.2 per cent. Now, the average frequency in *Geraint and Enid* (300 lines) is 18.8 per cent; all of *Guinevere* (692 lines) has 19 per cent; 500 lines of *Merlin and Vivien* show 22.6 per cent; *Lancelot and Elaine* (1000 lines), 26.6 per cent. Among the first group of *Idylls*, then, the treatment of the verse in this respect is freest and lightest in *Lancelot and Elaine*. Of *The Coming of Arthur* Tennyson stated that its form was "purposely more archaic than that of the other *Idylls*,"[5] resembling, in this particular the *Passing*, which included the earlier *Morte d'Arthur*. It is therefore interesting to find that, in the verse of the

---

[5] Eversley Ed., p. 453.

opening poem, extra-syllables have been restrained to 9.4 per cent, which brings it very close to the 8 per cent of the "old Morte"; while 198 lines written to introduce the latter into its place in the *Idylls* have 13.5 per cent.   On the other hand, *The Holy Grail*, written about the same time, has 23 per cent, *Pelleas and Etarre*, 22 per cent; a little later, extra syllables reach highest frequency in *The Last Tournament* (first 500 lines), 30 per cent; *Gareth and Lynette* (1000 lines) is a close second with 28.6 per cent; and *Balin and Balan*, added long afterward, has only 20 per cent.

Besides the increase in the absolute number of extra syllables introduced in the verse of the *Idylls* there is an increase in the number of lines in which the normal rhythm is noticeably disturbed by the use of more than one extra syllable in a single verse or by the presence of some added variation from the normal stress or pause. We then get movements as highly contrasted with the normal iambic rhythm as the following,

> The sound of many a heavily-galloping hoof[6]

in which *three* extra syllables set up a strongly anapaestic movement.   In the following verse,

> And the sword of the tourney across her throat[7]

although there is but one supernumerary syllable, this, combined with a weak first measure and inversion of the second gives us again, a strongly anapaestic effect.   Or the movement may be shifted as in the following,

> Even the shadow of Lancelot under Shield.[8]

Here, beginning inversion plus *two* extra syllables has resulted in a light dactylic movement through the early portion of the line.   Again, in the verse,

> Crimson, a slender banneret fluttering,[9]

---

[6] *Geraint and Enid,* 447.
[7] *Pelleas and Ettarre,* 446.
[8] *Gareth and Lynette,* 1289.
[9] *Ibid.,* 891.

although there is only one extra syllable, this is ingeniously combined with the beginning inversion and the weak fifth measure to produce a distinctly dactylic movement.

Inversion alone, without any change of syllabic number, gives a trochaic-dactylic character to the following,

> Felt the light of her eyes into his life
> Smite on the sudden.[10]

It might be well questioned whether some of these are legitimate blank verse cadences; but at any rate they are exceptional, even in the *Idylls,* and merely serve to illustrate the extremes to which Tennyson occasionally pushed his departures from the normal iambic rhythm of the verse. Far more significant are the habitual devices for modifying the verse end and the medial pause and for retarding or hastening the run of the metre. Among these the most noticeable developments in the blank verse of the *Idylls* are the increased use of counter-caesural inversion, the increased frequency of weak measures, the increase of epic caesurae, and of double endings, the final tribrach, and perhaps most characteristic of all, a device which I shall call for lack of a better term, the *weak feminine caesura.*

The counter-caesural inversion produces a distinctive modulation of rhythm which Tennyson practiced with increased freedom in the *Idylls.* Its abundance amounts to an idiosyncrasy in *Guinevere,* of which the first two hundred lines contain nine or ten examples. There are at least five in the first thirty-five lines. Of the following examples, the first four are from *Guinevere,* the others from various sources.

> The white *mist, like* a face-cloth to the face
> Clung to the dead *earth, and* the land was still.[11]
> Climbed to the high *top of* the garden wall[12]
> So from the high *wall and* the flowering grove[13]

---

[10] *Coming of Arthur,* 56–7.
[11] *Guinevere,* 7–8.
[12] *Ibid.,* 25.
[13] *Ibid.,* 33.

Smote by the fresh *beam of* the springing east[14]
And in the wild *woods of* Broceliande[15]
Till all the white *walls of* my cell are dyed[16]

It is probably significant that in connection with the usual frequency of counter-caesural inversion in the early passages of *Guinevere,* we have a very large number of beginning inversions, 49 in the first 200 lines, together with 4 caesural inversions. Weak measures, also, which are of high average frequency throughout the *Idylls* are especially prominent in *Guinevere,* where we find 72 in the first 100 lines; 73 in lines 101–200; 62 in the last 100 lines of the poem.[17] *Merlin and Vivien,* one of the more even of the *Idylls* in syllabling and stress, has 55 weak measures in the first 100 lines, 53 in lines 101–200; 60 in its last 100 lines. A characteristic passage of *The Holy Grail* (lines 100–199) has 59 weak measures; *Gareth and Lynette* (lines 1280–1379) has 51. In these several passages, weak fifth measures run from 2 to 10 per cent and weak first measures from 2 to 11 per cent. As in the earlier verse, the stress most frequently fails in the fourth measure.

In the above mentioned passages, to which may be added all of *Gareth and Lynette,* double endings and epic-caesurae usually run from 1 to 3 in each 100 lines, but sometimes are so massed as to become characteristic. Thus all of *Gareth and Lynette* (1394 lines) has 49 double endings and 31 epic caesurae, or 3.5 per cent of the former and about 2 per cent of the latter. Yet passages of 100 lines are found in which double endings run to 5 or 6 per cent,[18] and others having as high as 7 per cent of epic caesurae.[19]

---

[14] *Passing of Arthur,* 382. This, taken over with the old *Morte d'Arthur,* is one of *three* examples in the 1842 poems.

[15] *Merlin and Vivien,* 2.

[16] *Holy Grail,* 119.

[17] It should be recalled that the average frequency in the 1842 poems was only 48.7 per cent. The average for *Dora,* by far the highest among the 1842 poems, was 63 per cent.

[18] E. g., *Guinevere,* 593–692; *Gareth and Lynette,* 1–100, 501–600, 701–800.

[19] *Gareth and Lynette,* 901–1000; *Holy Grail,* 100–199; *Last Tournament,* 1–100.

Mr. Saintsbury has expressed the opinion[20] that Tennyson
depreciated the blank verse of the *Idylls* by a too free use
of the tribrach; but a careful examination hardly sustains
this view.   In the passages studied, tribrachs appear from
2 to 7 times in each 100 lines; perhaps 5 per cent would be
a fair guess for the running average of the *Idylls*.   He did,
however, develop a fancy for the light double ending produced by employing the tribrach in the final position of the
verse, as in the following examples:

> Bearing all down in thy precipitancy[21]
> A huge man-beast of boundless savagery[22]
> And when the damsel spake contemptuously[23]
> And fain would I reward thee worshipfully[24]
> Furrowing a giant oak, and javelining[25]
> They twain were wedded with all ceremony[26]
> If he would only speak and tell me of it[27]

The two last examples bring us very close to Tennyson's
ordinary double ending which is almost always so light as
to give it very nearly the character of a final tribrach.

But the most subtle device employed by Tennyson for giving
legerity of movement to the verse of the *Idylls* is that of
placing the medial pause with great frequency within a weak
measure.   If we note the effect of his typical epic caesura
as in the following examples from *The Holy Grail*,

> Coming upon *me—O* never harp nor horn[28]
> Rose red with beatings in *it, as* if alive[29]
> Far in the spiritual ci*ty": and* as she spake[30]
> Far in the spiritual ci*ty; and* come thou too[31]

[20] *Nineteenth Century Literature*, p. 268.
[21] *Gareth and Lynette*, 8.
[22] *Ibid.*, 622.
[23] *Ibid.*, 786.
[24] *Ibid.*, 809.
[25] *Merlin and Vivien*, 933.
[26] *Marriage of Geraint*, 839.
[27] *Geraint and Enid*, 54.
[28] *Holy Grail*, 112.
[29] *Holy Grail*, 118.
[30] *Holy Grail*, 162.
[31] *Holy Grail*, 483.

and if we compare these with examples of the plain feminine caesura dividing the weak measure, we shall feel, I think, that a somewhat similar effect is produced without the license of the supernumerary syllable:

> Come victor. *But* my time is hard at hand[32]
> Black, with black bann*er, and* a long black horn.[33]
> As if for pit*y? But* he spake no word
> Which set the horror high*er: a* maiden swooned;[34]

In the last example, it will be noticed, the first line has the weak feminine caesura, the second line, epic caesura. In one hundred lines of *Gareth and Lynette* which embrace this passage, out of 53 feminine pauses, 22 fall within a weak measure. An examination of several hundred lines of various *Idylls* shows this to be about the usual proportion. In a great many cases, where the sense pause is slight, particularly when it falls, as Tennyson frequently contrives to have it, in the midst of the weak fourth measure, the result is to slur the medial pause. In other cases, it has the effect of lightening a full-stop or a half-stop in the midst of the verse as in the following example, where it has a fine expressive effect:

> Low on the border of her couch they sat
> Stammering and star*ing. It* was their last hour,[35]

It will be seen that most of the devices enumerated above tend toward a lighter syllabling of the blank verse of the *Idylls* than that which Tennyson had worked out with so much care in his 1842 blank verse. The abundance of weak measures alone is sufficient to distinguish the prevailing rhythms of the *Idylls* from the deliberate, full-syllabled movements of the earlier poems. Probably Tennyson was not fully aware of the degree to which he had allowed his blank verse to become emaciated in this particular. He wrote more rapidly, and he aimed, in general, at a more sprightly and more casual style which he emphasized by lighter,

---

[32] *Holy Grail*, 481.
[33] *Gareth and Lynette*, 1331.
[34] *Gareth and Lynette*, 1358–59.
[35] *Guinevere*, 100–101.

"feminine" rhythms of the verse. One suspects, also, that his ear may have been to some extent seduced, in this later period, through his contemporaneous practice in less exacting, and particularly in triple, metres. Thus he was led at times to the introduction of *direct*[36] rhythms into his blank verse, whereas he had formerly restrained himself to modulations of the iambic movement.

The difficulty is that these conscious variations of rhythm and the equally conscious return, in set passages, to the full-toned iambic, are frequently obtrusive. When we meet in the *Morte d'Arthur* such a line as this,

> So strode he back *slow* to the wounded king

the expressive effect of the inversion which throws a modest emphasis on the word "slow" is artful, but it is not obtrusive. But when, in *Lancelot and Elaine*, we meet the following,

> First as in fear, step after step, she stole
> Down the long tower stairs, hesitating:[37]

though the double inversion, or hovering accent upon the last word is tremendously artful, it is perilously near being too much so. We suspect the poet of making the verse play tricks upon us. And when these devices are frequent, and when, too, we encounter so studied and obvious a balance of phrase and pause as the following,

> Fainter by day, but always in the night
> Blood-red, and sliding down the blackened marsh
> Blood-red, and on the naked mountain top
> Blood-red, and in the sleeping mere below
> Blood-red.[38]

the design upon us becomes quite too evident, and we have that uncomfortable sense of over-sophistication in the style of which Ruskin complained. The blank verse of

---

[36] By "direct rhythm." I mean such a desertion of the fundamental iambic movement as we have in the anapaestic verse quoted above,
"The sound of many a heavily-galloping hoof."
[37] *Lancelot and Elaine*, 340–41.
[38] *Holy Grail*, 472–6.

14

the *Idylls*, then, is not less fertile in device than the blank verse of the earlier poems, it is even more artful; but its art has the misfortune of being less happily applied, and it has the unhappiness, above all, of attracting attention to itself. Manner, for lack of perfect inspiration, has declined into mannerism.

Tennyson never completely recaptured the earlier charm of manner, though in some of his later poems he imitated very closely the technical characteristics of his earlier blank verse. Immediately after the completion of the first series of *Idylls* he turned to those studies of contemporary and lowly life which he collected and printed, in 1864, under the title, *Idylls of the Hearth*, though this title was shortly discarded and the volume published under the simpler one, *Enoch Arden etc.* The *Enoch Arden* volume contains almost the last attempts of Tennyson to apply his idyllic and decorative manner to subjects drawn from contemporary domestic life. Besides the title piece, *Sea Dreams* and *Aylmer's Field* belong to this class. *Sea Dreams* had been printed in *Macmillan's Magazine* four years earlier.[39] *Enoch Arden* had been completed in the summer of 1862, and *Aylmer's Field* was written in 1863. All three poems are in blank verse; but in spite of the tendency to ornate treatment, the stories are not won to the realm of Tennysonian magic. Elements of realism and violence give to each of these poems that odor of melodrama which clings about much of Tennyson's later work. These characteristics in the spirit of treatment are indicated in the versification. That substitution of a *natural* for a formal rhythm, and the ''over-expressiveness'' which took hold of his later blank verse is present here. The controlled manner of the 1842 idylls is absent. These poems have the metrical freedom and apparent self-consciousness of the later blank verse of parts of *The Princess* and of *The Idylls of the King*.

Among the blank verse poems of this issue were *Tithonus*, which Tennyson had dug out of his old papers and finished off for Thackeray, four years before.[40] Because of Ten-

---

[39] January, 1860.

[40] First published in the *Cornhill Magazine*, January, 1860.

nyson's statement in regard to the date of its composition I have included it in my review of the blank verse poems of 1842,[41] but it may be worth noticing that, in spite of its general resemblance to the 1842 poems, it has a larger proportion of extra-syllables than any other poem of that group. The other poems in blank verse were, "Dear, Near, and True," which has a few violences of metre suggestive of Tennyson's later practice, and the *Specimen of a Translation of the Iliad in blank verse*, the structure of which indicates that for this purpose Tennyson would have favored a severe structure of verse not unlike that of his early models.

The year 1868 must have been one of no little activity. In May, *Lucretius*, one of the finest of Tennyson's later classical studies and one of the most sumptuous examples of his blank verse of any period, appeared in *Macmillan's Magazine*. The same year was printed with the title, "The Birth of Arthur," a "trial edition" of the four *Idylls of the King* which were published in the volume entitled *The Holy Grail and Other Poems*, in 1870. To the same year also belongs the first trial book of *The Last Tournament*, though that poem was not actually published until three years later. Finally, toward the close of the same year "thirty-six years after the first two parts had been put into type, Tennyson again took *The Lover's Tale* in hand."[42] Annoyed by the continual piracies of R. A. Shepard, Tennyson had resolved to prepare the poem for the press; it was greatly altered, a third part, afterwards called *The Golden Supper*, was added, and the whole was actually put into print this year; but the problem of working over an immature poem and making proper adjustment of style and metre to an earlier theme was a perplexing one, and the poet was still dissatisfied with the result, or at least was not satisfied of the expediency of publishing the poem, and it did not, as a whole, come to actual publication until eleven years more[43] had elapsed.

---

[41] See above, Chap. VI, p. 121.

[42] Wise, I, p. 53.

[43] For the changes made in *The Lover's Tale*, between 1833 and 1879, see above, Ch. III, pp. 77–85. For the changes made between 1869 and 1879, see Wise, I, pp. 55–73.

THE DRAMAS

For a period of about ten years after the virtual completion of the *Idylls* in 1872, Tennyson was chiefly occupied with the composition of his dramas. *Queen Mary* was published in May, 1875; about a year later, it was produced at the Lyceum Theatre, by Henry Irving, and ran a little less than a month. *Harold* came from the press in 1877, and, after another interval of two years, *Becket* reached, in 1879, the phase of a "trial edition." *Becket* was refused by Irving, and its publication was delayed for some five years. It finally appeared, with many changes and additions, in 1884, and achieved its stage production in 1893, the year after Tennyson's death. Similar delays occurred in the publication of the other plays. Thus, *The Falcon* was privately printed in 1879, *The Cup* and *The Foresters* in 1881, *The Promise of May* in 1882. But *The Falcon* and *The Cup* first reached publication together in 1884. *The Promise of May*, after a bad reception on the stage, was unobtrusively and apparently with reluctance included in the volume entitled, *Locksley Hall Sixty Years After, Etc.*, 1886. *The Foresters* reached the stage in the United States in 1892, eleven years after the first "trial edition", and was published in England the same year.

Tennyson's late foray into the region of formal drama may be regarded as a development out of his growing effort to touch life more directly and more vigorously. It is surprising, but not unaccountable. The history of the plays indicates that he was not sparing of his labor in the attempt to make his achievements in this department worthy of his success in departments for which he was more richly endowed. To the composition of his dramas, he brought a matured intelligence and an accomplished and sophisticated gift of literary execution, and he succeeded, by their application, in producing a series of works which are not negligible, however they may fail to elevate him to the character of a native dramatist. Though he shows little real dramatic instinct, he mastered his historical materials and compounded them with a strong sense at least of spectacle and of static values; and he clothes them in language which, while it lacks dramatic magic, is dignified and worthy.   He subdued to a considerable degree his native tendency to elegiac and idyllic elaboration.   In so doing, he sacrificed no little beauty; but he achieved a very respectable imitation of the condensed vigor which drama should possess.   In the more violent scenes there is occasionally the shrieking key which he was prone to break into when he attempted to touch character and action vitally, but in most of the scenes of most of the dramas he escapes it.

Metrically, the dramas follow naturally enough after the period of the *Idylls*.   During that decade, as we have seen, he had been occupied almost constantly with composition in blank verse.   The freedom which grew upon him in that period was naturally accelerated with some suddenness when he turned to the composition of drama.   Not only did an extension of metrical liberty fall in with all his tendencies at this time; these were augmented by his theoretic apprehension of the metrical traditions of the drama.   Significantly, his most violent break with his own idyllic form of verse is to be found in his first play, *Queen Mary*.   In metre, as in other respects, this is perhaps the most violent of the plays. The normal verse pattern is more frequently sacrificed here than in the later plays.   Extra-syllables, epic-caesurae, double and triple and even quadruple endings are freely admitted, expanding the individual verse frequently and far beyond the normal syllabic content.   Short lines, phrases from one to nine syllables in length, are freely admitted, outside the normal verse scheme.   The later plays have fewer irregularities, partly, perhaps, because of a less excited and more dignified tone.   Thus, in *Becket* we have less irregularity than in *Mary*; in *Harold* less than in either; while *The Cup,* which is classical in theme and setting, is also classical and restrained in tone, and the versification is correspondingly regular and severe.   *The Promise of May*, which presents a theme and setting from contemporary life and represents

Tennyson's strongest set toward realism, is almost entirely in prose, and the language occasionally passes into dialect; while those passages which are in verse are chiefly reflective or idyllic in tone and the versification is regular by way of bolder relief against the prose which constitutes the body of the play. Summarily, whatever we may think of the wisdom of Tennyson's economy in devoting the greater share of his energy for ten years to creation in dramatic form, we have in this phenomenon one supreme exemplification of the trend of his development, a development which is conclusively demonstrative of the close relation between form and matter in his work, and of his mature sophistication in the fitting of metrical means to literary ends.

Tennyson had now lived out the span of life allotted by the Psalmist. He was destined by strength to make it more than four-score; and during most of this time he remained vigorously at work; though he executed no large plan, he continued to publish more and more liberally in magazines, and, every two or three years, brought forth a volume of miscellanies. Before completing his series of dramas, he had brought out, in 1880, his volume of *Ballads and Other Poems.* Four others were to follow: *Tiresias and Other Poems,* in 1885; *Locksley Hall Sixty Years After, etc.,* in 1886; *Demeter and Other Poems,* in 1889; and *The Death of Œnone, Akbar's Dream, and Other Poems,* shortly after the poet's death, in 1892.

The core of these later volumes is the group of poems to which Tennyson gave the name Ballads. His first published poem in this style appears to have been *The Grandmother.* Tennyson read this poem to some friends in July, 1858; it was printed in *Once a Week,* July, 1859, under the title *The Grandmother's Apology.* The poem was written in the six-stress free-syllabled metre, whose flexibility and adaptableness to realistic and quasi-prosaic statement he had discovered during the composition of *Maud.* In this poem, and in all subsequent poems in the same style and metre, the six-stress verses rhyme in couplets, and this is the only important deviation from his practice in *Maud.* *Northern Farmer—*

Old Style was written in the same metre and here the attempt
to portray his characters in the language of their ordinary
daily life is carried to the farther extent of imitating the
Lincolnshire dialect, with which the poet had been familiar
in his boyhood.   We first hear of this poem as early as 1851.
Northern Farmer—New Style was privately printed under
the title, *Property,* in 1864, but was first published in the
Holy Grail volume, 1869–70.[44]   The proof sheets of this poem
show considerable care and effort on the poet's part to trans-
form his language and style to that of the dialect he was
representing: "muther" for "mother", "proputy" for
"property", "oop" for "up", and "bees" for "flies" are
examples of dialect spelling and diction which were thought
of only after the copy had gone to press.   In the 1880 volume,
he presented five additional poems of this type, of varying
intensity and distinction, but similar in subject matter and
method, several of them being in dialect.   These were *The
First Quarrel, Rizpah, The Northern Cobbler, The Village
Wife, or The Entail,* and *In The Children's Hospital.*   In
the same metre, but of different poetical cast was *The Voyage
of Maeldune.*   His predilection for the metre is indicated by
the fact that he runs into it in one passage of his lines *To
Princess Frederica, etc.*   *The Revenge* is in a similar metre,
but adds to the free-syllabling, freedom of verse length and
rhyme distribution, and a free use of the rest pause; while
in some sections a more regular anapaestic movement prevails.   *The Defense of Lucknow* may be characterized as similar to the poem just described.   The 1885 volume had four
pieces in the six-stress metre and of similar character: *The
Wreck, Despair, To-morrow,* and *The Spinster's Sweet-Arts.*
The Flight is said to have been of early composition and is in
couplets of seven-stress verse like those of the early poem,
The May Queen.   *The Charge of the Heavy Brigade* is in
irregular triple movement, somewhat after the fashion of
The Revenge.

---

[44] The volume was dated 1870, though actually issued in December,
1869.   (Wise).

Two poems of the 1889 volume are of the Ballad type and in the six-stress metre, *viz.*, *Owd Roa* and *Happy;* two poems of a different cast, *Parnassus* and *Beautiful City* are, one partly, the other wholly, in this metre; while two, *Forlorn* and *Politics,* are in broken arrangements of the septenarius. The 1892 volume has three poems, *The Bandit's Death, The Church Warden and The Curate,* and *Charity,* in the six-stress metre, which possess also the other characteristics of this group; *The Dawn* and *The Dreamer,* though different in subject and key, are chiefly in six-stress metre.

Meantime Tennyson seems to have become interested again, about 1885, in the possibilities of the *Locksley Hall* metre. *Locksley Hall Sixty Years After* was published in 1886, but two poems of the preceding volume show his inclination to revive the metre. *To Virgil* has precisely the same movement, extended to nine beats instead of eight. *Frater Ave atque Vale* is in the eight-stress trochaics of *Locksley Hall.* The 1889 volume, again, has traces of the same movement. Thus *Parnassus* begins in six-stress metre, but in Section III slips into regular eight-stress trochaics. *By an Evolutionist* has verses of three, five, six, and seven stresses in triple movement, while two of its sections are in the regular eight-stress trochaics, which differ from those of *Locksley Hall* only in rhyming alternately. *Vastness* is in eight-stress verse throughout and rhymes in couplets; but a dactylic movement has been substituted for the trochaic of *Locksley Hall.* For the "Hymn" in *Akbar's Dream,* Tennyson contrived a stanza out of the eight-stress trochaic of which he was very proud. In this stanza, lines 1, 2 and 4 rhyme together while the third verse is mute, acatalectic, and unstopped. Two other pieces in the 1892 volume, *Faith* and *The Making of Man* are in the same metre and stanza. The long rolling metre of the lines *To Virgil* is repeated in *God and The Universe.* The verse of *Kapiolani,* though irregular, is similar to that of *Vastness;* it is dactylic in movement and extends, normally, to eight-stress, though many of the verses are shorter; finally, it is rhymeless, except that the various sections of the poem, which are of unequal length, close on a rhyming syllable.

Shortly after the completion of the first group of *Idylls*, Tennyson began to experiment in unrhymed metres other than blank verse. The *Enoch Arden* volume contained several *"Experiments"* in which he tried his hand at the representation of classical metres in English. *Boädicea* is an attempt to reproduce, in accentual verse, one of the movements of Catullus. Tennyson was anxious lest the ordinary reader might be unable to give the proper metrical effect to his lines, and he gave the significant instruction: "Read it as prose and it will come right." The other poems of this group are experiments in quantity: *On Translations of Homer,* in hexameters and pentameters; *Milton,* in Alcaics; and an address to "indolent reviewers," headed simply, *Hendecasyllabics,* an imitation of Catullus. All of these poems are interesting and clever attempts to make the natural vocalization of the syllables, according to their sense, fall in with their native quantity to produce the cadences of classical poetry. They are chiefly interesting as an exhibition of Tennyson's ingenuity in fitting the natural prose cadences of an English sentence to a fixed and artificial scheme of rhythm. They are indications, also, of his continued interest in metrical novelties and problems. They do not at all indicate that he considered classical models of any direct practical efficacy for English poetry.

Later, his interest in unrhymed metres appears to have been re-awakened by contact with Anglo-Saxon poetry. His spirited rendering of *The Battle of Brunanburgh* in unrhymed dactylics and trochaics is perhaps the best adaptation of the old alliterative verse to be found in modern English poetry. This translation appeared in the collection of 1880. The 1889 collection has two studies in similar metre. *Merlin and the Gleam* is mainly in trochaics and dactylics, two-stress lines, and has caught from the Brunanburgh poem the fine unstayed effect of the trochaic or dactylic verse, together with the device of the occasional four-stress verse and the close of the period upon a stressed syllable. It is not, however, alliterative, and anacrusis is more frequent. *On the Jubilee of Queen Victoria* is in systematic unrhymed trochaic and dactylic metre and shows, in addition, the effect of his constant study of classical measures. Two kinds of metre alternate in the poem. The opening and each successive odd section is composed of three unrhymed, five-stress trochaic verses.[45] The eleventh and concluding section is double; that is, it runs to six instead of three, verses. The even sections have each from eight to eleven unrhymed three-stress verses; each verse is, without exception, trochaic in the first measure and dactylic in the second and third. These are Tennyson's experiments in unrhymed trochaic and dactylic metres. In the meantime had come the revival of his interest in long metres of the *Locksley Hall* type which has been noticed. Finally, in his very last volume, the two principles combine to create the extraordinary metre of *Kapiolani*.

Another method of suggesting the cadences of alien poetry is to be found in some of Tennyson's late mutations of the quatrain. In the 1889 volume, he revived the ingenious stanza which he had long before invented for his address *To the Rev. F. D. Maurice*.[46] The history of this stanza is suggestive. First, he invented the stanza of *The Daisy*. In this stanza, all the verses except the third rhyme together, the third verse is silent, with feminine ending; while, for the third iambus of the fourth verse, the anapaest is systematically substituted. In *To the Rev. F. D. Maurice*, this movement was changed to one intended to suggest that of the Horatian Alcaic; the change is made by the simple device of introducing systematic beginning-inversion in the fourth verse, thus opening the verse with two dactylic measures. This stanza he employed in the poem *To Prof. Jebb*, introducing *Demeter and Persephone*. In his last volume, Tennyson carried this imitation one step farther. *To the Master of Balliol*, introducing *The Death of Œnone*, is composed in a stanza which has been developed out of the former. The non-rhyming third verse is reduced to five syllables, a trochee plus

---

[45] Five-stress trochaic blank verse is systematically used in Browning's *One Word More*, and, so far as I am aware, not elsewhere in antecedent English poetry.

[46] For earlier permutations of the quatrain, see above, pp. 102–106.

a dactyl, and the fourth verse passes over frankly into trochaic-dactylic movement, being compounded of a trochee, two dactyls, and a catalectic foot at the close. The short third verse may have been suggested by the final dimeter of the Sapphic. The transfer of the dimeter to this position overcomes an effect of that strophe which caused Tennyson to express a distaste for it, comparing it to "a pig with a curl in his tail." It will be noticed that all of these ingenious stanzas occur in poems of address to friends and were not invented for standard use.

None of the later volumes, except *Locksley Hall Sixty Years After, etc.*, is without its group of poems in the formal iambic metres in which Tennyson's first great triumphs were won. *Ballads and Other Poems* contained six pieces in blank verse. Two of these, *Sir John Oldcastle* and *Columbus* are monologues similar in scope and method to *Ulysses* and *Lucretius*, somewhat more familiar in style, and far inferior in distinction and beauty. *The Sisters* is similar in subject matter to the Ballads of the same volume; the poem is one of Tennyson's last attempts to treat a contemporary story of the kind in blank verse and it is only slightly idyllic in tone and decoration. The inserted songs are in rhymed lyric metre, a feature in which it is unlike the earlier idylls, but resembles *The Brook* and *Sea Dreams.*[47] The volume contained four sonnets of variable excellence.[48] Among the significant matters to be noted in regard to this volume are the considerable proportion of poems in the homely and realistic style suggested in the title of the collection, the considerable number of poems of address, and the considerable number, eight in all, which had appeared in *The Nineteenth Century*, an indication of the increasing habit of magazine publication.

The *Tiresias* volume, five years later, had five blank verse poems. Two of these were unimportant poems of address.

[47] Other poems in blank verse are the *Dedicatory Poem To The Princess Alice*, the translation, *Achilles Over The Trench*, and the reflective poem, suggested by the birth of his grandson, *De Profundis*.

[48] *Prefatory Sonnet to the 'Nineteenth Century,'* *To the Rev. W. H. Brookfield, Montenegro*, and *To Victor Hugo*.

The title piece was avowedly the work of earlier years and is
in general like the earlier poems on classical themes; it has
a noble smoothness, with something of the combined austerity
and vehemence of Tennyson's later style. The verse is of
the earlier pattern, though a few violences of syllabling occur
which would not have been tolerated under the 1842 standard.
This volume contained *Balin and Balan,* the last of the *Idylls
of the King.* In the verse of this poem, as we have seen,
Tennyson retrenched somewhat the liberties of the later
Idylls.

The Ancient Sage is in the poet's later vein as to both style
and content. The verse is unlike that of the earlier poems, for
though generally severe in syllabication, it is free as to stress
and pause. The lyric passages inserted in the poem revive the
quatrain of four-stress and three-stress iambics rhyming alternately. It is interesting that some of the most magical
touches to be found in the later volumes are in these quatrain
passages. When one lights on such melody as the following,

> How far through all the bloom and brake
>   That nightingale is heard!
> What power but the bird's could make
>   This music in the bird?
> How summer-bright on yonder skies
>   And earth as fair in hue?
> And yet what sign of aught that lies
>   Behind the green and blue?

or, on such a passage as this,–

> The years that when my youth began
>   Had set the lily and rose
> By all my ways, where'er they ran,
>   Have ended mortal foes;
> My rose of love forever gone,
>   My lily of truth and trust,
> They made her lily and rose in one
>   And changed her into dust.

one feels a reawakening of the genius which made *The Miller's
Daughter* and *The Vision of Sin,* and ''Come into the garden,
Maud.'' Several poems in this volume were in this metre;

the lines, *To E. Fitzgerald,* accompanying *Tiresias;* the *Prologue to General Hamley,* and the *Epilogue,* accompanying *The Charge of The Heavy Brigade;* and the *Prefatory Poem to My Brother's Sonnets.* In the last particularly, the metre is managed with more than a suggestion of the old Tennysonian magic.[49] In this volume we mark a strong inclination to reminiscence and reversion; there are four poems in the six-stress metre; there is a larger body of blank verse somewhat like that of the 1842 period; there is a revival of the quatrain of four-stress and three-stress iambic, and a revival of interest in the *Locksley Hall* metre.[50] Numerous poems of earlier composition are brought forward for publication. Memorial and occasional poems and poems of personal address continue to increase in number. The habit of periodical publication has continued.

Each of Tennyson's two latest volumes, like the *Tiresias* volume before them, takes its name from a poem of classical theme. *Demeter and Persephone* and *The Death of Œnone* are workmanlike studies in blank verse upon legends drawn from the classic stock. It is odd that the term, *studies,* should still seem appropriate to any of Tennyson's work. But it is nevertheless true that there is something experimental and tentative about these poems. They are not written from any inward necessity; they are deliberate studies after the manner of his own early work of the same kind; with deliberate correspondences and differences. The poet is still conscious of his technique. In versification, he returns to his earlier severe standard; as to characteristics of syllabication, stress, and pause, the blank verse is hardly distinguishable from that of 1842. But ornamentation is consciously reduced, and the style, seeking directness and austerity, becomes relatively harsh. Much of the old melody and most of the old glamour have departed. Tennyson has, with only partial

---

[49] In the 1889 volume, also, Tennyson revived the *In Memoriam* stanza. In this form he wrote the elegiac poem upon the death of his son Lionel. *To the Marquis of Dufferin and Ava;* and in the same stanza a poem addressed to W. G. Palgrave, entitled, *To Ulysses.*

[50] The next year brought forth *Locksley Hall Sixty Years After.*

success, imitated his earlier manner of imitating the classics. In a sense the wheel has come full circle; he is again playing with metrical and other toys; the difference is that now his career is behind him, not before him.   In addition to the title poem, the *Demeter* volume contained two pieces in blank verse, *The Ring,* presenting in dialogue a story of contemporary life, and *Romney's Remorse,* a monologue of semi-historical foundation.   In the last volume, *Akbar's Dream* presents somewhat more novelty of theme than the other blank verse poems.   *The Death of the Duke of Clarence and Avondale* belongs to the class of memorial poems, which has been else-where noticed.   *The Death of Œnone* and *St. Telemachus* are narratives whose analogues had long before appeared.   In all of these poems Tennyson returned to the severe blank verse pattern of his earlier idylls, but he did not recapture their charm of melody and texture.

The foregoing outline of the contents of Tennyson's latest volumes and of his metrical practices, though not meticulously exhaustive, serves to indicate the manner in which Tennyson employed the literary playtime of his old age.   Here, as everywhere, his choice and treatment of metres in suggestive of other characteristics of his work.   We observe a desire to follow knowledge,—the knowledge of his chosen art in its most distinctive department—"like a sinking star" to its utmost horizon. At the same time, we note an equally constant tendency to look back to forms and principles which he had followed with success in early years.   From the time of *Maud* onward, there is a strong predilection for the three-stress or six-stress verse unit and for irregular and "direct" rhythms. There is, too, a more frequent use of long metres and triple movements; particularly there is an increased choice of trochaic and dactylic movements, and, in some cases, this may be regarded as a yielding, at times when there was no dom-inating inward impulse, to the direct imitation of classical rhythms.   In much, in most, of the later work, we may ac-cept this experimentation in theme and metre as the play of an artist whose message, even in art, was long ago delivered; or we may describe it as the continued industry of a workman who loves his tools too much to put them away, but to whom they have become toys rather than tools.

Still, when his call is highest—and sometimes the call came, even "sixty years after"—the old voice is heard. At such times the metre responds; the slow iambic of his best days takes possession, and we get the old resonant dream music:

> What sound was dearest in his native dells?
> The mellow lin-lan-lone of evening bells
> Far—far—away.

Or shall we place in evidence that miracle among octogenarian lyrics, *Crossing the Bar*, closing our study with a piece of late but standard Tennyson,—a piece which Tennyson, with masterly insight, desired should always be printed at the end of his poems?

> Sunset and evening star,
>   And one clear call for me!
> And may there be no moaning of the bar,
>   When I put out to sea,
>
> But such a tide as moving seems asleep,
>   Too full for sound and foam,
> When that which drew from out the boundless deep
>   Turns again home.
>
> Twilight and evening bell,
>   And after that the dark!
> And may there be no sadness of farewell,
>   When I embark;
>
> For though from out our bourne of Time and Place
>   The flood may bear me far,
> I hope to see my Pilot face to face
>   When I have crossed the bar.

Not only is this poem strikingly regular in movement; it is peculiarly beautiful in symmetry and balance, for its very irregularities are balanced,—as in the hovering accents at the beginning of the first and ninth lines, respectively, and the rest pauses of the fourth verses of the second and third stanzas. Late as it is, *Crossing the Bar* is a sister of ''Break, Break, Break,'' ''Tears, idle tears,'' and ''Sweet after showers ambrosial air.'' We note for the last time, that Tennyson's genius lay, not in the invention, but in the *modulation* of rhythms. Where he is simplest in the outline of his forms, he is subtlest and best in their decoration.

APPENDIX A

TENNYSON'S EARLY DICTION

Language of the Early Poems

Arthur Hallam's statement in a letter of 1831, that he was alleviating his legal studies by "culling for Alfred, from the old fellow Blackstone, such poetic words as 'forestal' ", lends a hint of the fact, corroborated by the internal evidence of the poems, that Tennyson was, at this time, accumulating a studied poetic vocabulary. This poetic language he aimed to make surpassingly rich and strange. The theory back of it was anything but that which Wordsworth propounded in his first Preface, namely, that the language of poetry should be that of common, daily life. Tennyson's method consisted partly in taking words that had always been sequestered to poetical uses, partly in adopting rare words from Shakspere and Milton, partly in appropriating words to special poetic use after the analogy of these, as, for example, by the use of latinisms in a special or primitive sense. Partly, it consisted in the introduction of archaic and folk words after the fashion of preceding poets of the romantic school. There was no absolute novelty in this method; but few English poets seem to have been so enamored of words for their own sake, as was Tennyson at this period, and few have compounded so complete and elaborate a special vocabulary for poetic uses.

In the early poems, Tennyson did not always succeed in assimilating these words to their context, and the reader is too frequently annoyed by a suspicion that the poet is introducing a word because he thinks it a fine word and not because it is the necessary word for the place. Investing certain vocables with an esoteric poetical connotation or

15

yielding to the lure of mere sound, Tennyson sometimes admitted them into contexts where they were of doubtful value. Frequently such words were removed in the revision of the poems, at a later period. Many of them disappeared through the suppression of the pieces in which they occurred.

Tennyson never completely outgrew this love of words for their own sake. "Browning," he once said, *"cares nothing for the glory of words."* Hallam Tennyson tells us that his father "regretted that he had never used the word 'yarely' ". Certain words retained his allegiance through life and became fixed mannerisms of his style. It is possible that we are here on the scent of a vicious method of composition. Tennyson admitted that a word or phrase was with him often the germ of a poem. This is well enough; but what if a poem were written *for the sake* of a word or a phrase, or, not to make too great a leap at once,—a verse for the sake of a word, a passage for the sake of the line, and, finally, a poem brought into existence for the sake of expression, a subversion of the right poetic process? A. Hallam, when urging Tennyson to publish *The Lover's Tale*, used, as a part of his persuasion, the argument that Tennyson would not readily find "as good a framework for the many beauties of that poem." It seems tolerably certain that a number of the longer poems of the early volumes, *The Palace of Art*, for example, and *A Dream of Fair Women*, served as "frameworks" for the introduction of series of minute "studies" in verbal artistry. We may believe that Tennyson, in time, outgrew this method of composition and learned to hatch his poems from ideas and not from words; but he always continued the habit of composing bits for their own sake. Similes, snatches of music or description, purple patches, jewels five words or five verses long, were treasured up until such time as opportunity offered, to introduce them into a "framework" of larger design.

The early poems contain many amusing instances of affection for certain "poetic" words. One of these was the word "crisp," "crispèd," applied to the rippled surface of waters. It is a word which has been for centuries almost exclusively devoted to poetry. It is found in Shakspere, in

Ben Jonson, in Collins, in Byron, and, most familiarly of all in Dekker's best known song "Canst drink the waters of the crispèd spring?"[1] This noticeable and obviously "poetic" epithet occurs about a dozen times in Tennyson, down to 1833, viz., in *Claribel, Supposed Confessions, We are Free*, in the 1830 version of *Mariana in the South*, three times in *The Lover's Tale* (two cases excised in the published version), in *An Unpublished Sonnet*,[2] in *A Fragment*, (published in the *Gem*, 1831,) and finally, in *The Lotus Eaters*, where it still remains finely expressive: "To watch the *crisping* ripples on the beach."

Of similar extraction is the Homeric epithet, "ambrosial," much used by Milton, though not by him introduced into English poetic diction. Nine times occurring in *Paradise Lost*, twice in *Paradise Regained*, once in *Comus*, it was much repeated by eighteenth century verse-makers, Pope, Young, and Cowper, among others. Byron shows his comic appreciation of its "poetic" conventionalism, by its use in his satire on the "ambrosial Waltz." One of Tennyson's earliest fragments introduces us to "ambrosial glooms". Later, we have in *Claribel* the oak-tree "Thick-leaved, ambrosial", in *Isabel*, "ambrosial orbs of rich fruit-bunches," and in *Eleanore* an "ambrosial smile." "Ambrosial breaths" and "ambrosial pulps" both disappeared from *The Palace of Art*, in the 1842 version, as did "ambrosial dew" from *Œnone;* but in the latter poem the epithet thus saved is restored by applying it, in the later version, to the hair of Aphrodite, where it is reminiscent of a passage in Virgil. In *Œnone,* also, the apples "smelt ambrosially". In Tennyson's later poems, the epithet is more frugally managed, but it adorns some famous passages as, in *The Princess*, "The broad ambrosial aisles of lofty lime," and in the "Sweet after showers ambrosial air" of *In Memoriam*.

Another of these conventional epithets is "divine". It is common in English poetry before Milton; but it was by

---

[1] In Milton, also, *P. L.* IV, 223 ff., a passage particularly admired by Tennyson. I am reminded by Professor Dodge.

[2] *Memoir*, I, 80.

him consecrated to the service of poetry.   It occurs over *sixty*
times in his poems, and usually with the *hyperbaton* which
suits its accent to iambic verse.   It came to Tennyson with a
long list of credentials; Popists and romantics alike perpetuated it through the eighteenth century.   Milton's famous
"human face divine" perhaps did more than any other
phrase to lend it prestige.   To this may be added the "bright
eyes divine" of *Christabel* and the "maiden eyes divine"
of the heroine of *St. Agnes' Eve*.   Tennyson's Madeline
has also "eyes divine"; the second Mariana, has "melancholy
eyes divine," and Eleanore, "lineaments divine."   Like "ambrosial," this epithet had a place in *The Palace of Art*, but
the "naked shape divine" of Venus disappeared in the revision.   *Œnone* retains its "snowycolumned range divine";
"many a woven acanthus wreath divine" in *The Lotus Eaters*
was allowed to stand, though "ancient heights divine" was
excised.

Many other examples might be cited, of the same general
class, words of fine sound and rich association suggestive of
remote times or climes, keen sense excitements, fragrance,
colour, light, or warmth.   Such are *amber, amorous, azure,
bloomed, cedarn, charmed, chrystal, chrystalline, enchanted,
flavorous, fringed, honeyed, impearled, odorous, orient, sheeny,*
etc., etc.   To these might be added many stock substantives
with the things they name, and some archaisms or classicisms,
such as, *what time, then when, there where, now while,* etc.

Now, Milton was not the first, in the majority of cases, to
employ given individual words of this class for poetic purposes.   They will be found abundantly in Spenser, Peele,
Marlowe, Shakspere, Chapman, Drayton, Drummond, Beaumont, and Fletcher, in half-a-hundred Elizabethans; but it
was Milton who first learned to talk exclusively in such a
dialect, and who made that dialect the peculiar possession
of English poetry for all time.   "Such phrases in Milton as
'Fanning their odoriferous wings'," Tennyson said to his son,
late in life, "are undoubtedly commonplace now, but Milton
introduced the style."   Again, in the same conversation:
"Our English language alters quickly.   This great line would

be almost commonplace now: 'The dismal situation, waste and wild.' " Tennyson meant, no doubt, that the words, "dismal" and "situation" have, through vulgar and careless usage, lost their distinction and hence drag the line down with them. This is true of many a passage in Milton and the older poets, where a nice consciousness of words in their etymological sense is necessary to an enjoyment of their poetic connotation.

It is obvious then, that an indiscriminate pillage of Milton could not be otherwise than fatal to a modern poet. Tennyson had too much literary tact to fall into this error, even had he not had too much imagination to need, and too nice a literary conscience to wish, profit from such plunderings. He placed the Miltonic language under contribution: but he recoined what he took, richly alloying it with metal from countless other sources, and put forth, in due time, a specie bearing his own crown imperial. A capital illustration of Tennyson's methods may be observed in his management of the epithet "ambrosial" in Œnone. Here, as we have seen, the epithet was, in the course of revision, deleted from one passage of description and transferred to another. As the text now stands, the "ambrosial hair" of Aphrodite, together with the context, is redolent of Virgil's description of Venus at her parting from Aeneas in the first book of the Æneid. Thus, the epithet has been applied, not only with a sense of its associations in English poetry, but, in addition, with a full sense of its Virgilian provenience.[3]

---

[3] Since this passage seems to have been overlooked by collectors of "classical echoes" in Tennyson it may not be out of place to reproduce the lines which provided him with several reminiscences:

Dixit et avertens rosea cervice refulsit,
Ambrosiaeque comae divinum vertice odorem
Spiravere; pedes vestis defluxit ad imos,
Et vera incessu patuit dea..........

Ipsa Paphum sublimis abit sedesque revisit
laeta suas, ubi templum illi centumque Sabaeo
ture calent arae sertisque recentibus halant.
Æneid, I, 402–405, 415–417.

Reminiscences of (the "Sabaeo ture" of) this passage are noted below, p. 237. Compare, also, The Lover's Tale,

And onward floating in a full dark wave
Parted on either side her argent neck.

Tennyson's treatment of the class of words cited above is striking and suggestive; but there is an even larger class of words, less hackneyed in preceding poetry and employed only once or twice by Tennyson himself. Sometimes these words have a touch of archaism about them, sometimes they are dialectal; some of them are latinisms; some, apparently, are coinages. In the use of these, Tennyson was frequently unhappy, and they were often suppressed in revision.

Take the phrase, for example, "Purfled wimple," (*Lilian*, 1830.) This was changed in the 1842 version to "gathered wimple." The change suggests that Tennyson may not, in the first instance, have very clearly understood the meaning of the word, "purfled," thinking it meant, pleated, puckered, or the like. He may have picked it out of Chaucer or Spenser though it is probable that it was suggested to him chiefly by Milton's "purfled scarf".[4] This passage with its "crispëd", "odorous", "rosy-bosomed," etc., Tennyson doubtless knew by heart. From it, he drew the motto which stands at the opening of his suppressed poem, *The Hesperides*,

> Hesperus and his daughters three
> That sing about the golden tree.

The passage is, indeed, one of the Spice Islands of English poetry, rich, fragrant, mystical. More than once in Tennyson, some vagrant sweetness reminds us how close we are to those enchanted shores.

"Pleached" (meaning "plaited") is another epithet whose history gives us an insight into Tennyson's methods. The word was not used by Milton, and Tennyson probably adopted it out of Shakspere, where it occurs several times;[5] though in this case, Keats may have given an intermediary hint. Tennyson has it in a number of the early poems; but later revisions and suppressions removed it entirely from his vocabulary, except for the compound, "self-pleached" in *A Dirge*. The phrase "cool impleached twilights", in

---

[4] *Comus*, 995.

[5] Variously compounded, as "thick-pleached", "even-pleached", "impleached".

Timbuctoo, smacks unmistakably of Shakspere. *Ode to Memory* (1830) had,

> With pleached alleys of the trailing rose,

but "pleached" was exchanged for "plaited", in 1842. *The Lover's Tale,* early version, had "the *pleached* ivy-tress," changed in the 1879 version to "plaited." "*Pleached* with her hair" is found in a suppressed Sonnet, "The palled thunderstricken", etc.

At the risk of tediousness, I shall mention one further example which is of unusual interest for the light it throws upon Tennyson's methods at this time. In *A Dirge,* occurs the word "eglatere." This can have come from only one place in English literature, *viz.,* from *The Flower and the Leaf* in Speght's Chaucer. "Eglantine" had been thoroughly incorporated into English poetic diction, by Spenser, Shakspere, Milton and Keats. In his search for verbal novelties, Tennyson must have lighted upon the unique form "eglatere," in Speght, probably an erroneous spelling in a poem erroneously attributed to Chaucer.[6] It may be too ingenious to suppose that there is also a subtle indication of Chaucerian influence in the identical rhyme of this passage:

> The woodbine and eglatere
> Drip sweeter dews than traitor's tear.

Illustration must cease, though it might be continued at great length. A list of verbal oddities follows. These are, variously, archaisms, dialecticisms, latinisms, coinages, or affectations. *Almondine, anear, angerly,*[7] *anight, annoy, atween, balm-cricket, battailing, bight, birk, blenched, blosmy, bordure, brere, brilliance, burn, clips, clothed on, coverture, breaded blosms, embattail, dight, empery, evocation, eyne,*[8]

---

[6] See Skeat's note, *The Flower and the Leaf.* In spite of this authority, however, one must notice the closeness of the French form, *eglantier.*

[7] Shakspere and Keats.

[8] Rhymed with "between".

fere, frequent with,[9] *glistering, ivy tod,*[10] *joyance, kine, low-embowed,*[11] *lowlihead,*[12] *margents, marish, more lovelier, rivage, parlance, pleasance, profulgent, reboant, reflex,*[13] *refluent, respectant, roseries, roundelay, salient,*[14] *shame fall-'em, tanling, trenchant,*[15] *Turkis, welaway, wolds, yesternight, yronne.*

This list does not claim completeness, nor does it contain a large number of words which are strictly poetic in character, but not sufficiently strange to warrant their inclusion in such a list.   *Bowery,* for example, is so frequently employed as to amount to a mannerism of diction.   The same may be said of *pillar'd, diapered, diamonded, silver, silvery* (in numerous compounds), *hornëd* (applied to various landscape features), *silver, vagrant, crowned, crowning, ridged, faery, hollow, sallow,* etc.   The list might be considerably extended. Other mannerisms were the archaic spelling of many words: *antient, Atlantick, brier* (for *briar*), *chrystal,* etc.; the excessive use of syllabic ''ed''; a predilection for substantive compounds with *under,* as ''under roof,'' ''under-sky,'' ''under-flame,'' ''under-stream,'' etc.; great freedom in the compounding of epithets and, in the early text, the affectation of no hyphen, with such results as ''diamondeyed,'' ''lily-leaved,'' ''fulleyëd,'' and the like.

It would be easy to exaggerate the affectations of Tennyson's diction in this period; but his vigorous efforts to enrich the modern poetical vocabulary were not by any means uniformly happy.   It was fortunate, on the whole, that his subsequent revisions and suppressions tended toward a more conservative, a simpler, and more natural, language.   Doubtless one would be credited who should declare that Tennyson's

---

[9] A latinism, copied from Milton or Shelley, or both.

[10] Spenser, *Shep. Cal.*   Coleridge, *Ancient Mariner.*   Shakspere and Fletcher *T. N. K.*

[11] *The Mystic* (1830) ''low-embowed eld.''   cf.   *Il Penseroso,* ''high-embowed roof.''

[12] Spenser and Chaucer.

[13] For image, reflection, (a mannerism).

[14] A latinism; (of the heart or the blood).

[15] Literal, (swords).

real successes, even in the early volumes, lay in those poems and parts of poems in which he adhered to a simple diction and depended for poetic effect upon the sheer force of his imagination. This is not, however, the fact. To be sure, *Mariana*, which is the most perfect piece in the 1830 volume, and received practically no touch of later revision, is remarkably free from these preciosities of diction. At the same time, the *Recollections of the Arabian Nights,* almost as successful, is embroidered with them from end to end.

PARALLELISM AND REMINISCENCE

It is clear that this was the time when Tennyson first gave himself passionately to the old masters of English poetry. He belonged, now, to a group whose subsequent achievements in scholarship testify to their critical grounding. Among them were Spedding, the editor of Bacon, Kemble, the editor of *Beowulf,* Monckton Milnes, and other brilliant youngsters. Tennyson's reading in Chaucer, Shakspere, and the others must have profited immensely from such association. That his acquaintance with the older writers was curious, if not critically thorough, has just been shown; the general ardor of his intimacy with the elder poets and dramatists is attested by many anecdotes in the *Memoir,* and elsewhere. Evidence of their influence upon the substance and form of his poetry may be adduced if we gather together the numerous examples of parallelism and reminiscence in the early volumes.

In the 1830 volume Shakspere plainly leads all the rest, or is second only to Milton, if second even to him. In reminiscences of subject matter, in specific words and phrases of which some examples have been given above, in those parallels which contain an unmistakable transfusion of some particular passage, and in vaguer infusions of the manner of the master, Shakspere is ever present in this volume.

It has been often pointed out that the names of many of the women are drawn from Shakspere; but I am mistaken if Tennyson did not, in a few instances, get something more than the names for these "fancy-portraits," from that source. The titles suggestive of Shakspere are "Claribel", "Juliet", "Rosalind", "Isabel", "Mariana", and "Kate".[16] The first two poems contain nothing except the name which has any connection with Shakspere,—Isabel very little. Rosalind has much in common with the heroine of *As You Like It*. Kate may have something of "The Shrew," and the likeness is strong to the Kate of Stephano's song:[17]

> But none of us cared for Kate,
> For she had a tongue with a tang,
> Would cry to a sailor go hang.

Compare,

> For Kate hath an unbridled tongue
> Clear as the twanging of a harp.[18]

Nor should Lady Percy be quite forgotten. Some have seen in the phrase "gilded flies" and context a reminiscence of *King Lear*.[19]

As for *Mariana*, I have seen no criticism of that poem which recognizes how far it is an amplification of an undeveloped *motif* in *Measure for Measure*. "The dejected Mariana" of "the moated grange," wronged and slandered, but still, after five years, in vain "washing with her tears the marble Angelo," suggests more than vaguely the scene, situation and mood which Tennyson wrought out so successfully. There is, too, a verbal reminiscence in the line "Upon the middle of the night."[20] The song *The Owl* is a direct imitation of "When icicles hang by the wall,"[21] *A Dirge* is a sheer trans-

---

[16] Collins, *Early Poems*, p. 306.
[17] *Tempest*, II, ii.
[18] *Kate*, C. 306.
[19] *King Lear*, IV, vi, 14. Cf. also *King Lear*, V, iii, 13.
[20] Cf. Keats, *Eve of St. Agnes*, "Upon the honeyed middle of the night" and *M. for M.* IV, i, 35. "Upon the heavy middle of the night".
For "grey-eyed morn" Collins suggests "The grey morn smiles" etc., from *Romeo and Juliet*, thus misquoting it. Note also Chapman's,
> "And haste thee where the grey-eyed morn perfumes
> Her rosy chariot with Sabæan spices."
> *Bussy D'Ambois*, V, i.
[21] *L. L. L.* V, ii.

fusion of the Dirge in *Cymbeline,*[22] and contains some
verbal reminiscences from this and other Shaksperean sources,
such as "pleached", "long purples",[23] "gold-eyed kingcups
fine".[24] In *The Merman* the "merrily" of the refrain was
obviously suggested by Ariel's song.[25] "Ridged sea", as in
King Lear,[26] appears in the song "We are Free", and *The
Sea Fairies:* "ridging", applied to the sea, appears in *The
Lover's Tale,* and *Ode to Memory* has "ridged wolds." Also
we have "trenchant swords",[27] "golden prime",[28] "stilly
sound",[29] "glistering" is at least Elizabethan. "Broadim-
based[30] beach" though not in Shakspere, is precisely in his
manner. A peculiar use of "flatter," in a primitive sense,
suggests Shakspere, possibly encouraged by Keats.[31]

In the 1833 volume, "Full-sailed verse"[32] suggests a line of
Shakspere,[33] though classical parallels have been pointed
out.[34] Œnone's "My eyes are full of tears, my heart of
love" varies only slightly from a Shaksperean line. [35] "Tirra

---

[22] IV, ii, extravagantly admired by Tennyson to his dying hour.
[23] *Hamlet,* IV, vii, 170.
[24] Cf. *Cymbeline,* II, iii, 26. (Collins)
[25] *Tempest,* V, i, 92.
[26] *Lear,* IV, vi, 71.
[27] To (————————) ; *Timon of Athens,* IV, iii, 115.
[28] *Rec. of Arab. Nts.: Rich. III,* I, ii, 248.
[29] *Ibid., Henry V,* IV, Prol., 5. Coleridge was fond of this epithet.
        Poetic works. (*Passim*).
[30] Apparently Tennyson's coinage; missed by the *New Eng. Dict.* Tennyson has "Broad-based" several times.
[31] "*Flattering* the golden prime
        Of good Haroun al Raschid."
                                    Recollections of Arabian Nights.
"In deep or vivid colour, smell and sound
        Was *flattered* day and night.
                                    Palace of Art (1833 Version.)
cf. Shakspere:
        "Full many a glorious morning have I seen
        Flatter the mountain tops with sovereign eye—"
                                    Sonnet 33.
and Keats:
        "*Flattered* to tears this aged man and poor"
                                    St. Agnes Eve.
[32] *Eleanore.*
[33] *Sonnet* 86. "Was it the proud full sail of his great verse."
[34] Mustard, *Classical Echoes in Tennyson,* p. 140.
[35] 2 *Henry VI,* II, iii, 17. "Mine eyes are full of tears, my heart of
grief."

lirra'' in *The Lady of Shalott* is from *A Winter's Tale*.[36]
Cleopatra in *A Dream of Fair Women* is of course drawn
chiefly after Shakspere's heroine in *Antony and Cleopatra*.

The abundance and variety of these parallels clearly indicate that Shakspere was a chief feeder of Tennyson's imagination during this period, and an important source of his
poetical language.

In much the same manner, Tennyson was saturating himself in the poetry of Milton. So thoroughly is his verse suf-
fused with the colors of Milton's descriptive poetry that the
phrases actually taken by him direct from Milton only feebly
illustrate the extent to which he has submitted his technique
to the Miltonic discipline.

The poem of the 1830 volume which reminds us most in-
sistently of Milton is the *Ode to Memory*.[37] This poem is
full of ideas and of color, subtly drawn from *Il Penseroso*,
much as Collins drew from it in the *Ode to Evening*. The
landscape is from nature and far more real than Milton's;
but the tone and diction of the poem are richly Miltonic.
The retreat of "retired leisure" at the close,

> Whither in after life retired
> From brawling storms
> From weary wind
> With youthful fancy re-inspired
> We may hold converse with all forms
> Of the many sided mind.

amounts to a restatement of the latter portion of Milton's
poem. The line, "My friend, with you to live alone" had
hardly been, had not Milton sung,

> These pleasures, Meláncholy, give
> And I with thee will choose to live.

---

[36] Act. IV, Sc. II. "The lark that 'tirra-lirra' sings."
  Lady of Shalott, 1833. "Tirra-lirra, tirra-lirra,"
                                        Sang Sir Launcelot.

[37] Disturbed by the confident over-statements of Churton Collins as to
the influence of Coleridge discernible in this poem, I was glad to find a
coincidence with my own view—strongly, although incidentally, expressed
in the notes of Mr. Verity. (*Milton's Early Poems*, London). In
this case, as in others, Collins's phrase, "modelled on," is objectionable,
implying too full and conscious an indebtedness on the part of Tennyson,
in this instance to Coleridge's *Song of the Pixies*. See above, p. 31.

"Storied walls" recalls "storied windows"; let one compare the shore-sounds of the two poems and he will be convinced. "The thick-fleeced sheep from wattled folds" is such a transfusion of "The folded flocks penned in their wattled cotes,"[38] of *Comus* that it would puzzle a critic whose memory of the passages might be a little dim to tell which is Milton and which Tennyson. "Orient", "amber", "what time", "livelong", had been the common inheritance of the Miltonic school for sixty years; but one can rather feel than prove how utterly Miltonic is the timbre and poetic sheen of such a bit as the following, in which there is perhaps no reminiscence of a specific passage:

> What time the amber morn
> Forth gushes from beneath a low hung cloud.

Specific reminiscences of Milton in the early volumes are, "A courage to endure and to obey",[39] "The clear-pointed flame of chastity",[40] "eyelids of the morn",[41] "the dark hyaline",[42] "Spread his sheeny vans for flight",[43] "Sabaean spice",[44] "The day down-sloped was westering in his bower",[45] "horned valleys",[46] "amber round", "fleecy

---

[38] *Comus*, 344.

[39] *Isabel.* The obverse of Milton's "and courage never to submit or yield." *P. L.* I, 108. The sentiment suggests Shelley, *Prom. Unbound.* IV.

"Gentleness, Virtue, Wisdom, and Endurance," etc.

[40] *Isabel.* Cf. *Comus*, 425. "The sacred ray of chastity," and other comparisons of chastity to light.

[41] *To*— "Ray-fringed eyelids of the morn," cf. *Lycidas:* "Opening eyelids of the morn." cf. also *Comus*, 890: "rushy-fringed bank." "Fringed" was one of Tennyson's early favorites, e. g., *Madeline*, of her eyes, "little clouds sunfringed."

[42] *Elegiacs.* Classic, through Milton and Shelley, cf. "The clear hyaline" *P. L.* VII, 619. *Prom. Unbound.* II, v. 21.

[43] *Love and Death. P. L.*, II, 927. "His sailbroad *vans he spreads for flight.*"

[44] *Adeline. .P. L.* IV, 162, "Sabean odors from the spicy shore." But Chapman's "Sabæan spices" is closer (see above, p. 234, note 20.).

[45] *Mariana* (1830 version, one of the few lines retouched.) Cf. *Lycidas*, "Towards Heaven's descent had sloped his westering wheel."

[46] *Supposed confessions.* Classic, through Milton. Cf. *P. L.* 831. "The horned flood." The precise phrase occurs in *In Memoriam.* Cf., also, *Audley Court*, "To where the bay runs up its latest horn."

night'',[47] "that deep-wounded child of Pendragon''.[48] The imitation of many Miltonic epithets has been noted in the paragraphs on diction. The resemblances to Milton in *Timbuctoo* are noted in the account of Tennyson's early blank verse. A piece of blank verse, on the Colossus of Rhodes, entitled *A Fragment*, printed in *The Gem* (1831), is Miltonic in many respects: in attempted vastness of effect, in its spiced Orientism, in its names. The use of proper names and the style (paraphrastic) of scriptural allusion, are not infrequently in the manner of Milton. In his sonnets, particularly in *To J. M. K., Alexander, Buonaparte*, and most of all, *Poland*,[49] the manner is that of Milton. The sonnets which most resemble those of Milton, however, are in the 1833 volume; but there Milton's influence is supplemented by that of Wordsworth. The sonnets of the 1830 volume, which were much poorer,[50] suggest the influence of Coleridge and Shelley.

The tradition is, that Wordsworth, Coleridge, Shelley, and Keats were the modern poets in the ascendant among Tennyson and his friends at this period;[51] but direct reminiscences of them, particularly verbal reminiscences, are not plentiful. Of Wordsworth's *Intimations* we have a few distinct traces, as in the lines,

> Every heart this May morning in joyance is beating[52]
> O'er the deep mind of dauntless infancy;[53]

Some of the sonnets and such poems as "Nature as far as in her lies'',[54] and "Of Old Sat Freedom on the Heights'',[54] are like Wordsworth in their reflective matter and moral tone, but the likeness seldom amounts to a verbal echo.

The same principle prevails in such passages as derive from

---

[47] *Margaret* (1833 version). Cf. *Il Penseroso*. (of the moon)
       "Stooping through a fleecy cloud."
[48] *Palace of Art* (1833). Compare this entire stanza with *Comus*, ll. 999–1002.
[49] A direct imitation. Cf. "Avenge, O Lord."
[50] See chap. II, p. 32.
[51] *Memoir*, I, 45.
[52] *All things will die*.
[53] *Ode to Memory*.
[54] Not published until 1842, though then placed among the 1833 poems.

Coleridge. "Ribbed sand"[55] recalls "the ribbed sea-sand"
of *The Ancient Mariner*.[56] "Myriad-minded"[57] was probably
already proverbial. *Recollections of the Arabian Nights* owes
considerable in theme and tone to *Kubla Khan*:[58] and even
more suggestive of specific passages in Coleridge's dream poem
are some of the lines in *An Unpublished Sonnet*,[59] of about
1831. It is not remarkable that this sonnet was never published during the poet's lifetime, for its finest lines were
transferred to *The Lotos-Eaters* and *The Palace of Art*, not
without some loss.

>   And give up wholly
> The spirit to mild-minded melancholy.

is not improved when diluted to form the following couplet.

>   To lend our hearts and spirits wholly
>   To the influence of mild-minded melancholy.[60]

and the finely paired epithets "dark and holy" in the line,

>   And all the haunted place is dark and holy

seem less fittingly applied to "heaven", as follows:

>   Beneath a heaven dark and holy.[61]

In *The Palace of Art* the passage,

>   No nightingale delighteth to prolong
>   Her low preamble all alone.

---

[55] *Ode to Memory*.

[56] One of the passages claimed by Wordsworth.

[57] *Ode to Memory*, cf. "Our myriad-minded Shakspeare." *Biog. Lit.* Ch.
XV. *Shakespeare and Other Dramatists*, 72.

[58] Overstated, however, by Collins.

[59] *Memoir*, I, 100. Compare

>   "Thro yonder poplar alley,
>   Below, the blue green river windeth slowly,
>   But in the middle of the sombre valley
>   The crisped waters whisper musically,
>   And all the haunted place is dark and holy."

with the remarkable passage in *Kubla Khan*,

>   "But oh that deep romantic chasm which slanted
>   Down the green hill athwart a cedarn cover!
>   A savage place! as holy and enchanted
>   As e'er beneath a waning moon was haunted" etc.

[60] *Lotos-Eaters*, 5. Two lines above, "crisping" reappears.

[61] *Lotos-Eaters*, 7.

thriftily preserves a line which Hallam said was "worth an estate in Golconda":

> The nightingale with long and low preamble.

Finally, we may note that both passages recall a bit of Beaumont and Fletcher which Milton, too, remembered, while writing *Il Penseroso:*

> Then stretch our bones in a still gloomy valley:
> Nothing's so dainty sweet as lovely melancholy.

Note, too, that these excellent bits when transferred to their final positions hardly suggest at all the passages in Coleridge and in Beaumont and Fletcher of which they smacked so strongly in the suppressed sonnet. Doubtless this was accidental; but it looks like clever bookkeeping.

Resemblances to Keats are more frequently analogous than literal, a hazardous kind of likeness from which to argue an indebtedness. The heroine of *The Eve of St. Agnes* may have suggested the name of *Madeline.* They have nothing else in common except "eyes divine." The compound, "argent-lidded"[62] is slightly suggestive of "azure-lidded",[63] "blush'd *angerly*",[64] is much like "flush'd *angerly*",[65] and both are archaic. In

> *Flattering* the *golden* prime
> Of good Haroun al Raschid,[66]

the use of "flattering" is sufficiently queer to suggest Keats' curious

> Music's *golden* tongue
> *Flattered* to tears.[67]

In a general way the physical sensations of the poems may have owed something to Keats' tender appeal of the same

---

[62] *Rec. Arabian Nights.*
[63] *The Eve of St. Agnes.*
[64] *Madeline.*
[65] *Hyperion.*
[66] *Rec. Arabian Nights.*
[67] *The Eve of St. Agnes.*

kind. There is a predilection for such words as "lush", "flavorous", "pulps", etc.; and what Spedding deprecatingly called the "creature comforts" of the early volumes can be fairly paralleled in Keats. There are a few touches which seem due to Keats, in the 1833 volume. Collins finds Tennyson's "yellow-banded bees"[68] sufficiently like the "yellow-girted"[69] ones of Keats. But grant analogous methods of description and the likeness of phrase may easily be coincidental. "Unheard melody"[70] is harder to accept as a coincidence. "Large Hesper glittered on her tears"[71] seems a belated reminiscence of Keats'

> Where no insulting light
> Could glimmer on their tears;[72]

it was not in the 1833 version, but was added later. A similar image and phrase occur in the early version of *The Lover's Tale* and in *Tithonus*. In general, it is fair to say that, though literal parallelisms to either Coleridge or Keats are few, the atmosphere of a number of the most successful poems is more like that of those two transcendent romanticists, the quality of aestheticism there regnant is more like that found in *Christabel* and *The Eve of St. Agnes*, than it is like anything else that had preceded in English poetry.

The problem of Tennyson's indebtedness to Shelley is complicated by the fact of their common debt to Milton in both phrase and versification. Such phrases as "translucent wave", "odorous winds", "the clear hyaline",[73] may have descended to each in a direct line from Milton, or they may have come to Tennyson through Shelley. Milton's fine use of "winnow", especially in the passage,

> with quick fan
> Winnows the buxom air,[74]

---

[68] *Eleanore.*
[69] *Endymion,* I, 253.
[70] *Eleanore.* Cf. *Ode on a Grecian Urn.*
    "Heard melodies are sweet, but those unheard are sweeter."
[71] *Mariana in the South,* 1842 version.
[72] *Hyperion,* II, 6.
[73] Tennyson, "the dark hyaline".
[74] *P. L.* V. 270.

16

seems to have haunted them both. Its frequency in Shelley amounts well nigh to a mannerism and it occurs at least twice in Tennyson's early poems: first, in *Timbuctoo* where the entire context is reminiscent of the Miltonic context; and again, in *The Kraken*. In both passages, also, there are Shelleyan characteristics of diction. There are few definite borrowings from Shelley, though we are reminded of specific passages, here and there, as "I faint, I fall",[75] "It will change but it will not fade",[76] "desire," "dawn", "snake", "blosmy" are words often used in both poets; Tennyson reproduces quite closely Shelley's manner in the personification of Loves, Hopes, and Desires; and he has Shelley's predilection for enchanted boats and shallops, e. g., in *Recollections of the Arabian Nights*. Like Shelley's are the ideas of *The Poet* and of some of the early sonnets, afterward suppressed, especially "Shall the hag Evil die with child of Good?", "The pallid thunderstricken sigh for gain", and the three entitled, *Love*. But there is also an extensive indebtedness for imagery to *Paradise Lost*, Satan's interview with Sin and Death, and the subsequent flight through Chaos.

To summarize the foregoing statements: it is clear that suggestions of Coleridge and Keats in the poetry of these volumes are comparatively intangible, affecting, for the most part, the general conception and method of some of the poems, leaving rather stouter evidences than the influence of Shelley, but hardly more than that of Wordsworth; while, if we consider the source and character of his poetic diction, making allowance for the modifying force of Tennyson's own faculty and purpose, if we consider either quantity or clearness of reminiscent theme and phrase, and if we consider the pervading atmosphere of the poems, regarding the successful

---

[75] *Confessions of a Second-rate Sensitive Spirit.* Cf. *Indian Serenade,* "I die, I faint, I fail."

So, also, *Eleanore.* "I faint, I swoon," said to be reminiscent of Sappho.

[76] *Nothing Will Die.* Cf. *The Cloud.* "I change but I cannot die."

equally with the unsuccessful, and allowing for his own time and temperament, the conclusion is irresistible, that the real study of Tennyson in this period was in the elder poetry, and that Shakspere and Milton were the real masters of his style. Reminiscences of nineteenth century poets or clear marks of specific passages in them are comparatively rare in these volumes. In the 1833 volume, they are rarer than in the earlier one, and after this, the reminiscences of all English poetry become far more remote and infrequent. The poets of antiquity and of the sister literatures continued to be levied upon: but as Tennyson possessed himself of his own style, and as he began to feel some fair assurance of a position among the masters of his own speech, he became correspondingly sensitive to debt and rigidly excluded anything which might be imputed as an obligation to his peers.

APPENDIX B

NOTE ON THE ORIGIN AND INFLUENCE OF THE METRE OF LOCKSLEY HALL

If, as is likely, the metre of *Locksley Hall* was of Tennyson's invention, it constitutes one of his most striking extensions of English rhythm.[1] Browning, indeed, used the same line in his *Home Thoughts from the Sea,* said to have been written as early as 1838. This antedates by four years the publication of *Locksley Hall.* But Tennyson as we have seen

---

[1] Some critics (*e. g.,* Professor Mustard, *Classical Echoes,* p. 157) seem to have taken seriously the theory advanced by E. Koeppel (*Englische Studien,* xxviii, 404–5) that this metre was suggested to Tennyson by the Latin translation of the Arabic originals, printed with Sir William Jones's prose translation of the seven poems of the *Moällakat.* We have Tennyson's own statement that the idea of the poem was suggested to him by the translation: but no obligations are acknowledged to the metre of the original. (*Memoirs,* I, 239) Herr Koeppel's grounds for ascribing such an influence are flimsy. He says: "Ich erinnere mich in einer englischen zeitschrift oder zeitung gelesen zu haben, dass ein weit gereister gesuch— wenn mich mein gedächtnis nicht täuscht, der bruder des mit Tennyson befreundeten Francis Palgrave—dem dichter sagte, er sei durch das breit rollende metrum von *Locksley Hall* an den schwung und tonfall der arabischen poesie gemahnt worden, worauf sich der dichter erstaunt zu einem gewissen zusammenhang bekannt habe." What the "englische zeitschrift oder zeitung" referred to may be, I do not know; but a passage in Palgrave's "Personal Recollections" refers to an interview between Tennyson and Palgrave's brother, William Gifford, which answers roughly to the foregoing. Palgrave says, "he now, meeting Tennyson for the first time, ventured to remark on the truth of that poem (*Locksley Hall*) to Arabian sentiment and manner. The conjecture proved correct: Locksley Hall had, in fact, been "suggested by reading Sir William Jones' prose translation of the old Arabian *Moällakat.*" (*Memoir,* IV, p. 277.) Nothing was said of the metre, "das breit rollende metrum von *Locksley Hall.*" The article of Koeppel offers interesting evidence of the probable presence of Sir William Jones' works in the library at Somersby; but it is a large step from such proof to the picture of the poet with the Latin transliteration before his eyes and the unfamiliar syllables resounding in trochaic rhythm "wie sie der dichter in der einsamkeit seines studierzimmers vor sich hingedonnert haben muss".

The most that could be postulated, with even a fair plausibility, in re-

had employed it in sporadic couplets[2] of *The Lotus Eaters*
and had even anticipated it in the 1833 version of that poem.
Moreover, it is not easy to believe that two English poets
could have happened coincidently upon so extraordinary
a rhythmic novelty within a few years, and we are set per-
force upon an inquiry as to the probable priority of one
or the other.[3] The priority probably lies with Tennyson.
Unfortunately, it is not possible to establish with much cer-
tainty the date of the composition of *Locksley Hall*. A large
number of the poems of 1842 are mentioned in the letters of
Tennyson and his friends from 1834 on, but *Locksley Hall*
is not one of this number. If the memory of the poet was
accurate in the following anecdote, recorded by his son in
1890, the poem must have been composed comparatively early.
"Two undergraduates were walking together some time after
he himself left Cambridge. One of the two mentioned
'Tennyson'. The other replied, 'O do not mention that
man's name. I hate him. I was the unhappy hero of

---

gard to the influence of the *Moällakat* upon the metre of *Locksley Hall*
would be that the poet's eye might have been caught by the long look of
the sentences in the English paraphrase. If Tennyson had a desire to
know the "schwung und tonfall" of the originals, he probably availed
himself of the careful explanation of the metre which lay directly under
his eye. At the close of the page preceding Sir William Jones's prose
translation of *Amriolkaïs* is the following paragraph:

"The metre is of the first species, called *long verse*, and consists of the
bacchius or amphibrachys, followed by the first epitrite; or in fourth and
eighth places of the distich by the double iambus, the last syllable being
considered as a long one; the regular form taken from the second chapter
of commentaries on Asiatic poetry, is this:

<blockquote>
'Amator puellarum miser saepe fallitur
'Ocellis nigris, labris odoris, nigris comis'"
</blockquote>

(Works of Sir W. Jones, IV, 248. The commentaries referred to in this
passage are in Vol. II, p. 347.) Transferred into English metre these
verses would give us some such movement as the following:

$$x \overset{'}{-} x \mid x \overset{'}{-} - \overset{'}{-} \parallel x \overset{'}{-} - \mid x \overset{'}{-} x \overset{'}{-}$$

Any combination of the measures indicated in Jones's description gives
us a verse of fourteen syllables. It is obvious that this could not
possibly have suggested to Tennyson the eight-stress trochaic rendering
of the transliterations upon which Herr Koeppel bases his theory.

[2] See above, p. 42, note.

[3] If, as some have thought probable, the metre was suggested by that
of the *Pervigilium Veneris* the two young poets might conceivably have
derived it from the same source, about the same time. Even this theory,
however, involves a rather daunting coincidence.

Locksley Hall. It is the story of my cousin's love and mine, known to all Cambridge *when Mr. Tennyson was there,* and he put it into verse'."[4]

Coming from an undergraduate, the words which I have italicized obviously imply a recent residence at Cambridge on Tennyson's part, and taken in connection with the remainder of the sentence may, but do not necessarily, imply that the poem was written while he was still at the university. Tennyson's note on the line, "Let the great world spin forever down the ringing grooves of change", states, "When I went by the first train from Liverpool to Manchester (1830) I thought that the wheels ran in a groove.—Then I made this line." Though our knowledge of Tennyson's methods hardly forbids us to regard the composition of a line as the genesis of a poem, it would be much to postulate, from his memory of a single line, the genesis of a new and unusual metre. The first anecdote, however, gives reason for believing that *Locksley Hall* was well-known, as were many of the poems, long before it got into print and for surmising that scraps of it may have reached Browning's ears before he left England on the voyage which produced *Home Thoughts,* in 1838. There is no good reason to suppose that Tennyson could have made the acquaintance of Browning's poem previous to its publication in *Bells and Pomegranates* in 1845. With these facts before us, Tennyson's own statement may be held to settle the matter. "Mr. Hallam said to me that the English people liked verse in Trochaics, so I wrote the poem in this metre."[5] The two poets must be thought to have happened independently upon the metre, or Browning, whether he caught the suggestion from *The Lotus Eaters* or *Locksley Hall,* must be regarded as the first and the greatest of Tennyson's imitators.

Whatever may be thought of Browning's relation to *Locksley Hall,* certain it is that the novel rhythm immediately found distinguished imitators. Before the year was out

[4] *Memoir,* II, 379.

[5] *Memoir,* I, 195. Apparently in hand, then, before Hallam's death. Or is the reference to Arthur Hallam's father?

in which the poem was published, Thackeray introduced its metre into one of the earliest and best of his ballads, enlarging the couplet to a triplet, apparently for the sake of enhancing the burlesque effect. *King Canute,* which is best known on account of its position in *Rebecca and Rowena* (1849), first appeared in *Miss Tickletoby's Lectures on English History* contributed by Thackeray to *Fraser's* in 1842. Later he wrote in the same metre, one of the *Ballads of Policeman X,* viz., *Damages Two Hundred Pounds,* and also, *The Ballad of Eliza Davis.* Schipper mentions,[6] as the only example in English of the acatalectic eight-stress trochaic, Thackeray's *Sorrows of Werther,* which is, however, printed in half-lines. But Browning has the same metre in his *Christina,* also printed in half-lines, while the same metre, with interrupting rhyme and the second half-line catalectic, is found in his *Soliloquy of the Spanish Cloister.* The couplet arrangement and the two-syllabled rhyme characterize the song, "There's a woman like a dewdrop," in *A Blot in the Scutcheon,* 1843. Browning came closest to the rhythm of *Locksley Hall* in *A Toccata of Galuppi's,* though the rhymes are in triplets. *La Saisiaz* has the couplet arrangement, but the rhythm is much modified by a freer variation of the caesura and by other metrical irregularities characteristic of Browning. Most of these poems, it may be noted, were later than Mrs. Browning's imitations of the *Locksley Hall* metre discussed below. Swinburne, too, tried his hand at this metre in several poems in his *A Midsummer Holiday.*

The metre of Mrs. Browning's *Lady Geraldine's Courtship* (1844) was obviously modelled after that of *Locksley Hall.* The rhythm is essentially the same, although its effect is considerably disguised by a cross-rhyme quatrain arrangement, and the first and third lines are made acatalectic by consistent two-syllabled rhymes. In the "Conclusion" of the poem this scheme is still further modified by the introduction of interior rhymes in the first and third verses. A

---

[6] *Englische Metrik.* 2, 378.

very similar scheme to this last, disguised only by the manner
of printing, is to be found in *The Lost Bower*, which appeared
in the same volume. These poems immediately crossed the
Atlantic and created there the rhythm of Poe's *The Raven*
(1845) and its congeners. A few illustrations will make these
relations much clearer. The second stanza of *The Lost Bower*
runs

> Green the land is where my daily
> Steps in jocund childhood played,
> Dimpled close with hill and valley
> Dappled very close with shade;
> Summer-snow of apple-blossoms running up from glade to glade.

With this we may compare the following from the "Conclusion" of *Lady Geraldine's Courtship*.

IV

With a murmurous stir uncertain, in the air the purple curtain
Swelleth in and swelleth out around her motionless pale brows
While the gliding of the river sends a rippling noise for ever
Through the open casement whitened by the moonlight's slant
    repose.

VII

Said he—"Wake me by no gesture,—sound of breath, or stir of
    vesture!
Let the blessèd apparition melt not yet to its divine!
No approaching—hush, no breathing! or my heart must swoon to
    death in
The too utter life thou bringest, O thou dream of Geraldine!"

VIII

Ever, evermore the while, in a slow silence she kept smiling;
But the tears ran over lightly from her eyes, and tenderly:—
"Dost thou, Bertram, truly love me? Is no woman far above me
Found more worthy of thy poet-heart than such a one as *I*?"

X

Ever, evermore the while in a slow silence she kept smiling,
While the silver tears ran faster down the flushing of her cheeks;
Then, with both her hands enfolding both of his, she softly told him,
"Bertram if I say I love thee—'tis the vision only speaks."

Let any competent reader analyze and compare this poem and Poe's *Raven* observing the character of the rhythm, the nature and frequency of the rhymes, the use of alliterations and repetition, the manner in which quotations are introduced, the rhetorical devices, the setting, the characters, even some of the phrases and even more the weird, mystical atmosphere of the poems,— and then judge whether in Poe's fantastic story of the origin of his poem, with its rubbish about "originality", his statement in regard to the stanza was altogether ingenuous: "nothing even remotely approaching this combination has ever been attempted."[7]   Longfellow, whom Poe constantly accused of plagiarizing from Tennyson, would doubtless have been the first to acknowledge his own indebtedness for the metre of *The Belfry of Bruges* and *Nuremberg*, to *Locksley Hall*, which they followed by the short space of four years. But perhaps the earliest of its American imitators was Lowell in *The Present Crisis* (1844), earliest, that is, among eminent writers, for this note makes no pretension to exhaustiveness.

---

[7] *The Philosophy of Composition.*